Profiles In Banking

A History of
First National Bank of Glens Falls
and its years of service to
the North Country

By
Joseph E. Barnes

© 1990 by Joseph E. Barnes.

**Published by the First National Bank
of Glens Falls, NY, a subsidiary of
Evergreen Bancorp, Inc.**
Printed in the United States of America

Credits   Edited by Arthur S. Fisher
              retired editor *The Glens Falls Times*

              Typeset, Printed and Bound
              by Coneco Laser Graphics, Inc., Glens Falls, NY

              Printed on 70 lb. Finch Fine
              by Finch, Pruyn and Co. Inc., Glens Falls, NY

Dedication

This book is dedicated to the countless thousands of people, past and present—customers, shareholders, directors, officers, other employees, and special friends who have contributed so much to the success of our first 137 years as the leading banking association of the North Country.

CONTENTS

PREFACE

Corporations and organizations quite often record their history on special anniversaries like their centennial or their sesquicentennial—while this is not a special occasion, it seems like a good opportunity to record the history of this institution. In reading what another bank had done to commemorate a special event, it reminded me that we had a responsibility to take advantage of the people who had great recollections and for so long had an interest or an association with this bank, to perpetuate the records while the opportunity was present. With that in mind, I turned to Joe Barnes, who was not only a successful writer but a gentleman who had been associated with First National for more than forty years, to undertake the task of pulling together information from a wide variety of sources and weaving it into a publication which would record the more than 135 years of this proud institution. This has not been an easy task; Joe Barnes labored long and diligently in searching the files, minutes of the organization, personal accounts and any other resource that was made available to him to tell the story of First National and the role that this institution has played in providing financial services for people and businesses in the development of the North Country, beginning in 1853.

Joe Barnes has decided to tell the story of The First National by recounting the tenure of the eleven presidents that this bank has had; Joe worked with five of those eleven individuals.

I have enjoyed knowing more about the history of those who have contributed so much to the organization; my reading has raised a lot of questions . . . questions that probably can never be answered simply because the answers have been lost in time. One question that came to mind was related to Augustus Sherman, who was one of the founders and second president of this bank. Mr. Sherman, eighteen months earlier, was one of the principal organizers and a director of the bank that was to become known as the Glens Falls National Bank and Trust Company. What happened between December of 1851 and July of 1853 that took Augustus Sherman from one of the original directors of our principal competitor to become an organizer and director of this bank? Why Mr. Sherman would have left one bank to join the other is one of those interesting questions that shall probably remain unanswered. Then, too, there is the question of what were the circumstances surrounding the first president, William McDonald. He served for five years as the founding president, resigned or was not reappointed, and lived for a number of years thereafter in the area but was not associated in any way with the bank. Following Mr. McDonald, it is interesting to note that Mr.

Sherman, Jerome Lapham, William McEchron, Byron Lapham, Arthur Sherman and Maurice Hoopes all died while they were still active with the bank. It wasn't until Hubert Brown took early retirement in 1962 that a First National Bank president ever retired. Perhaps we can conclude that in the first hundred years, there may have been such a fascination for the job that no one ever wanted to retire . . . or could it be that the company didn't have a very attractive retirement plan? These answers are also lost in time.

The company, our directors, and all of our employees are grateful to Joe Barnes for this labor of love. He has woven together stories of old, legends, the lives of some very interesting people, as well as the times that made First National what it is today and what it has meant to those who have lived and worked in the North Country during the time this institution has been in existence.

I would like to publicly disclaim any responsibility relating to the reported record of the undersigned as it was Joe Barnes' idea. However, I confess that I found it generous and flattering and for that, I am eternally grateful.

William L. Bitner III
Chairman of the Board &
Chief Executive Officer

THE PRESIDENCY OF WILLIAM McDONALD
1853-1858

The year was 1853—a very good year in which to establish a new bank, which would later become known as The First National Bank of Glens Falls, New York.

The promise of prosperity permeated the world of business, at that time, in a village thriving with activity surrounding the Feeder Canal—the transportation link that, in 1832, had unlocked the potential of the area.

It was very befitting that William McDonald was elected President of the new banking institution, chartered by the State of New York as the Commercial Bank of Glen's Falls. (Note the original spelling as Glen's.)

Mr. McDonald was perceived as a man of vision and perseverance. It is said that to him, more than any other man, is due the credit for opening up the resources of Glens Falls and vicinity.

As a member of the State Assembly from Warren County, he had obtained, in 1821, a survey and an appropriation for the construction of the Feeder Canal. He was so highly regarded that only seventeen votes were cast against him in town in his bid for return to the Assembly the following year.

McDonald's foresight proved correct. The hamlet of Glen's Falls prospered and in 1839 was incorporated as a village with 1270 inhabitants. Because of the nearby vast forest lands, the production of lumber was naturally the most prominent industry, closely followed by lime, lath, black marble, and grist mills that surrounded the falls.

The founders of the Commercial Bank correctly felt that McDonald's prestige, power, and presence would enhance the stature of the new bank. He had foreseen that the canal would become the highway for starting local products on their way to world markets, thus bringing great prosperity to the area. The founders reasoned that now there was both need and opportunity for financial services beyond what then was available locally.

At that time in history, in most communities, the general store was naturally the center of its business life, and every merchant performed, in some fashion, the functions of a banker. The country storekeeper's trade was based principally on a system of barter. Whatever money there was usually found its way into his pockets. Thus he naturally became the banker for the community.

Notes were given for trifling amounts, even for a few shillings. The storekeeper accepted these notes for payment for groceries and other commodities. Men who had credit would pay small accounts by orders for certain commodities directed to the store-keeper. When nothing else would suffice, the storekeeper would be asked to advance cash in small amounts.

There were many such merchant bankers throughout the State of New York. Formally chartered state banks were few and far between. In fact, it appears that no legislation for banking was passed by the New York State Legislature until 1782 when the City of New York had less than 25,000 inhabitants.

By 1851, the Feeder Canal and the Big Boom on the Hudson River had made it possible for Glen's Falls to become the lumbering capital of the nation. Boats loaded with lime, lime-stone, and black marble from local quarries added to the traffic on the canal and the prosperity of the community.

It was apparent that the community needed proper banking facilities to accommodate its fast-growing commerce at the state, national, and international trade levels. One bank had already opened its doors on December 1, 1851. It was chartered as the Glen's Falls Bank, eventually to become the Glens Falls National Bank and Trust Company, and a longtime competitor of First National.

So it was that in December 1852, two men set out to solicit subscriptions to the proposed new bank. One traveled North, the other South. One of these men was Augustus Sherman, who became the second President of the bank, in 1858.

Records do not reveal the name of the other solicitor.

Their goal had been to obtain $150,000 capital.

When the solicitors returned in January 1853 and reported the results of their efforts, it was revealed that the total of the subscriptions secured amounted to $136,400.

At a meeting of the incorporators, at which the men reported, it was suggested that rather than delay progress until the full $150,000 was subscribed, some of the subscriptions be reduced to make the total equal to a more preferable capitalization of $125,000. The two men stubbornly refused, maintaining that too much effort had been expended in securing subscriptions to now have them reduced. It finally was decided to accept all subscriptions and capitalize the bank for $136,400 with 2728 shares at $50 par value.

Of the 429 original investors, only seven men purchased 100 shares or more. The two largest investors, William McDonald and Dr. Bethuel Peck, each purchased 160 shares; Keyes P. Cool, 150 shares; and four others, C. F. Austin, G. A. Austin, A. A. Cheney, and Augustus Sherman, 100 shares each. Most of the original investors purchased ten, twenty, or forty shares of stock. Jerome Lapham was among them with a purchase of ten shares. Keep in mind that annual incomes of $500 to $2,000 prevailed in those days.

A section of the bank's Articles of Association provided for, ''a Board of Directors which shall consist of not less than nine and not more than thirteen persons, each of whom shall own at least twenty shares of the capital stock of the association, a majority of whom shall reside in the County of Warren, and all of whom shall reside in the State of New York.''

The first thirteen Directors elected were James C. Clark, Keyes P. Cool, Lewis Hunt, William McDonald, James Morgan, Bethuel Peck, Hermon Peck, Joseph Russell, Augustus Sherman, all of

Glens Falls; Erskine G. Clark, Sandy Hill; Quartus Curtis, Queens-bury; William W. Rockwell, Hadley; and William H. Warren, Moreau.

At the first meeting of the Directors on March 21, 1853, Keyes P. Cool was appointed Chairman of the Board and James C. Clark, Secretary of the Board.

Lewis Hunt, Augustus Sherman, and James C. Clark were appointed a committee to obtain a Banking House. Hunt was chairman. Within a month, they gave E. Hubbard a binder of $200 toward the $2,581 purchase of the Sherwood Building adjacent to the Glens Falls Hotel on the west side of what was then known as "The Four Corners," later as "Fountain Square," and still later as "Bank Square." In 1990, the original bank location is now known as the "Old Braydon and Chapman building" on the corner of Glen Street and Hudson Avenue and is currently occupied prima-rily by Domino's Pizza Parlor.

The formal election of William McDonald as President took place at a meeting of the Board of Directors on April 19, 1853. Dr. Bethuel Peck was elected Vice President. It was also "approved and carried that the chairman appoint a committee of three to put the Banking House in order."

However, the bank had considerable difficulty finding a Cash-ier. The minutes of a meeting of Directors on April 26 reveal that a letter had been received from one John J. Lee declining to be an applicant for the position. At the same meeting, the Board decided to offer the position to Isaic Fowler of Ballston Spa. He also declined.

Subsequently Isaiah Scott, Cashier of the Bank of Vergennes, Vermont, indicated that he would be receptive to an offer. At a meeting on May 5, 1853, the Secretary of the Board was instructed to inform Mr. Scott that the Board of Directors had accepted his proposition to take charge of the newly formed bank as Cashier upon the terms proposed by him. This included, together with fees as a Notary Public, an annual salary equal to $1,500. As Cashier, he also served as Secretary to the Board and kept the minutes of the meetings (handwritten in a large, bound book). On July 12, 1853, Charles Thompson was elected teller.

By-Laws for the bank were adopted on July 26. One of the original was that "all employees be required to take an oath of faith to the bank and promise to preserve secrecy in all matters of business conducted by the bank." Although amended many times, the original by-laws are still in effect, and the rule of secrecy is still in force.

It is interesting to note that Article Four of the original By-Laws stated, "All of the Clerks and Servants of the Bank, except the President and the Vice President and Directors, shall give bonds to the Bank, be approved by the Board with one or more sureties in such sums as the Directors by resolution shall determine and their salaries and involvements shall in like manner be determined by the Board and the same shall be paid quarterly."

On November 13, 1853, Orange Ferris, Esq., was appointed as the first attorney for the bank.

On July 11, 1854, "Mr. Charles Thompson was elected teller for the present year at an annual salary of $600." Paradoxically that was the same as the salary for an entry-level employee in 1936. However the waiting period before receiving any pay, in the '30s, was only one month rather than the three months practice in the 1850s.

The bank opened its doors for business about August 1, 1853, confident that there was plenty of business for two banks. One month earlier, the other bank had reported total deposits of $75,000. Within twenty-two months, the newly formed Commercial Bank had deposits totaling $90,000 and total resources of $355,000.

Originally, the banking hours were from 9:00 A.M. to 4:00 P.M. except on Sundays, Christmas Day, New Year's Day, and the 4th of July, which were specified holidays. Later the hours were changed to 10:00 A.M. to 2:00 P.M., then 8:30 A.M. to 4:00 P.M.. Several changes have taken place since those days to meet the changing needs of banking service in the community.

In 1853, the year the bank opened, the New York Clearing House was also first opened. Another sign of an expanding nation was that Chicago was first reached by rail that same year. Locally, Col. Zenas Van Duzen founded extensive sawmill and lumbering operations at the Feeder Dam.

At the first annual meeting of stockholders on February 7, 1854, eleven of the original thirteen Directors were re-elected to the Board. William A. Fonda of Glens Falls replaced James C. Clark, and Jeremy Rockwell of Glens Falls had replaced William W. Rockwell of Hadley, in September 1853, having purchased his brother's shares of stock.

From time to time, weekly notations in early Board Minutes stated simply, "Discounting attended to, the Board adjourned," or "Board met as usual and adjourned."

By 1854 the whole nation was surging ahead. It was the year in which a detachment of U.S. Marines, led by Commodore Perry, landed in Japan and secured a favorable trade treaty from Japan, thus opening the country for Occidental trade.

At the bank's annual meeting in February 1855, Augustus Sherman was elected Vice President and continued to serve as a Director. Henry Ferguson, Levi Hatch, and Enos Howland became new members of the Board.

The following year, 1856, found Ira Harris, Ruliff Kipp, and Charles Richards replacing Enos Howland, Bethuel Peck, and Hermon Peck on the Board.

In 1856, the Republican Party was founded with John C. Freemont as its first presidential candidate. But he was beaten by James Buchanan, the first bachelor President of the United States, and who preceded Abraham Lincoln.

William McDonald, the bank's first President, continued in office until he resigned at a meeting of the Board of Directors on November 30, 1858, because of advanced age and the need for more time for his private affairs. He died September 11, 1870 at the age of 86.

William H. Warren also resigned on November 30. Their vacancies were filled by Linus B. Barnes, who had joined the bank in August, and by James Morgan, who rejoined the Board.

By now, only five of the original thirteen founders were still on the Board of Directors. Some others had come and gone, so that a total of twenty-four men had served on the Board during its first five years.

Augustus Sherman was duly elected President at the November 30, 1858 meeting, and Linus B. Barnes, Vice President.

Directors during Presidency of
William McDonald, 1853-1858

* **Erskine G. Clark	1853-1866
*James C. Clark,	1853-1853 Sep
*Keyes P. Cool	1853-1857
*Quartus Curtis	1853-1854
Henry Ferguson	1855-1864
**William A. Fonda	1854-1866
Ira Harris	1856-1860
Levi Hatch	1855-1864
Enos Howland	1855-1856
*Lewis Hunt	1853-1854
**Ruliff Kipp	1856-1891 May 2 died
* **William McDonald	1853-1858 Nov 30 resigned
Pres 1853-1858	
* **James Morgan	1853-1854
VP 1861-1873	1858-1873 Oct 25 died
U. G. Paris	1858-1858
*Bethuel Peck	1853-1856
VP 1853-1856	
*Hermon Peck	1853-1856
Charles Richards	1856-1856
Jeremy Rockwell	Sep 1853-1853
*William W. Rockwell	1853-1853 Sep
*Joseph Russell	1853-1858
Isaiah Scott	Jly 1854-1859 May 1 resigned
* **Augustus Sherman,	1853-1884 Dec 13 died
VP 1855-1858	
Pres 1858-1884	
Daniel Sweet	1857-1864
*William Warren	1853-1858 Nov 30 resigned

24 men served on the Board during the term of William McDonald
  6 of whom were still Board members at the time of conversion to a
  National bank in 1865
1 who succeeded him as President

 * Member original Board
** Member 1865 conversion to FNB

Augustus Sherman.

THE PRESIDENCY OF AUGUSTUS SHERMAN
1858–1884

When fifty-seven-year-old Augustus Sherman assumed the role of President of the young and thriving bank, he was already thoroughly familiar with its operation, having been one of the principal organizers, an active member of the Board from inception, and Vice President for the past three years.

The Presidency was a role he played well from November 30, 1858, until his death on December 3, 1884, two months short of his 84th birthday.

His twenty-six years of service, as President, have proven to be the longest, to date (1990), of any of the bank's eleven Presidents during its 137-year history.

It is worth noting at this point that Augustus Sherman was also one of the founders of the Glen's Falls (National) Bank in late 1851. No explanation has been found as to why he set out a year later to form another bank, the Commercial Bank of Glen's Falls.

During his term of office, he wrestled with problems brought on by the Civil War, the loss of the bank building in the great fire of 1864, the transition of the bank from a state to a National Bank, the Financial Panic of 1873–74, another devastating fire that leveled part of the business district of the village in 1884, and sundry other problems.

He was already a man of considerable stature in the area when he became President. But he was not a person who had been "born with a silver spoon in his mouth."

According to all accounts, Augustus Sherman was truly a

19

self-made man in every sense of the word. His only opportunities for a formal education were derived from winter attendance in such schools as the sparsely settled lumber districts in the area could afford. This was in addition to one winter of schooling in his native Arlington, Vermont, from which his parents moved to Kingsbury when he was five years old. So it is not clear as to when he received that schooling.

Early in life he learned the lessons of exhaustive rough manual labor working with his father in the mingled pursuits of farming and lumbering. By the time he was fifteen years old, he was hauling horse-drawn loads of lumber, alone, to Albany, attending both to sales and purchases, with the care and thoughtfulness of an adult.

With the opening of the Feeder Canal, he was, if not the first, among the first to place a boat on its waters for the transportation of lumber.

His first venture in the lumbering business, on his own, was at age nineteen, running an old English mill, with two saws, which stood on a small stream that empties into the Hudson near Fairfield (now Luzerne). At the same time he was running a grist mill nearby. Later on, he moved his operation to the Feeder Dam and with increased facilities began the manufacture of lumber on a larger scale. Thus, he laid the foundation for the princely fortune he subsequently attained.

Year by year, with increased means at his command, his lumber operations became more and more extended until they assumed colossal proportions. His lumber land investments resulted in lucrative returns. He seemed to have the gift of the golden touch.

A vigorous man, he had other talents, too. He was the father of thirteen children, nine by his first wife, who died in 1848, and four by his second wife, whom he married eight years later when he was fifty-five years old.

Possessed of rare good judgment and strong common sense, his investments, numerous and varied as they were, prospered in every direction. Subsequently, he obtained, according to local historian Dr. A. W. Holden, an aggregate fortune equal to, if not greater than, that of any person in Warren County.

Fourteen years before he became bank President, Augustus Sherman built a home at the corner of Glen Street and Hawkeye Street. In his honor, the street name was changed to Sherman Avenue. His home became the first building in Glens Falls to be named to the National Register of Historic Places. It is still a gracious building and provides a meeting center for Senior Citizens and others.

At the same meeting at which Augustus Sherman was elected President, James Morgan and Linus Barnes were elected to the Board to replace William McDonald and William Warren, who had assigned and transferred all their bank stock. Morgan was returning to the Board after having been absent for nearly four years.

Within two months, Isaiah Scott, the Cashier, gave notice that "he wished to leave the Bank on May 1, 1859." Charles Thompson, the teller, did likewise. These were the two key operating people in the bank.

Frederick A. Johnson Jr. was hired immediately as Cashier and Emmett T. Johnson as teller to familiarize themselves with the details and effect a smooth transition.

In 1861, James Morgan replaced Linus Barnes as Vice President. Also Gustavus Austin was replaced on the Board by Charles Fowler of Chestertown when it was realized Austin was ineligible because of his residency in Vermont. In October of that year, Henry Crandall was rendered ineligible for Board duty by the sale of his stock and was replaced by Lifelet (Eliphelet) Harris.

The winds of war were blowing, and in 1861 President Abraham Lincoln declared war, asking for "75,000 volunteers to put down the rebellion in the South." It was called "The War of Rebellion," later known as the Civil War. The next four years proved to be the darkest in the nation's history. Before the war was finished, Lincoln had to call for an additional 300,000 troops.

In the meantime the bank wanted to keep abreast of the expanding means of communication, and in 1863 contributed to a telegraph line between Glens Falls and Fort Edward.

Bank business was expanding too, and the Cashier was instructed to employ a Boy (Yes, a capital B, according to the minutes) as additional help in the bank. "Boy" was a job title in those days.

In addition to accepting deposits and making loans, one of the most important functions of a bank in those days was printing currency ("bank notes"). The value, or "discount rate" of the bank notes changed almost daily, in accordance with the bank's reputation, its location, and the amount of notes in circulation at any given time.

There was a high degree of currency stability in New York State and Ohio because each bank honored bank notes of other banks within these states at the same discount rate. In fact, the systems of these two states became the models used by the federal government in 1863 when it passed the National Currency Act.

Salamon P. Chase, Secretary of the Treasury at that time, estimated that there were seven thousand different kinds of currency circulating in the United States. Legislation, sponsored by Chase in 1863, authorized Congress to charter national banks and bring stability to the currency market. It gave those banks the exclusive right to issue a uniform national currency called "national bank notes," based on the market value of the federal government bonds pledged as security by each bank. In 1865, Congress levied a 10% tax on all other currency.

National bank notes, which were soon called "greenbacks," remained the major form of currency in the United States until 1913. The note-issuing privilege conferred on national banks by the 1863 act expired in 1935. A few notes issued by First National and other nationals are still outstanding. These will be paid at face value if presented through any commercial bank to its Federal Reserve Bank.

This is a facsimile of an old $20 bill issued by the First National Bank on March 17, 1905. It is signed by bank officers, Byron Lapham, President, and A. W. Sherman, Cashier, as well as officials of the U.S. Treasury. The number 980 is the charter number for First National Bank of Glens Falls as a national bank.

Notice that the bill is secured by "United States Bonds or other securities" deposited by the bank, with the Treasurer of the United States.

Currency of the period was larger than it is today (1990). It measured 3 1/8 x 7 7/16 inches. Current bills measure 2 5/8 x 6 1/8.

(This facsimile courtesy of John E. Rafferty)

The minutes of February 24, 1864, reveal that "The matter of getting new plates for five and ten dollar bills was postponed for the present." Conjecture would lead us to believe that the Directors already were considering the feasibility of becoming a national bank.

Of more immediate concern to Glens Falls was the great fire of May 31, 1864 which leveled 112 buildings, including all but three in the village center. It emphasized the urgent need for a reliable water system. The bank was destroyed with a loss of $4,000, of which $2,000 was covered by insurance. Cash, records, and other valuables were saved. The fire started in the Glens Falls Hotel, next door to the bank, and the Commercial Bank building was next to burn. The other bank was just two doors away, and it too soon burned to the ground.

The Commercial Bank resumed business in temporary quarters in the Glens Falls Insurance Company's building on Glen Street, which was located on the lower corner of what is now Lapham Place. The only indication in the minutes that the old building had been destroyed is a resolution which appeared later authorizing the Cashier "to rent offices upstairs in the new building to Morgan and McEchron for $125 a year." The "new building" was the one erected on the site of the old banking house and which the First National continued to occupy until 1915. Years later, it was greatly remodeled, and with a third story added, is still (1990) standing on the corner of Glen Street and Hudson Avenue.

FIRST NATIONAL BANK, GLEN'S FALLS.

In 1864, business was booming in the area, and a paper mill was erected by the Glen's Falls Paper Mill Company, which was the forerunner of one of the greatest paper companies in the world, the International Paper Company. It was on the factory site now (1990) covered by the James River Corporation in South Glens Falls.

In December 1864, Frederick A. Johnson Jr. resigned as Cashier. Emmett T. Johnson was promoted from teller to replace his father, effective January 1, 1865. Emmett held that position for forty-two years, until his death February 3, 1907.

In 1864, Postal Money Orders were first issued.

By the close of 1864, the bank was able to report profits of $39,406 and deposits totaling $250,106, and resources of $524,000.

A sad commentary, reflective of the times, appeared in the minutes of January 28, 1865, referring in particular to Daniel Brown, who had been a Director for only one year. It reads, in part: "On the 24th day of December 1864, Daniel V. Brown and Edward Riggs were appointed a Committee by the citizens of this town to proceed to some southern city with funds—and authority to obtain recruits to fill the quota required from this town under the call of the President of the United States for 300,000 troops.

"And whereas—in the dispensation of Providence, it has seemed best that the Divine Will should be made manifest in a peculiar manner—in the death of Daniel V. Brown by the sinking of the *Melville* the vessel on which he with his associate were passengers, on the 8th day of January 1865, while in the performance of a high and honored duty, which the voice of our community and the call of his country imposed upon him."

Ironic that a villager filed a claim for $125 "for reimbursement of my gold watch which I loaned to Daniel for his trip."

The year 1865 would prove to be a very eventful one for the bank and the nation. Minor though it may sound, the first formal Discount Committee was formed on February 5, thus delegating the responsibility of reviewing and authorizing the loans made or rejected each week. The full Board was kept apprised of major loans but devoted most of its attention to ponderous matters confronting the bank and the community, among them the matter of converting to the new National Banking System.

On March 11, 1865: "President Augustus Sherman and Cashier, Emmett T. Johnson were instructed to proceed to Washington, D.C., to make necessary arrangements for changing the bank in accordance with the new national system."

Prior to this there had been much discussion and a flurry of activity pertaining to the filing and exchange of various documents, which had to be forwarded to Washington and to the New York State Banking Department while seeking authority for conversion to the national system.

Several pages were devoted to Certificates of Authority, Notice of Officers, Rules pertaining to same, Notices filed with the Comptroller of the Currency in Washington, D.C., the Depository Authority, and the Depositing Authority Treasurer of the United States Division of National Banks.

First National was required to "forward $50,000 in U.S. Stocks to the Treasurer of the United States as security for Government deposits of the 16th Congressional District."

Finally, Certificate of Authority No. 980, dated April 5, 1865, was received from the Comptroller of the Currency, and the bank changed its name from Commercial Bank of Glen's Falls to The First National Bank of Glens Falls, and began operating as a national bank under its new charter. The original of this historic document was suitably framed and is still carefully preserved in the bank's Board Room.

No. 980

Treasury Department,

Office of Comptroller of the Currency,

Washington, April 5th , 1865.

Whereas, by satisfactory evidence presented to the undersigned, it has been made to appear that "The First National Bank of Glens Falls" in the village of Glens Falls in the County of Warren and State of New York has been duly organized under and according to the requirements of the Act of Congress entitled "An Act to provide a National Currency secured by a pledge of United States bonds, and to provide for the circulation and redemption thereof," approved June 3, 1864, and has complied with all the provisions of said Act required to be complied with before commencing the business of Banking under said Act:

Now, therefore, I, Freeman Clarke , Comptroller of the Currency, do hereby certify that "The First National Bank of Glens Falls" in the village of Glens Falls in the County of Warren and State of New York is authorized to commence the business of Banking under the Act aforesaid.

In testimony whereof, witness my hand and seal of office, this Fifth day of April , 186 5

sgd Freeman Clarke
Comptroller of the Currency.

In conjunction with this conversion, it had been necessary for the owners of two-thirds of the capital stock of the Commercial Bank to authorize the Directors to make the necessary organization certificate to change and convert the bank into a national association under the provisions of an Act of Congress. Such a vote was easily accomplished since all but 369 of the total 2728 shares were at that moment owned by the members of the Board of Directors who had been buying up the stock as it became available. Five of those twelve men owned 2205 shares, and there now was a total of only twenty-four shareholders.

A resolution read, in part: "We do hereby make and execute this organization certificate with a capitalization of $136,400, which shall be divided into 2728 shares of $50 each as it is now divided in the said Commercial Bank of Glen's Falls."

They voted to have all the Directors continue in office and to become the original Directors of the reorganized bank. All of them did, other than Charles I. Fowler of Chestertown. There is no explanation as to why he was off the Board at the time of the actual conversion. He did reappear on the Board in 1866 replacing Erskine Clark.

The eleven men listed as Directors of the bank under its new identity as The First National Bank of Glens Falls and the number of shares each owned were as follows:

Augustus Sherman	Glens Falls	659 shares
James Morgan	Glens Falls	841
Jerome Lapham	Glens Falls	455
Samuel Pruyn	Glens Falls	160
Alexander Robertson	Glens Falls	90
Ruliff Kipp	Glens Falls	20
William McEchron	Glens Falls	20
William A. Fonda	Glens Falls	20
William H. Gayger	Glens Falls	54
Lifelet Harris	Queensbury	20
Erskine G. Clark	Sandy Hill	20

Of that group, three had been founders of the original bank, namely Augustus Sherman, James Morgan, and Erskine Clark. Two others, Jerome Lapham and William McEchron, were later to become Presidents of First National.

Currently, Augustus Sherman continued as President and James Morgan as Vice President.

It's worth noting here, that Alexander Robertson had also been a founder of the competing Glen's Falls Bank, yet became a Director of our bank in 1862.

Perhaps Glens Falls was affected by the national economic chaos that immediately followed the Civil War. But, if so, there is no evidence to suggest that First National experienced any difficulty coping with the situation.

The growing village of 3,600 people was busily engaged in lumber, lath, lime, marble, and grist mills, and girding itself for a post-war economic boom. Among other things, ground pulp (made from four-foot logs) was first used in 1867 for making paper, and it had a tremendous impact on our local economy.

Samuel Pruyn, a member of the First National Board, was actively involved with Daniel J. and Jeremiah W. Finch in expanding Finch, Pruyn and Company into the paper-making field. Successor generations of those families and their spouses have played important roles in the First National history, as will be explained in later chapters.

The railroad, a division of the Delaware & Hudson Canal Company, was extended in 1869 from Fort Edward to Glens Falls, establishing yet another link to widening markets.

As shown by old records, Augustus Sherman was associated either as a trustee, director, manager, or president in nearly all of the monied corporations in the area at that time. He was the first President of the Glen's Falls Paper Mill Company, as well as the Bald Mountain Lime Company. Also, he served as an active Director of the Glens Falls Insurance Company. In the late '60s and early '70s, he erected a costly block of stores and offices which bore his name, and which were described as "an elegant addition to the village, a monument sacred and equal to his memory." He was enjoying the well-earned fruits of his early toils and was considered a true patriarch of his times.

The late '60s and '70s were periods of growth and great prosperity. But prosperity also attracted elements other than legitimate businessmen. During the night of January 6, 1870, the neighboring bank (two doors away) was burglarized. On the following day, at a Special Meeting of the First National Board, a resolution was adopted to the effect that "in consequence of the misfortune of our neighboring banking friends, we tender to them the use of our safe and vault, together with other necessary accommodations, which in their present unpleasant and no less unenviable situation they may find themselves in need."

The Board evidently was impressed that its own quarters were scarcely less vulnerable, because five days later they voted to buy beds and bedding to have the teller and clerk sleep in the bank, and the Cashier was instructed to procure a watchdog. Cutler J. DeLong was the teller and E. W. Goodman the clerk. In consideration of their sleeping in the bank, the Directors increased their annual salaries to $1,200 and $500 respectively.

The Board of Directors had been reduced to only nine members by 1870 and remained so through 1875. There is little likelihood that it was a "rubber stamp" Board as evidenced by the vote on November 1, 1873, to fill the vacancy in the office of Vice President when James Morgan died. The tally was four votes for Jerome Lapham and three for Samuel Pruyn. T. J. DeLong replaced Morgan on the Board in January 1874.

A puzzling thing happened in 1872. Why did the Board of Directors fail to meet for eight consecutive weeks from late August to mid October, and again the first two weeks in November? There had been a similar, although shorter, seven-week gap in meetings in 1870. No explanation has been found.

Business was booming with shirt, collar and cuff manufacturers beginning to locate in the village after an adequate supply of water had been developed. This was about the time the Wilkie Reservoir was constructed on the slopes of West Mountain. The bank was continuing to pay an 8% semi-annual dividend to shareholders.

Little of a spectacular nature was noted in the minutes that related to the Financial Panic which swept the nation in 1873, although there were many notations relating to action taken on past-due notes of businessmen in the community. Compassion certainly was revealed in phrases such as "if possible make some arrangement for the payment or security of this note which has been so long overdue."

In the ensuing years, the bank continued to prosper and became known as one of the strongest financial institutions in Northern New York.

The bank protested to the Town of Queensbury that bank stock was exempt from taxation. Then on December 24, 1875, a dividend of 8% (free of all taxes) was declared.

Few bankers of that day were aware that Alexander Graham Bell had just obtained his first patent, in 1876, on an instrument that someday would become vital to their business. How could any bank operate today without telephones?

Scattered through the Board minutes are many interesting items. On June 30, 1877, the Board decided to sell "gold now on hand," and on December 10 of that same year approved the sale of an iron post to one M. Coffin for $5, the amount to be credited to profit and loss.

On November 21, 1878, the Board adopted a resolution which said, "Taking pride in the successful and honorable administration of the affairs of this bank by Augustus Sherman, its President for the past nineteen years, his picture be permanently kept in a suitable space in the Directors' Room, will be received, cared for and always regarded as a cherished keepsake by this bank." No further mention was made until March 10, 1883, when the minutes read: "The elegant picture of Augustus Sherman was received today through the politeness of Mrs. Sherman, to be hung as noted in previous minutes."

The following entry in the minutes of December 15, 1877, seemed strange: "Decided to divide up the combinations of our locks with Glens Falls National Bank and Sherman & Johnson (private bankers) instead of keeping them all with S. & J. as heretofore."

S. & J. was also Augustus Sherman's bank. In those days, "private bankers" engaged in the business of buying and selling stocks, bonds, specie, commercial paper, and U.S. government securities. Most would be classified today (1990) as investment bankers.

On November 25, 1879, the Cashier, Emmett T. Johnson, agreed with the Directors on the need to reduce bank expenses and voluntarily proposed that "the salary of the Cashier be reduced, after January 1, 1880, and be fixed at $2,000 per annum." To which the Board replied, "We recommend that the carrying out of such in our opinions to be a very commendable proposition on his part."

It is worth noting here that in 1879 *The Glens Falls Times* was established as the first daily newspaper in the village. One year later, electricity was first generated in a sawmill near Feeder Dam.

The rate of interest on deposits was set on September 11, 1880 at 2% in concurrence with the other bank. They each agreed to notify the other, in writing, thirty days in advance of any anticipated change in rates. Such collusion would be illegal in 1990.

In the early 1880s, the population reached 7,000 in Glens Falls, about 3,000 in South Glens Falls, and the nation topped 50,000,000. 1880 was also the year in which three young women graduated from Glens Falls Academy with New York State Regents Diplomas. One year later, a Union Free School District was organized—and still generates business for the bank.

A striking example of the slowness with which news traveled in those days is furnished by this item in the minutes for July 2, 1881: "On motion, the Cashier was requested to drape the front of the banking house in mourning for thirty days in case the rumored assassination of President Garfield, just received, proves true."

A notation in September 1881 stated: "A Night Watchman's Time Detector has been purchased and its use commenced this night. The key to be hung by a chain running through the front door of the Bank attached to a hook on the inside of the door." The watchman was paid $1.50 per night, that expense being shared by the banks, the Glens Falls Insurance Company and others in the village business district.

By 1882, Glens Falls had become widely known as the most industrious, wealthiest, and most progressive place of its size in the State of New York. This was the year the railroad was extended to Lake George, introducing more wealth to the area.

To those of you interested in long-term investments, perhaps it is appropriate to remind you that the Brooklyn Bridge was opened in 1883.

Fred T. Russell was hired as "Bank Clerk" on April 21, 1884, at a salary of $75 per year upon his furnishing the usual bond in the sum of $4,000. Before the turn of the century, he sometimes wrote the Board minutes and had authority to write bank drafts and make small loans. Old-timers remember stories of Fred as the "bachelor man-about-town" with a colorful carriage and a team of spirited horses. Fred was promoted to teller, and held that position throughout his sixty-three years in the bank. Well into his seventies, the old bachelor sometimes grew crotchety with the pace and volume of business at a teller's cage in the late 1930s. But he was very kind to new young people on the staff.

Fire, in April 1884, once more destroyed a portion of the village business district, this time on the East side. But, the same as before, better and more modern business blocks and residences rose on the sites of the old structures.

The death of Charles I. Fowler, who had served as a Director since 1861, was reported in the minutes of July 26, 1884, and a laudatory resolution recorded.

And before the year ended, there was another. The minutes of December 6, 1884, read: "RESOLVED that as a mark of respect and sorrow for the sudden and unexpected death of Augustus Sherman, late, the honored President of this bank, the members of this Board will attend a funeral in a body. That the Bank be suitably draped in mourning and be closed on the day of the funeral from noon until 3 o'clock p.m. That the employees of the bank be invited to attend the funeral with us and that a committee of three be appointed by the Vice President to prepare suitable resolutions of mourning and respect to be presented at the next regular meeting."

December 13, 1884: "Whereas Augustus Sherman, for twenty-six years the honored President of this Bank, *(twenty years as FNB, six years as the Commercial Bank)* has been suddenly and, although ripe in years, quite unexpectedly called to that bourne from whence no traveler returns. Therefore resolve that Mr. Sherman's relations with this bank as a Director and its President since its first organization (as a National Bank) are worthy of his high commendation and of enduring commemoration.

"In many respects he was a remarkable man and his was a remarkable career. Always kind and considerate of the views and opinions of his fellow Directors, always carefully weighing the reasons which others deemed sufficient for influencing and controlling their actions. Always ready to receive, and prompt to digest and act upon information from any source, his evaluation, his discriminating and excellent judgment was rarely at fault and has been of the greatest service throughout the whole history of the bank.

"To us personally, he was a friend. He has presided over this Board during all this long period in harmony and without jar. While exacting in his ideas of the industry, frugality, and enterprise which should characterize those engaged in the business affairs of life, he had a high respect for such attributes, especially in the young.

"To some extent they were regarded as necessary virtues. Never unmindful that by a little mindful accommodation, the deserving might be sustained, the young beginner be started on the road to business prosperity and great usefulness as that assistance such as the bank could give might tide over the unexpected, unforeseen or accident troubles occasionally occurring from time to time."

Directors during Presidency of
Augustus Sherman, 1858–1884

Alson B. Abbott	Jly	1877–1894	Aug 28 shotgun
Gustavus Austin		1861–1861	ineligible
Nathaniel Barker		1861–1861	
Linus B. Barnes	Nov	1858–1861	
VP 1859–1861			
Daniel Brown		1864–1865	Jan died
* **Erskine G. Clark		1853–1866	
Martin Coffin	Aug	1867–1891	Jan
Henry Crandall		1860–1861	Oct sold stock
Theodore J. DeLong		1874–1908	May 12 died
Henry Ferguson		1855–1864	
**William A. Fonda		1854–1866	
Charles I. Fowler		1861–1864	
		1866–1884	Jly 24 died
**William H. Gayger		1862–1898	May 29 died
**Lifelet Harris	Oct	1861–1867	
Ira Harris		1856–1860	
Levi Hatch		1855–1864	
**Ruliff Kipp		1856–1891	May 2 died
**Jerome Lapham		1860–1898	Nov 7 died
VP 1873–1884			
Pres. 1884–1898			
**William McEchron		1865–1906	Sep 2 died
Pres. 1898–1906			
* **James Morgan,		1853–1854	
VP 1861–1873		1858–1873	Oct 30 died
**Samuel Pruyn		1861–1896	June sold stock
**Alexander Robertson		1862–1869	
also founder at GFNB			
Isaiah Scott	Jly	1854–1859	May 1 resigned
Melville A. Sheldon		1876–1890	Jan 9 died in London

* **Augustus Sherman   1853–1884 Dec 5 died
    Pres. 1858–1884
    D. W. Sherman   1876–1894 Dec 10 died
    Daniel Sweet   1857–1864

27 men served during Presidency of Augustus Sherman
 3 were on the original Board
11 were on the Board at time of conversion to FNB
 2 would become future Presidents of the bank

 * Member original Board
** Member 1865 conversion to FNB

Looking north at corner of Glen and Bay streets long before construction of the Glens Falls Insurance Company building on the plot then surrounded by a white picket fence. The Episcopal Church is in the background left and is still in use in 1990.
(Courtesy of Dr. John E. Barnes)

Jerome Lapham

THE PRESIDENCY OF JEROME LAPHAM
1884–1898

Jerome Lapham presided over First National during a time of bustling activity and prosperity in the village and the nation. His term began while the community was still resurrecting itself from the ravages of the devastating fire of 1884.

Shortly after taking office, he asked that the Board of Directors again be increased, to thirteen members. It was. Three stalwarts of the day, Byron B. Fowler, Jonathan Coolidge, and William E. Spier, were selected and served with distinction. Byron B. Fowler served for fifty-one years until he died in May 1936 at the age of ninety.

A self-made man, Jerome had very little formal education other than grade school and one year at the Glens Falls Academy. Yet he became a member of the State Assembly after having been Town Supervisor many times, as well as having held all the minor posts in town government.

He was employed as a farm boy at the tender age of twelve. He worked as a canal driver, boat hand, teamster, and served a considerable apprenticeship in the mercantile business for James Morgan. He became a partner, invested heavily in a tract of forest land, then a canal freighting and transportation line, expanding it to eight boats.

With persistent effort, he reached an enviable height of financial success. By the time he was forty, he sold out his interest in the business and retired to devote his time to public service and improvements of the community. Three years prior to that, in 1860, he had been elected to the Board of the Commercial Bank.

A very public-spirited man, he shared both his time and money in the interests of his fellow-man. In 1864, when the community was required to raise $100,000 to pay volunteers (to prevent a military draft), the Commercial Bank contributed $16,400, the other bank $13,400, while Jerome Lapham, alone, contributed upwards of $10,000.

It was not until he was sixty-one years old that Jerome Lapham became President of the bank. He had been on the Board for twenty-five years, and Vice President since 1873, having replaced his old partner, James Morgan, in that position.

Strange circumstances surrounded Morgan's death. It is claimed that two strangers appeared at Morgan's door in the late evening telling him that his horses were creating a disturbance. He lit a lantern and entered the barn to investigate. The stable burst into flames. Morgan was found burned to death, next to one of his favorite horses. No one else was known to have seen or identified the strangers.

Jerome Lapham combined his stewardship of the bank with the needs of the community. He joined other trustees of the Glens Falls Academy in their efforts to provide opportunities for education equal to that of the best English and classical academies of the day. He was the ideal person to be selected as the first President of the Glens Falls Board of Education, from 1881 to 1886, and remained a member for the rest of his life.

Among other things, he pressed for more development of the enormous water-power capacity from the falls; the financing of a horse-drawn trolley car system between Glens Falls, Hudson Falls, and Fort Edward; improved fire protection methods and equipment in the village, including the personal bankrolling of the Jerome Lapham Fire Engine Company. He was involved in anything that would improve the standards of scholarship, culture, and business life in the area.

In June of 1887, First National opened an account with the National Commercial Bank of Albany for the purpose of clearing checks and other instruments. Many benefits accrued to both banks in a strong relationship that prevailed for more than eighty years.

At the end of December 1887, the minutes deal with the first internal defalcation ever experienced by the bank. It was a situation where a bookkeeper also was responsible for a supply of cash. The employee was fired. And rules were established to forever prevent the commingling of such duties.

In 1888, the bank purchased a new time lock for the safe for $125, replacing the one then in use.

Soon, another first was recorded. "F. F. Pruyn, teller, was granted a ten day vacation in 1888." Apparently vacations were unheard of for workers in those days. Periodically, thereafter, Pruyn was granted varying short vacations. But there was no mention of vacations for others.

It's worth noting that during this period, the wealthy were constructing, for themselves and their posterity, attractive large and valuable mansions in the village. Employment was high. Business flourished.

There were many notations in the minutes regarding various actions taken to safeguard the interests of the bank in relation to loans, drafts, and mortgages.

In those days, the Directors also closely involved themselves in any decisions regarding the hiring of any person, as evidenced by this excerpt from the minutes of September 8, 1888: "The President, Cashier, and Mr. Abbott were appointed a committee to consider application of Walter P. Leavens and if found in their judgment a desirable selection to fill the clerkship vacancy occasioned by the resignation of H. G. Crandall, to engage his services at once. Also look up any other Boy or boys suitable for the position and report."

The following week, "The committee was granted additional time to look up a Boy to fill the vacancy."

The bank was actively granting loans to out-of-town firms. The Cashier traveled to New York City to buy short-term business paper for $10,000, $20,000, and $40,000 at 6% and U.S. 4% bonds.

The Board busied itself seeking more collateral and additional endorsement on notes when warranted.

Politeness prevailed in the bank's dealings with its loan customers, as evidenced by a phrase seen often in the minutes: "Tell Mr. _____ we prefer that his note for $1,000, due the 26th, be paid in full rather than attempt to renew it." A much gentler touch than the stereotypical flat "No."

On the other hand, firmness would be applied sometimes to those in high places, as revealed on June 13, 1891: "Resolved that the Cashier be instructed to notify Mr. Darwin W. Sherman (an FNB Director) that his account is overdrawn $3,473 and that he be requested to conform to the regulations of the bank regarding the keeping of his account."

In December 1891, the Board granted a line of credit to the Glens Falls Savings and Loan Association.

Only two increases in salary were granted in 1892, of $100 to each of the bookkeepers. No other raises. Yet, within a month, the Cashier corresponded with the Department of Treasury in Washington to ascertain if National Banks were allowed to declare dividends other than semi-annually, in January and July. Then on June 25, a regular semi-annual dividend of 8% was declared, followed two days later by a Special Extra Dividend of 50%.

Later that year, answering a proposal from a Washington, D.C. lawyer, the Board advised the lawyer, "that should he succeed in recovering a portion of the assessments that have been levied annually since 1875 by the U.S. Treasurer for expenses of redemption of circulating notes at this Bank, we will return him one-third of the amount recovered. Should he not succeed, no expenses to be incurred by this bank." No record found, so apparently he failed.

Two years later, another legal firm solicited a $10 contribution from the bank to stop the further collection of that tax, as explained in the following letter:

A. S. PRATT & SONS,

NATIONAL BANK ATTORNEYS,

THE SUN BUILDING.

PUBLISHERS OF
PRATT'S DIGEST OF NATIONAL BANK LAWS, $2.
PRATT'S MANUAL OF GENERAL BANKING LAW, $2.
"HOW TO ORGANIZE A NATIONAL BANK," 25 CENTS.
THE BANKERS' ECLECTIC (MONTHLY), $2.

Washington, D. C. _____ Jan. 26, 1894. _____ 189

Dear Sir:

    The suits brought for the purpose of testing the validity of the statute under which the tax is collected on the notes of the National banks are now on the calendar of the Court of Appeals of the District of Columbia, and will be reached next month.

    If successful, these suits will stop the further collection of that tax. We have competent legal advice that the chances of success are excellent.

    About $2500 more is required to pay counsel fees, and as your bank would be largely benefited by a favorable decision, we write to ask if you will contribute $10.00 towards this expense.

    If you contribute, briefs of counsel, with statement of the case will be sent you.

    Any further information you may desire will be furnished you.

    Very truly yours,

[signature]

E. T. Johnson Esq. Cash
First Nat'l Bank
Glens Falls. N.Y.

JEROME LAPHAM, President.
Wᴹ Mᶜ ECHRON, Vice Prest.
E. T. JOHNSON, Cashier.

980.

CAPITAL $ 136,400.
SURPLUS $ 150,000.

THE FIRST NATIONAL BANK,

Glens Falls, N.Y. _____ 189__

Sample of bank stationery in 1892 showing signature of Jerome Lapham

In 1893, the Merchants National Bank of Glens Falls opened for business. First National increased from 2% to 3%, the interest paid on Special Deposits. And the Board enacted another increase, of a different nature, when they "Decided to require the employees of this Bank to furnish a bond of indcmnity in the amounts as follows: Cashier, $15,000; Teller, $8,000; 1st Bkkeepr, $5,000; 2nd bkpr, $4,000; Boy, $2,000."

Emmett T. Johnson, who had served as Cashier since January 1865, was elected to the Board at the annual meeting in January 1894, and also retained his position as Cashier.

Near the end of that summer, the community was shocked by the death of Director Alson B. Abbott as described in the newspaper article reproduced on the next page.

An 1892 view of Fountain Square before Merchants National Bank replaced Peck Grocery on corner of Ridge and Glen streets. Glens Falls National Bank occupied first building on the left. Third building (narrow two-story) was home of First National Bank until 1915. Note the first utility poles and electric power lines in the village.

(Courtesy of Dr. John E. Barnes)

RESULT OF THE INQUEST

The Coroner's Jury Brings in a Verdict in Accordance With the Facts.

Mrs. A. B. Abbott is resting a little easier today, after the sudden shock of yesterday, and her friends say she exhibits a remarkable fortitude in bearing her terrible affliction. In compliance with her wishes the funeral will be held from the house on Thursday afternoon at 2 o'clock. The Rev. John R. Crosser will officiate.

Coroner F. B. Streeter decided yesterday afternoon, after consultation with the immediate relatives, to hold an inquest. The following gentlemen were empaneled as a jury: M. L. Wilmarth, foreman; Henry Cronkhite, John D. Wright, Hiram Holley, Charles A. Hovey, John L. Landon and James C. Root. They viewed the remains, and examined Alson M. Abbott yesterday afternoon, and then adjourned until this morning at Dr. Streeter's office.

Only two witnesses were examined this morning, Dr. T. I. Henning and Albert W. Harris. The doctor's testimony was short and merely developed the fact that Mr. Abbott was dead when he arrived, a few moments after the accident.

The testimony of Albert Harris was that of an eye-witness of the greater portion of the incidents which led to the accident. He said Mr. Abbott was in plain view from where he sat waiting for Alson, and that several times he looked up and saw Mr. Abbott busy with the gun. He said that Mr. Abbott went into the little office to fix the gun for Alson; it was a single-barreled breech-loading gun, and was out of repair; Mr. Abbott was in plain sight all the time in front of the desk in the office. There was no door between the room in which he sat and the office; portieres were hung, but they were spread wide apart. As he heard the report of the gun he jumped to his feet and saw Mr. Abbott fall to the floor; did not stop to see how badly he was hurt, but ran immediately for a physician.

After a consultation by the jury, which lasted two minutes, they brought in a verdict that the late A. B. Abbott came to his death as the result of the accidental discharge of a shotgun, while he was engaged in cleaning it.

At a meeting of the officers and directors of the First National Bank of Glens Falls, held this morning, the following was unanimously adopted:

While sharing with the whole community the shock of sorrowful surprise at the sudden removal from the sphere of his usefulness, we by the closer relations into which we have been brought with Mr. Abbott, are especially affected with a sense of loss. With the community at large we have recognized his consummate abilities, brilliant and accurate scholarship, public spirit, and honorable bearing but by reason of the more intimate association we have come to have a high regard for the kindliness of spirit, the dignified courtesy of manner, thoughtful consideration of the feelings and interests of others, strict integrity of character, and his connection with this bank—his conscientious and valuable service, extending over the long period of his association with us.

We extend our sympathy to the deeply afflicted family of our deceased friend, and in token thereof direct that a copy of this minute be forwarded to Mrs. Abbott; and that we attend the funeral services in a body.

The Board of Directors of the Glens Falls Insurance Company held a special meeting at the company's office this morning, when the following minute was adopted:

The sad and sudden death of Hon. Alson B. Abbott early yesterday morning brings us together to record another vacancy in our membership. Mr. Abbott was elected a member of this Board of Directors in January, 1878, and for more than sixteen years since, has continuously served in and with this body, in promoting the interests of this corporation. His scholarly equipment, large reading, studious habits, quick perception, aptness of expression, and earnestness of conviction and purpose; his genial manner, warm friendship and decided integrity of character, contributed much to the deliberations and decisions of this Board, and added delightful qualities of fellowship and personality which will be a lasting remembrance of our deceased associate.

It is ordered that our flag be floated at half mast from the company's building; that this Board attend his funeral in a body; that these minutes be entered in the record of proceedings, and that a copy be sent his bereaved family with our sincere sympathy.

In 1895, the New York State Armory was completed on Warren Street and continues to be a highly visible landmark in Glens Falls.

Evidence of the bank's conservative stance can be seen in minutes later that year when the Board decided to grant a merchant $75,000 on his line of discount, "he furnishing as collateral security—mortgages on his store, his homestead, and timberland in addition to security we now hold."

In those days, mortgages were short-term instruments as were notes. Most notes were written for one, two, or three months. Some would be granted for as long as six months.

This excerpt from the minutes of April 18, 1896 seemed a bit incredulous: "Harry H. Whipple engaged as clerk, commencing April 13. Salary to be decided hereafter." No further mention of his salary appeared until September 26. "Committee on Salaries reported the salary of Master Harry A. Whipple, as Clerk, fixed at $75 per year commencing last April 1." So it appears, Whipple worked six months before being advised or getting any salary.

The first mention of safe deposit boxes for customers was made in February 1897 when the bank decided to buy a set of such boxes from Herring, Hall, and Marvin Co. for $425. Rental was $2.00, $4.00, $6.00 a year.

In April of that year, a loan of $1000 was granted using Bolton and Lake George Telegraph stock as collateral.

When a company did not pay its obligation, here's what could happen: "The Safe, Desks, Chairs, etc. bid in by the Bank on judgment against the Conkling Ore Co. at $50 were sold to the G. F. Portland Cement Co. for $100."

The form letter, reproduced below, is self-explanatory. Also shown is a copy of a notice posted in the bank lobby and published in a local newspaper.

--Form 571.
(Ed. 7-22-'96—5,000.)

IMPORTANT

Treasury Department,

OFFICE OF THE

COMPTROLLER OF THE CURRENCY,

Washington, D. C., October 15, 1896.

Address Reply to
"COMPTROLLER OF THE CURRENCY,"
. . . . . D. C.

To the Cashier.

SIR: You are respectfully informed that the shareholders of a national bank may amend its articles of association at a meeting *specially* called for the purpose.   Where the articles of association (not the by-laws) make no provision for the length of notice, each shareholder must be given thirty days' notice, either by publication in a newspaper or by mail, of the meeting, and the notice must mention the article or articles to be amended.

If at such *special* meeting a resolution be adopted amending the articles of association, a *certified* copy of the amendment, *under seal of the bank,* together with a copy of the notice given shareholders, showing date of issue, should be promptly forwarded for the files of this Office.

If you contemplate changing in any manner the articles of your bank at the *next annual meeting,* you should give notice as above, irrespective of any provision in the by-laws to the contrary.   If this course is not pursued, the proceedings, so far as amendment of articles is concerned, *will be illegal.*

Great trouble and delay result from failure on the part of the banks to strictly observe the rules relating to amendments, and if you will act in accordance with the suggestions herein contained it will result in mutual advantage to your association and this Office.

Respectfully yours,

James H Eckels

Comptroller.

NOTICE.

The annual meeting of the stockholders of the First National Bank, Glens Falls, N Y., for the election of directors, will be held at their banking office, on **Tuesday, January 11, 1898,** at 10 o'clock a. m.
12-10d4toew   E. T. JOHNSON, Cashier.

DEC 10 97

Here's an indication of the type of investments being made by the bank in the late 90s. June 25, 1898: "Cashier reported the sale of $10,000 Union Pacific 4% @ 97 3/4 and purchase of $10,000 Chesapeake & Ohio 4 1/2's, at 83 1/2. Also the purchase of Louisville & Nashville and the purchase of $10,000 Atchinson."

Resources of the bank were reported as $1,728,000; deposits, $1,380,000; capital, surplus and profits, $298,000.

A Special Meeting of the Board was held on November 7, 1898. The minutes read: "Convened for the purpose of passing suitable resolution on the death of our lamented President, Mr. Jerome Lapham, who died on Saturday, November 5, 1898, at 10 o'clock p.m. THAT the bank be closed during the hours of the funeral on Wednesday, November 9th, and that the Directors and employees attend the funeral in a body."

On November 12, 1898, William McEchron was unanimously elected President, and Byron Lapham elected Vice President.

Looking north on Glen Street across Fountain Square in the early 1880s.
(Courtesy of Carol J. Lauer)

Directors during Presidency of
Jerome Lapham, 1884–1898

Alson B. Abbott	Jly	1877–1894 Aug 28 shotgun
Merritt Ames		1896–1911 May 30 died
Martin Coffin	Aug	1867–1891 Jan resigned
Jonathan M. Coolidge		1885–1912 Nov 12 died
VP 1907–1912		
Theodore J. DeLong		1874–1908 May 12 died
Byron B. Fowler		1885–1936 May 2 died age 90
VP 1913–1936		
**William H. Gayger		1862–1898 May 29 died
Emmett T. Johnson		1894–1907 Feb 3 died
Teller		
Cashier 1864–1907		
**Ruliff Kipp		1856–1891 May 2 died
Byron Lapham		1891–1929 Feb 25 died
VP 1898–1906		
Pres. 1906–1929		
**Jerome Lapham		1860–1898 Nov 5 died
VP 1873–1884		
Pres. 1884–1898		
**William McEchron		1865–1906 Sep 2 died
VP 1891–1898		
Pres. 1898–1906		
**Samuel Pruyn		1861–1896 June 13 sold stock
		replaced by Warren Weaver
Melville A. Sheldon		1876–1890 Jan 9 died
VP 1887–1890		in London
Arthur W. Sherman		1894–1916 Feb resigned
replaced George Parks	Jly	1917–1930 Jly 3 died
2nd VP 1905–1906		
VP 1906–1907		
Cashier 1907–1929		
Pres. 1929–1930		
Darwin W. Sherman		1876–1894 Dec 17 died

William E. Spier		1885–1901 May 9 died
William H. Weaver	June	1896–1902 Oct 16 died
H. McKie Wing		1895–1933 Jan 9 died age 86
		in California

19 men served on Board during Presidency of Jerome Lapham
 5 of whom were Directors at time of conversion
 2 who would become Presidents of the bank

** Member 1865 conversion to FNB

View of the William E. Spier mansion on Glen Street just north of the Episcopal Church. The area behind the fence is now (1990) part of a parking lot for employees of Continental Insurance Company.

Note the stately elm trees which lined all the main streets and others of the city. In time, they formed cathedral-like domes here and there.

The elms became infected with Dutch Elm Disease. Hundreds of trees had to be cut down by foresters in the 1950s, 1960s, and 1970s.

(Courtesy of J. Erwin Barnes)

William McEchron

THE PRESIDENCY OF WILLIAM McECHRON
1898-1906

William McEchron, like his two predecessors, had carved out a name for himself and a fortune from the lucrative lumbering business and related activities. He was respected as a leader in every worthy movement in the community and was well known for his many philanthropic contributions.

He gained a reputation for looking quietly at all sides of a problem, preferring to listen until the more vociferous had worn themselves out. When he spoke, others listened.

He was born in "old" Saratoga, (now known as Schuylerville). The family moved to Fort Edward when he was eight where he went to the Common Schools, as they were then called. Later he was sent to the Argyle Academy. He was a descendant of Donald McEachron (note spelling) and Anna McDonald, who came to this country in 1738 with Scottish settlers of the Argyle Patent in Charlotte (now Washington) County.

When he assumed leadership on November 12, 1898, at age sixty-seven, he was the last of those who had been on the Board at the time the bank converted to a National Bank in 1865. Now there were three banks in the village square, a trust company farther up Glen Street, two banks in Hudson Falls, one in Fort Edward, and soon to be one in South Glens Falls, offering more competition.

Growth was rampant in the area, providing more and more opportunity for the banks and the community.

The industrial situation had changed. Grist mills and the marble quarries were now playing minor roles having been replaced by the gigantic plants of the International Paper Company and Finch, Pruyn and Company, which were turning out about 200 tons of newspaper and 120 tons of ground wood pulp daily. The Imperial Wall Paper Company was establishing its roots on lower Warren Street. Production of lime was still vigorous. Most of this activity took place along the shores of the river. Elsewhere in the village, shirt, collar and cuff factories were producing for world-wide markets. The Terra Cotta Works, a firm which made brick and fancy tiles, was located at what was then considered a remote spot off the Ridge Road. Mr. McEchron was a Director of that company.

March 1899 was a busy month for First National. The bank borrowed $50,000 from GFNB at 3%, $50,000 from the National Commercial Bank of Albany at 4%, and $50,000 from the National Park Bank of New York at 3 1/2%—on three-month notes signed by the President and the Cashier. It was common practice in those days for strong banks to borrow from each other whenever they found opportunities for sound investments at higher rates of return.

On July 29, 1899, "The Cashier was directed to ship to New York $10,000 in gold coins, and $10,000 in Greenbacks, and obtain a $20,000 Ctf for same."

The village now boasted a population of 14,600 and the nation would exceed 76,000,000 in the 1900 census.

In the summer of 1900, architect E. B. Potter was engaged to prepare plans for changing the interior of the Banking House. No further mention in the minutes and no photos of the interior lobby have been found.

However, we did discover an old photo of the work area behind the teller windows, as shown on the opposite page. We have been unable to find anybody who can identify any of the four bankers, or the customer, in this scene.

When was this photo taken?

Who knows? Some contend it was in the 1880s: others believe it was shortly after the turn of the century. In any event, it had to be before the bankers vacated the old building in 1915.

Work area of the old bank.

Why was the bookkeeper wearing a hat? Note how he was standing on a wooden platform; the bow ties, the overflowing wastebasket, the window open for ventilation, the massive books in which to maintain customer accounts, the gas lamps, which antedated electric lights. Electricity was available in the village in the 1890s, and it's assumed that the bank switched to electric lamps during that period. If so, the 1880s seems like a plausible date for the photo.

Also note the large general-ledger book on the center table, in which the bank's records were summarized and hand posted daily. This same size book was still being used in the early 1940s.

Abandoned lime rock mines (or quarries) which had produced fortunes for enterprising businessmen in the 1800s.

(Courtesy of Penny B. Sandora)

Fractional currency was issued by a special act of Congress in 1854, but the public disliked the small size of the paper money, and its use soon dwindled.

An 1899 issue of a $5.00 silver certificate honored the American Indian on its face.
(Courtesy of Nelson E. and Viola L. Smith)

The above check reveals the frugality of customers and bankers at the turn of the century. No point in printing new checks. Simply overwrite the old date.
(Courtesy of George F. Reger Jr.)

The first typewritten minutes appeared in the minute book in early 1901. Since it was a bound book, the typewritten sheets were pinned to the pages. No paper clips were available at that time. Straight common pins pierced the sheets and the pages.

Gray E. Safford was first employed as a clerk for the summer of 1902. An interesting notation was found penciled in the margin of a minute book. ("This is where Gray E. Safford began his banking career.") Another notation was found ("Inscribed by G. E. Safford, 1941") which stipulated that "in the winter of 1903-04, GES was re-employed as clerk on an annual basis."

In October 1902, a resolution was adopted when Director William H. Weaver died. It is difficult to imagine that he contributed much to the Board. He had replaced Samuel Pruyn when Pruyn sold his stock in June 1896. But in the ensuing six years, Weaver attended only one meeting a year, two of those to attend the funerals of other Directors. Weaver had been a close personal friend of William McEchron, and a Director of the National Commercial Bank of Albany, and, as a lumber broker, an important link with Albany during the heyday of McEchron's involvement in the lumbering business.

In November 1902, the First National borrowed $50,000 from Glens Falls National at 4%, and five days later bought $50,000 International Paper Co. receivables. A week later, they borrowed another $50,000 at 4 1/2% from National Commercial Bank of Albany.

Early in 1903, minutes stated: "Decided to change our Agent at Washington, D.C., from J. D. Patten to the Riggs National Bank of Washington, D.C. This change made at the suggestion of the National City Bank of New York in their letter on file." Dealing with government agencies was a problem even back then.

In order to obtain New York State deposits, the bank was required to furnish a $30,000 bond as security through Fidelity & Deposit Company of Maryland in December 1903.

A few months later, the bank bore the cost of obtaining new Indemnity Bonds on employees as follows: "Cashier, $15,000; teller, $10,000; bookkeeper, $10,000; 2nd bookkeeper, $5,000;

Whipple, $5,000; M. Potter, $4,000; and Safford, $2,000." Previous to this, each employee had to pay for and provide his own bond.

Perhaps influenced by Mr. McEchron, the first *paid* fire department was organized in the village in 1903. On the other side of the coin, the old plank toll road from Glens Falls to Lake George ceased to exist the following year. The toll had been twelve cents for one horse, double that for a team.

Thinking of the old wooden plank toll road brought to mind a vision of all the lumber required for that nine-mile stretch of highway. But, in those days there was a great abundance of lumber available locally. As evidence, we found that William McEchron, as secretary of the Big Boom Association, had compiled some mind-boggling figures that put the lumbering industry in perspective during the last half of the 1800s. His tally revealed that 2,461,800,000 (TWO BILLION) feet of lumber flowed through the boom from 1851 to 1878. No wonder fortunes were made by men who later became bankers.

YMCA building on Glen Street before a street (known in 1990 as Lapham Place) was cut through to the left. The bank's white marble structure was erected on the site occupied by the house shown in the left corner.

(Courtesy of June E. Walsh)

Each spring, a virtual sea of logs, jammed the Hudson River from shore to shore at the Big Boom, a giant herding pen for the logs. All logs had been felled by axe and hand-cut with crosscut saws in the Adirondacks. Horses were used to skid the logs into piles on the ice and along the riverbanks.

The end of each 13' 9" log bore the mark of its owner. Rivermen used long pike poles to sort the logs into individual company holding booms.

Also still going strong were the thirty lime kilns that produced the purest, whitest lime found on the continent, when properly calcined. Some 400 to 500 men were employed cutting stone from the quarries, stoking 30,000 cords of wood a year to keep fires going night and day, and drawing 250 to 300 barrels of lime from kilns every seventy-two hours.

Newspaper advertising was entirely foreign to the bank until May 1904 when "It was decided to place an ad in *The Toiler* for three months at a total cost of $12.50." Perhaps the best advertising the bank enjoyed was the high regard the community held for William McEchron, its President. It was he who, prior to becoming President, had been the key person to influence others to form a YMCA in the village. It was planned at first as a friendly sort of place to counteract the influence of the numerous saloons in town.

Mr. McEchron motivated others into action when he said, "I will be happy to erect a building for the YMCA." And he, together with his friend, William E. Spier, planned to do so. They proposed the massive five-story brick and brownstone structure which still stands on the corner of Glen Street and Lapham Place.

Actually it turned out that McEchron and Spier soon conspired to enlist financial support from wealthy lumberman Jones Ordway, and were surprised when Ordway said, "I will be happy to provide a building for the YMCA."

Ordway, (or Ordaway, as his name is spelled on the stately column marking his family lot in the Bay Street Cemetery), contributed the main gift of $50,000 (a huge sum in those days). And so it was, that the three of them provided not only a structure, but a fully-equipped interior as well. It included an auditorium bearing the name "Ordway Hall," and an impressive gymnasium.

Mr. McEchron served on the YMCA Board as long as he lived and left, in his will, the "Y's" first endowment bequest.

He was also a very liberal contributor to the old Methodist Church on Warren Street, and in a very meaningful sense, to the new beautiful edifice on Bay Street.

Along in the 1890s, there was a movement among the Methodists to erect a larger church building to accommodate their need for more space. Mr. McEchron was a trustee, and a member of the Quarterly Conference. He said, "If the people will build such an institution, (meaning a new church), I will give $50,000 to start the work going."

And he did.

The congregation raised another $100,000 through direct pledges. The Warren Street property was sold to the Roman Catholic Church, Mr. McEchron making it possible by a gift of $5,000 to the Catholic Church. He was a true Christian both in spirit and practice.

In due time, St. Mary's Academy was erected on the site of the old Methodist Church on the corner of Warren and Church Streets.

The cornerstone for the new church on Bay Street was laid in June 1905. It was dedicated, free of debt, September 20, 1907. But the man, whose generosity had made the beautiful edifice possible, was not there to witness the ceremonies. He had already gone to his heavenly reward.

During his lifetime, his concern was not for the young alone. He also donated the large white house on the corner of Prospect and Warren Streets as a home for "old ladies." It had been the former home of the bank's first President, William McDonald.

His own beautiful home on the corner of Ridge and Maple Streets was later donated to a worthy cause and has been used for many years as a community Health Center.

Liberal as he was, his granddaughters could not tease him into installing two different telephone systems in their house. There were two systems in town. They wanted to be able to talk with "all" their friends.

He was frequently a delegate to various State and District Conventions, a member of the Canal Investigating Commission in 1898-99, and an active Director of the Glens Falls Insurance Company.

In June 1905, the bank "Decided to purchase through Spencer Trask & Co., $45,000 of American Telephone and Telegraph Co. five-year gold notes due 1907 at 1 3/4 premium, 4% basis."

A month later the Bond Committee became concerned about the proper safekeeping of securities belonging to the bank. Arthur W. Sherman was sent to New York and rented a safe deposit box at the National Park Bank for $125 a year.

Near the end of the year, Arthur W. Sherman was elected Second Vice President of the bank with a salary of $1,500. His duties were not defined other than "he is hereby instructed to keep a record of the absence of any of the employees of the bank during the ensuing year. Also to ask all employees to try and arrive at the Bank in time for business at 8:30 a.m."

It is not clear why the problem of tardiness kept popping up from time to time in Board minutes.

Hardly worth mentioning, but in March of 1906, the secretary started pasting typewritten minutes into the official minute book. Among them was a resolution to send $15 to the New York State Bankers Association for the purpose of the bank paying its share toward the expense of the association.

Another long-time relationship was born for the bank in 1906 when the Cashier was authorized to obtain a Bond of $200,000 as security for New York State deposits, "said Bond to be procured of the Agency of C. W. Cool." (Now the Cool Insuring Agency, Inc.) Its present chairman, Warren E. Rouillard, has been a member of the bank's Board of Directors since October 1970.

The first mention of an examination by outside examiners appears in the minutes of June 16, 1906. It stated, "Letters from the Comptroller at Washington calling attention to the Bank Examiner's report were read as was also our reply." In the absence of any negative comments, it can be assumed the report was a favorable one.

What was then described as the "new" High School Building was erected on Glen Street in 1906. And historians of the day credited Glens Falls with having one of the best Union School Systems in the country, standing second to none.

Testimony to the bank's profitability was seen in the minutes of July 7, 1906: "Decided to transfer from Profit & Loss to Surplus a/c $264,552." Resources of the bank, at the beginning of the year, were reported as $2,990,000; deposits, $2,463,000; capital, surplus and profits, $450,000.

The minutes of May 12, 1906, briefly mentioned "Mr. McEchron is sick, but the doctor reports his symptoms are better." He attended only one meeting after that, and died on September 2, 1906.

Katherine Cunningham justifiably extols the virtues of her grandfather in her book *William McEchron, 1831–1906, Homely Recollections,* published in 1962. She reveals a great deal about the McEchron family life.

She also proudly quotes from the bank's minute book which, at the time of his death, speaks of "a feeling of sadness closely akin to that of a family from which a beloved member has been taken. And in this case, that member was one upon whom all depended, to whom all looked for guidance and counsel, for courage and support.

"We, who have been so closely associated with him in his business life, bear loving witness to his kindness, his gentleness, his courtesy, his generosity, his helpfulness, his patience, and his integrity. In business, as in his private life, he was ever a Christian gentleman, and his influence will long be felt by those who have in any way come into close relations with him."

Directors during Presidency of
William McEchron, 1898–1906

Merritt Ames		1896–1911 May 30 died
Charles W. Cool		1905–1932 Sep 24 died
Jonathan M. Coolidge		1885–1912 Nov 12 died
VP 1907–1912		
Theodore J. DeLong		1874–1908 May 12 died
Byron B. Fowler		1885–1936 May 2 died age 90
VP 1913–1936		
Emmett T. Johnson		1894–1907 Feb 3 died
Teller		
Cashier 1864–1907		
Byron Lapham		1891–1929 Feb 25 died
VP 1898–1906		
Pres 1906–1929		
**William McEchron		1865–1906 Sep 2 died
VP 1891–1898		
Pres 1898–1906		
Patrick Moynehan		1903–1920 Jan 19 died
		17 yrs to the day
Frederick H. Parks		1899–1906 May 25 died
Arthur W. Sherman		1894–1916 Feb resigned
replace George Parks	Jly	1917–1930 Jly 3 died
2nd VP 1905–1906		
VP 1906–1907		
Cashier 1907–1929		
Pres 1929–1930		
William E. Spier		1885–1901 May 9 died
William H. Weaver	June	1896–1902 Oct 16 died
H. McKie Wing		1895–1933 Jan 9 died age 86
		in California

14 men served on Board during Presidency of William McEchron
1 who had been a Director at time of conversion
2 who would become Presidents of the bank
** Member of Board during 1865 conversion to FNB

Time Frame
History in Headlines
On or about Wednesday, January 10, 1906

1/4   U.S. Bolsters Philippine Garrison.

1/9   South Glens Falls School Bids Received. None Accepted.

1/12   Plans Being Made for Wing Family 4th Reunion in Glens Falls.

1/12   National Collegiate Athletic Association Formed. Last Year 154 Injured and 18 Died Playing Football.

1/19   Luke Wright Named First U.S. Ambassador to Japan.

Commodities Then & Now (Year)		
	1906	1990
Dow Jones Ind	$98.09	$2,750.64
Gold, oz	20.67	391.19
Silver, oz	.61	5.04
Copper, lb	0.20	1.03

President: Theodore Roosevelt
Vice Pres: Charles Fairbanks

Prices Then & Now (Year)			
	1906		1990
Bread, loaf	$ 0.04	$	1.17
Milk, gal	0.30		2.02
Butter, lb	0.28		1.39
Gasoline, gal	0.05		.98
New Ford Car	600.00		10,995.00
Annual Income	1,074.00		25,050.00
New Home	3,395.00		91,945.00

On This Day in History

1738— Ethan Allen, American patriot is born.

1863—Florida secedes from the Union; joins confederacy.

Firsts, Fads, Things

Photocopier, victrola, nickelodeon Films becoming popular.

Major Events of the Year

San Francisco hit by major earthquake. Digging begins on Panama Canal. Voice and music radio broadcasts begin. President mediates an end to the Russo-Japanese War.

Winners in the Arts

Actor: Henry Miller in *The Great Divide*
Actress: Fay Templeton in
    45 Minutes from Broadway
Movie: *Dream of a Rarebit Fiend*
    Produced by Edwin S. Porter
Best Seller: *White Fang*
Big Movie: *The Kleptomaniac*

This Year in Sports

W. Series: White Sox beat Chicago Cubs. College Football Champion: Princeton. Stanley Cup: Montreal Wanderers. Kentucky Derby: Sir Huon. Football legalizes forward pass.

Byron Lapham

THE PRESIDENCY OF BYRON LAPHAM
1906–1929

Byron Lapham was elected President and Arthur W. Sherman Vice President on September 15, 1906, two weeks after William McEchron died. The office of Second Vice President was discontinued. Then during October and November, George Chahoon Jr., Walter P. Leavens, and William J. Townsend were elected Directors.

Byron Lapham was the son of Jerome Lapham, who had been President from 1884 to 1898. He was first elected to the Board in 1891, then became Vice President in 1898.

The roots of his association with leaders of the bank go back to 1866 when he graduated from Albany Commercial School and went to work for Augustus Sherman in a grist mill. Some time later, he bought the mill and operated it as Lapham and Company.

It's appropriate to mention here that Lapham's Vice President, Arthur W. Sherman, was the grandson of Augustus Sherman and had been on the Board since 1894. As Vice President, Sherman was paid $1,800 a year, just $100 more than teller Fred Russell. And, up to this point, there has been no mention of any salary for any President.

The fifty-three-year-old practice of allowing the Cashier to keep protest fees was discontinued when the revised Board decided, "The fees will go to the Bank as it is wrong in principle and contrary to custom to have any officer of the Bank receive the same." The Cashier's salary was set at $2,700. This was a raise of $100, the first in five years for Johnson.

Five weeks later, the following, seemingly innocuous entry, appeared in the minutes: "Cashier housed with a cold since last Thursday." Ten days later he died.

Arthur W. Sherman resigned as Vice President and was elected Cashier to replace Johnson. He was already a member of the Board. Jonathan M. Coolidge became Vice President.

As early as 1907, the Directors were exploring the feasibility of erecting a new building, but in May of that year canceled a proposal with Hoggson Brothers of New York. Inevitably, the idea would resurface within a few years.

The first mention of a sizable loss appeared in mid-year when the Directors decided to charge off $25,167.38 to Profit and Loss to cover loss in depreciation in the bank's Security Account.

In 1908 Glens Falls was proclaimed "the largest, richest, most progressive village in Northern New York." It was also the year when the signature of Governor Charles Evans Hughes (a Glens Falls native) created it a city, the 46th in the state, and the year the 46th state was added to the United States.

Charles W. Cool, a member of the First National Board, was elected the first Mayor of the city.

A grand chorus of prosperity sang out in the city, now identified as an important manufacturing center where were located some of the largest and finest plants of their kind in the world. The bankers dealt with manufacturers in many lines: lumber, paper, pulp, lime, Portland cement, shirts, collars, cuffs, ladies' shirtwaists, paper boxes, flour, Joubert & White buckboards, brick, ale breweries, lanterns, machinery and foundry products, confectionery, gold and silver refining, and more. All of this in addition to heavy mercantile business made diversity the order of the day for the bank.

All the main streets were paved with brick, asphalt, or macadam. Electric light and power were provided by the Spier Falls Dam. The best water in the state, for drinking or manufacturing, was supplied by gravity from reservoirs in the nearby Adirondack foothills.

During this period, more people were being added to the bank staff along with an adding machine and a second book-keeping machine.

The first mention of a loan relating to automobiles appeared in 1909 when the bank loaned $2,600 to Miller Brothers of the Glens Falls Garage Company. There would be many more loans to the garage for cars, but not to individuals.

1908 During this period, the motto was developed which guided First National for many years, "Prudence Points the Way".

In April 1909, the Board "voted to extend to Mr. Gray E. Safford the best wishes of the directorate upon his forthcoming marriage and to present him with $100 in gold coin as a further token of our appreciation and sincere regard which we hold for him."

During that year, the bank was actively granting loans to out-of-town business firms, from Albany to Port Henry, for as much as $50,000. Also the Board sentiment was "very strongly in favor of high-class investments even if the return thereon was not more than 4%."

The New York State Bankers Association held its convention at the Sagamore on Lake George July 15–16, with First National serving with other Glens Falls banks on the entertainment committee.

Starting in January 1910, the bank paid 2% interest on checking accounts with balances maintained at $1,500, and 3% on balances constant at $10,000 or more.

Some individuals in town were being granted loans of $40,000 or more on their signature alone. The Comptroller of the Currency criticized the bank for "excessive loans," but there was no evidence of loan losses.

In 1911, the bank renewed its contract with the Pinkerton's National Protective Agency and also contracted for an electric alarm system with the Electric Bank Protection Company, stipulating that the company conduct demonstrations of the system for the benefit of the public.

Shortly thereafter, the bank issued $50,000 more in bank currency. It also applied to the Board of Trustees of the U.S. Postal System to have First National designated depository of the Postal Savings Fund for Glens Falls. It was accomplished within a month.

The bank broadened its lending to include paper in amounts of $5,000 and $10,000 each from many well-known national firms of the day, such as Johns Manville, Bethlehem Steel, Swift Refrigerator & Transportation, Omaha Packing, Central California Canneries, Lord & Taylor, General Motors, and many others. The records also reflected the purchase of many accounts receivable from a variety of firms.

The volume of notes had increased to such an extent that only a segment of the demand notes, for instance A-B-C-D, were reviewed by the Discount Committee each week. The system kept the Board mindful of what loans were in file and was a means of control and audit over the Note Department.

It is worth mentioning here that one of its major customers, McMullen-Leavens Company, requested the right to mark its checks PAYABLE AT THE FIRST NATIONAL BANK OF NEW YORK. The company had become internationally famous for its shirts, and this was to facilitate acceptance by worldwide vendors and faster payment of its checks. The New York City bank was authorized to pay all such checks to the extent of $25,000 daily and charge the account of First National in Glens Falls. Walter P. Leavens had been a member of the Board since 1906.

The Cashier reported an overdraft of nearly $10,000 by JRL as being unacceptable. This was understandable since an overdraft amounts to an unauthorized loan. The Cashier was instructed to grant an interest-bearing loan of up to $15,000 to Mr. JRL. A year later the problem resurfaced and the customer had to be reminded that he must look after his account a little closer "as it is not the policy of this bank to allow chronic over-drafting on the part of any of our customers."

Another prominent member of the community had a note which had been renewed time and time again for the past several years without reduction of principal. The Board deemed it best that the note be secured in some manner or be paid off. The Cashier was instructed to talk with the customer and use his best judgment for the present.

Starting in November 1911, the bank published a "General Letter on Trade Conditions" and each month mailed a copy to its commercial customers and to any other customers who wanted it. The public response was very favorable.

After considerable discussion in March 1913, the Board decided to hire the bank's first stenographer at $50 a month.

Byron Lapham was the first President to encourage education for members of the staff. In July 1913, "the Cashier was authorized to re-imburse Messrs. Safford and Koech, $75.38 which they had paid to Wharton School of Finance of the University of Pennsylvania for their instruction to date. It was further agreed on the part of this bank to continue to defray the expense of this course to the finish should the boys desire to continue."

Koech had been hired in 1907 as a clerk at $350 a year. It was not until late 1913 that the spelling of his name appeared as Koch: J. Albert Koch Jr., who later became the bank's operating officer and Safford's whipping boy.

Business had been good again in 1913, and on December 20, the Board resolved "that every employee of this bank be presented with $25 as a Christmas Gift in appreciation of services rendered during the year."

By now the Board had concluded that a new building was essential and selected a site on the corner of Glen Street and Park Avenue (now known as Lapham Place), paying $33,000 to Messrs. Hovey and Lapham. An additional five-and-a-half feet of adjoining property was purchased from the Coolidge Estate for $3,625.

The bank's other major concern was to respond to a communication from Washington which in essence required every national banking association "to signify, in writing within sixty days, acceptance of the terms and provisions of Section 2 of the Federal Reserve Act, passed by the Congress of the United States on the 23rd day of December 1913."

After due consideration of the terms and provisions of the act, the Cashier was directed to notify the Reserve Bank Organization Committee of the acceptance by the bank of the terms and provisions of the Federal Reserve Act and of the intention of the First National Board to subscribe on behalf of the bank to the capital stock of the Federal Reserve Bank to be organized in the

District in which this bank will be located after the geographical limits to be served by such Federal Reserve Bank have been fixed by the organization.

In April 1914, the bank was notified that it was located in District 2, attached to the Federal Reserve Bank of New York, and that it was required to pledge 6% of its unimpaired capital and surplus, which amounted to $26,184. This meant that First National was obliged to buy 262 shares, at a par value of $100 each, of the capital stock of the Federal Reserve Bank of New York.

The creation, by Congress, of twelve regional banks under the Federal Reserve System was good. Local banks now had the privilege of borrowing funds from the Fed without shopping among many banks for the best rate. Soon they would not have to maintain as many compensating balances with correspondent banks for the purpose of clearing checks. Many could be cleared by the Fed. This, of course, made more funds available for lending and investing. Members of the system are required to maintain reserves (deposit balances) equal to a percentage of their total deposits.

By varying the percentage of reserves required, and the rate of interest charged to member banks for borrowing, the Federal Reserve System was better able to exercise a measure of control over the nation's monetary supply. (Not the national debt. It is Congress that controls the nation's fiscal matters.)

After hearing a report from the National Bank Examiner in the winter of 1914, the Board agreed there was too large a surplus of cash in the Teller area. They decided to set aside $100,000 in cash in the bank's own safe deposit boxes or by renting a box in some other vault in the city. The only persons having access to the box would be the President, Vice President, and Cashier.

When salaries were increased in mid-February, the Cashier Arthur W. Sherman, received a boost from $3,500 to $4,500 with the understanding that he would no longer draw a fee of seven dollars per week for his services at Board or Discount Committee meetings even though he was still a Director.

Because the bank securities were locked in a safe deposit box in New York City, it proved very inconvenient for the Cashier to journey to the city whenever the bank needed to pledge securities for loans or to sell them when conditions were favorable. He complained. Then the Board authorized him to transfer up to $185,000 to the bank's own vault for better availability.

Glens Falls Feb 14, 1914
Traveling in winter was not easy in those days as one can imagine from the above scene. The narrow, white, two-story building was the one occupied by the First National Bank from 1864 until June 1915.

(Arthur S. Fisher Collection)

Would the bank loan money to a woman in those days? Yes. Records reveal a loan of $30,000 to Helen E. Foulds on her signature alone.

Some customers were borrowing heavily, using shares of Glens Falls Portland Cement stock as collateral. And a line of discount was granted to the Imperial Wall Paper Company. Loans were being granted to the Glens Falls Hospital.

In early Fall of 1914, the bank began soliciting new accounts by mailing a special letter to selected prospects.

The minutes are not clear as to who made the first move. But in any event, President Lapham and Cashier Sherman held a conference with Maurice Hoopes, President of Finch, Pruyn & Company in relation to the company's bank account, which was carried with another bank. Mr. Hoopes stated that a change in the company's banking connections from the company's standpoint was desirable. If the business was thought desirable for First National to have, the company would be inclined to favor such a selection.

"The bank committee discussed the matter very thoroughly from all points of view, and each member (including Mr. Moynehan), upon being asked for his individual opinion, declared in favor of accepting the business of this firm, the account being thought by all to be very desirable and would prove of benefit to this bank." Then the President and Cashier were authorized to obtain this account if possible.

They did. But have you determined who made the first move?

As the Holidays approached, First National introduced a new service: Christmas Club for 1915. Public response exceeded the expectation of the Board.

As you can well imagine the bank was bustling with activity in 1915 in anticipation of the completion of its new building. During that same year, a new Post Office was erected on Warren Street and remained active for sixty-two years. The Sanford Street School was constructed. And the fire department bought its first motor-driven apparatus—a converted Buick touring car.

Much was happening, and the Board also had to remain alert to world conditions. In March it invested $20,000 in French Republic 5% coupon bonds, and $10,000 in German Imperial Bonds. Within two months, the Cashier was instructed to use his discretion in selling both bonds.

The Officers and Directors of the First National Bank

GLENS FALLS, N. Y.

Announce the removal from their old building to the new one, corner of Glen and Park Avenne

SATURDAY, JUNE 12th

and cordially invite your inspection of their New Banking Home from 2 until 10 o'clock, P. M., same day.

Open for transaction of regular banking business Monday, June 14th, 9 o'clock, A. M.

New Building of First National Bank

First National Bank, 104 Glen Street.—With its many natural advantages Glens Falls is advancing rapidly towards the front rank of American cities and the new bank building, which is being constructed by the First National Bank for its occupancy in the near future, typifies the spirit of growth and progress which is manifested in numerous ways throughout the city by the construction of modern and up-to-date office buildings and factories.

The site of the new building of the First National Bank is on Glen Street about two blocks above its present home and adjacent to the Y.M.C.A. building. It will, when completed, be the largest and most attractive building from an architectural standpoint in Northern New York. The foundation is being constructed entirely of reinforced concrete and the building proper is built throughout of granite and marble on a framework of structural steel. The majority of the marble to be used in the building is being brought from Vermont and the granite from South Carolina and in a few weeks the public will be able to see this beautiful addition to the many fine buildings of this city well on the way to completion. As mentioned above, the building will be entirely fireproof even to the doors, window frames and sashes which are to be of heavy wrought bronze. This plan of procedure has been carried out in all the plans, the furniture and fixtures called for being constructed of pressed steel and enamelled to represent mahogany.

The First National Bank when they enter their new quarters will be the possessor of the largest and most complete jewel and silver vaults in this part of the State as well as vaults containing safety deposit boxes for the safekeeping of valuable papers, stocks, bonds, etc. These vaults as well as the bank itself will be protected by the best and most expensive protective devices and service that money can buy. In the interior of the building, marble and tile will be used exclusively in the construction of partitions and walls while bronze railings will cut off the tellers' and cashier's cages from the part of the interior devoted exclusively to the use of the bank's customers.

The First National was incorporated as a state bank in 1853 and as a National Bank in 1865 and has grown steadily in the favor of the businessmen and residents of Glens Falls and the surrounding territory until it now has the largest capital stock, the largest surplus and the largest deposits of any bank in Northern New York. The institution has a capital stock of $136,400 backed up by a surplus of $470,000 with deposits of something more than $3,500,000. The officers are as follows:—President, Mr. Byron Lapham; Vice-President, B. B. Fowler; Cashier, Arthur W. Sherman; Teller, Fred T. Russell.

(Courtesy of Robert L. Eddy)

(From a contemporary publication)

Suffice it to say that even without the preceding description, one could see that the new edifice was a magnificent structure both in beauty and function. The structure was designed by Mowbray and Uffinger, New York architects. The exterior was of Vermont marble, and the interior of sienna marble and French caen stone.

Finally the big day arrived. The public was invited to an open house from 2:00 P.M. to 10:00 P.M. Saturday June 12, 1915, and the bank was flooded with visitors. Then at 9:00 Monday morning, the bank opened for regular business, with a total of eight men and two women on the working staff. This did not include the President or the Vice President. As of June 23, deposits totaled $3,658,599.86. Surplus and profits tallied $474,443.53.

The old bank building was sold to Miller Brothers for $20,000, the bank to remove the fixtures.

Strange that a half-century after taking over its assets, the Cashier asked for instructions concerning the redemption of currency issued by the Commercial Bank of Glens Falls. He was told to redeem at face value if thought to be genuine.

Now (in 1990) during the Diamond Anniversary of the white marble structure, we were reminded of a loan of $10,000 in 1915 to JHD, secured by 100 shares of Sandy Hill Iron & Brass Works stock. Coincidentally, the current President of that firm, Floyd H. Rourke, has been an active member of the bank's Board of Directors since 1972.

One feature of the bank's new building in 1915 was its Silver Vault in the cellar. It attracted business for the storage of valuable heirlooms, family silver, and the like when customers were on vacation, or extended trips. It also was used for the storage of valuable rugs, "guaranteed against burglary and fire only." Charges were a matter of agreement with the owner.

Arthur Sherman resigned as a Director on February 19, 1916, but continued as Cashier. Then in July 1917, he was again elected to the Board following the death of George Parks. It appears that Sherman resigned from the Board because too many Directors had been elected at the annual meeting.

The shiny face of prosperity was everywhere in 1916 as war raged in Europe and continued to spur wartime growth in the United States.

Then on April 6, 1917, Congress officially declared war against Germany. J. Albert Koch, a bank clerk, enlisted in the army and soon found himself in France. The bank promptly became heavily involved in making loans, secured by Liberty Loan Bonds, at 3 1/2%. A great rush of Liberty Loan subscriptions strained the capacity of the Cashier and the staff to handle the work load. The community subscribed to $764,650 through the bank for Liberty Loan Bonds, and it was necessary to order more small safe deposit boxes.

Byron Lapham was Chairman of the Warren County Defense Committee, and a member of the Liberty Loan Committee during the war. The bank itself contributed $4,000 to the Glens Falls War Chest Fund, subscribed to $300,000 in Second Liberty Loan Bonds, and another $150,000 in Third Liberty Loan Bonds; then $100,000 in Victory Loan notes.

During the busy months of 1918, the bank modernized its check processing operation with three new Burroughs statement posting machines. And Frank T. O'Neil, the man who was later to become the officer in charge of the Bookkeeping Department, resigned to enlist in the army.

What an episode that turned out to be for the feisty seventeen-year-old Irishman. Upon arriving at an enlistment center and boot camp near Niagara Falls, he and four other young friends from Glens Falls were promptly stricken with the flu. So rampant was the epidemic that the doctors placed them on cots, left a saucer of Aspirin, and hurried along to care for others. The men on either side of O'Neil died.

When O'Neil regained his mobility, he promptly dressed and headed for the exit. He was detained and told by the commanding officer: "Mister, you're not going anywhere. You're in the army now."

O'Neil was not averse to confrontation. He replied, "The hell I am. I never signed the papers." He took a train to Troy and then a trolley to Glens Falls.

The bank renewed its contract for advertising on four billboards along roads leading into the city, and for advertising space in local trolley cars, and on the screen at the Rialto Theatre.

The Board was delighted in May of 1919 when the National Bank Examiner reported. "No criticism of this bank's affairs." That summer, Gray E. Safford was elected Assistant Cashier, the first person to hold that title.

Many loans were still being granted, secured by Liberty Bonds and War Savings Stamps. Notes of from $5,000 to $50,000 from famous companies, such as R.J. Reynolds Tobacco, General Electric, Swift, Armour, Goodyear Tire, Firestone Tire, and others were commonplace in the First National loan portfolio in those days. So were loans of as much as $150,000 to the Chicago Daily News. One reason for such loans was that national concerns were willing to pay a 7 1/4 % discount rate, whereas the maximum rate, at that time, for notes originating within New York State was 6%.

Patrick Moynehan was a very active member of the Board and the Discount Committee. Paradoxically, his death occurred on January 19, 1920 on the very anniversary of his becoming a Director seventeen years previously.

Illustrative of First National's high regard for prized employees are minutes which read, "LeRoy H. Behan, a valued employee of this bank, finding it necessary to submit to a very serious operation, which was performed at the Glens Falls Hospital on April 19, 1920, the Cashier was instructed to pay all costs in connection with Behan's illness and charge the same to the Expense Account of this bank, and it is further understood that Mr. Behan will receive regular salary during his absence from the bank."

That action was many years before the bank developed formal employee benefit programs.

Owing to the high cost of living following World War I, every employee was granted a 5% bonus based on his or her salary on July 1, 1920.

Financing of a car in the 1920s meant that a customer would pay a heavy portion of the total cost and then give a three- or four-month note to the car dealer for the balance. The car agency would in turn endorse the note and discount it at the bank.

The advisability of increasing the Capital Stock of the bank was discussed in late 1920 and a resolution passed that the capital be raised from $136,400 to $500,000 consisting of 5,000 shares at $100 each. Each shareholder would surrender his present stock and give his proportionate amount of money representing the difference between $136,400 and $500,000. But it did not happen. No explanation was found as to why it was not consummated. Periodically other plans were advanced for increasing the capital. And ten years later, the capital was still $136,400.

E. W. West, President of the Glens Falls Insurance Company, offered an unrelated plan, whereby his employees could become stockholders of the insurance company. The bank supported the plan by agreeing to grant individual notes secured by the company stock. In time, there was $468,564 of such indebtedness on the books.

Business continued brisk, and the bank diversified its excess funds, in 1922 and 1923, by investing in quality stocks such as American Tel & Tel, American Sugar Refining, General Electric, Bethlehem Steel, and a host of leading railroads.

Within months it sold $325,000 of U.S. Liberty Bonds of different issues and invested in Government of Argentina 6% Treasury Gold Notes, Dutch East Indies Bonds, Federal Land Grant Bonds, Kingdom of Denmark, Republic of Bolivia, Switzerland, Sweden, and City of Copenhagen Bonds, and the Coffee Loan of Brazil.

At the same time, the Cashier proposed a miniature reproduction of the bank building to encourage savings accounts. 500 replicas, in bronze, were ordered at a cost of $1.10 each. Savings deposits increased and more banks were ordered. They are now collectors items and highly cherished.

In 1922, the bank's National Charter, No. 980, was amended and extended for ninety-nine years as explained in the official certification shown on the next page:

NO. 980
TREASURY DEPARTMENT
OFFICE OF COMPTROLLER OF THE CURRENCY
WASHINGTON, D.C., SEPTEMBER 27,1922

WHEREAS, the Act of Congress of the United States, entitled, "An Act to amend section 5138, Revised Statutes of the United States, relating to corporate powers of associations, so as to provide succession thereof for a period of ninety-nine years or until dissolved, and to apply said section as so amended to all national banking associations," approved by the President on July 1, 1922, provided that all national banking associations organized and operating under any law of the United States on July 1, 1922, should have succession until ninety-nine years from that date, unless such association should be sooner dissolved by the act of its shareholders owning two-thirds of its stock, or unless its franchise should become forfeited by reason of violation of law, or unless it should be terminated by an Act of Congress hereinafter enacted:

Now therefor, I,   D. R. CRISSINGER, Comptroller of the Currency, do hereby certify that THE FIRST NATIONAL BANK OF GLENS FALLS in the CITY of GLENS FALLS and State of NEW YORK, was organized and operating under the laws of the United States on July 1, 1922, and that its corporate existence was extended for the period of ninety-nine years from that date in accordance with and subject to the condition in the Act of Congress hereinbefore recited.

IN TESTIMONY WHEREOF, witness my hand and Seal of office this TWENTY SEVENTH day of SEPTEMBER, 1922.
Seal

D. R. CRISSINGER,
Comptroller of the Currency

The Christmas Bonus to employees had been $25 each in 1917, $50 in 1918 and 1919. It was 5% of yearly salary in 1920 and 1921. Then in 1922, the gift varied in accordance with length of service; $100, $50, or $25 with the exception that Gray E. Safford was given $150 "in appreciation of good and faithful service." The following year the standard was fixed at $100 and continued until 1971.

When it was erected it was believed the white marble building would provide plenty of space for expansion for fifty years or more. However, growth of business was such by mid-1923 that a one-story addition had to be erected at the rear of the bank in space that divided it from what was then known as the Lapham-Hovey Apartments. It housed the Bookkeeping Department with its noisy posting machines.

We have no intention of burdening readers with a series of official documents from governmental bodies. However, we thought there might be sufficient interest in the act which enabled First National to make Trust Services available to its expanding clientele to warrant printing the following:

FEDERAL RESERVE BOARD
Washington, D.C. March 4, 1924

Pursuant to authority vested in the Federal Reserve Board by Act of Congress approved December 23, 1913, known as the Federal Reserve Act, as amended by the Act of September 26, 1918, * * * The FIRST NATIONAL BANK OF GLENS FALLS, Glens Falls, New York * * *
has been granted the right to act, when not in contravention of State or local law, as Trustee, Executor, Administrator, Registrar of stocks and bonds, Guardian of estates, Assignee, Receiver, Committee of estates of lunatics, or in any other fiduciary capacity in which State banks, trust companies or other corporations which come into competition with national banks are permitted to act under the laws of the State of New York * * *

The exercise of such rights shall be subject to regulations prescribed by the Federal Reserve Board.

SEAL   FEDERAL RESERVE BOARD
Attest: by **D. R. Crissinger**
                                        Governor

_____
      Secretary

Even though the bank was well endowed with wealthy customers, developing sufficient business to warrant a full-fledged Trust Department took time.

Can you imagine several tellers operating from a common pool of money? That's how it was until 1924 when the Cashier was authorized "to make all necessary arrangements for the separation of the cash in such a manner as to give tellers, Russell, Behan, and Leicht their own cash to be handled solely by themselves and to be held responsible therefor and called to account for any errors."

Not only were business enterprises expanding in the 1920s, so were non-profit organizations. The bank recognized its responsibility to serve the needs of every facet of the community and contributed liberally to a wide spectrum of organizations, including the Sons of Italy building fund, the Hebrew Community building fund, to many area churches for their building expansions, and to the St. Mary's Academy building fund.

When Paul E. Lavine graduated from Glens Falls High School at age seventeen, in 1926—he became the twenty-fifth person on the staff that year, bringing the total annual payroll to $57,450. (more about Mr. Lavine, later)

The Cashier reported total deposits of $10,157,755.59 as of October 13, 1926—a new record for the bank.

The first instance of a loan being secured by Life Insurance Policies was recorded in January 1927. Many such loans would follow in later decades.

Prosperity abounded in the '20s and the bank was lending to more and more car dealers (then referred to as garages) on direct and indirect lines. It also granted a discount line of $100,000 to one individual for an Automobile Finance Company, which he had not yet named. Shortly thereafter, on one day the bank granted five loans of $50,000 each to five different wallpaper companies.

More reflective of the times, the Cashier reported, in May 1927, "The bank has on Call in the New York Market the sum of $200,000, secured by Stock Exchange Collateral with the usual margin."

Being watchful, prudent men, the Board authorized the Cashier in 1928 to submit a list of securities owned by the bank to Moody's Investors Service for their analysis and report.

That same year the Blanket Liability Policy, covering employees, was renewed with Glens Falls Indemnity Company to the extent of $25,000 each, and excess coverage was increased to $50,000. The Board also discussed introducing a service charge against unprofitable checking accounts to reimburse the bank for services rendered.

It seemed as if prosperity had come to everyone during the booming growth of the '20s. First National did its part toward meeting the financial needs of the community, including the encouragement of thrift habits at every level, even through a Savings Stamp program in the city schools. On "Bank Day," kids could insert coins and obtain matching stamps from a machine furnished by the bank. The youngsters pasted these stamps into individual savings books, and when full, took them to the bank for credit in their own personal savings account at First National.

Strange that the bank's first reported burglary was of the School Savings machine in Ridge Street School where two burglaries occurred within one week, netting the thief a little more than nine dollars.

Something more important was missing in 1928. I noticed that President Byron Lapham had not been recorded in attendance at any meeting since January 16: most unusual because he had a near-perfect attendance record for the past twenty-two years. No comments were found in the minutes to indicate that the eighty-year-old leader was ill.

However, various new authorities had been bestowed on the Cashier from time to time during the year. On January 24, 1929, Byron Lapham was again elected President. But his Presidency ceased, one month later, when his death was reported on February 25 after a long and fruitful career of which he and his heirs could be justly proud.

At the regular meeting of the Board of Directors of the First National Bank Glens Falls, N.Y., March eleventh, nineteen hundred and twenty-nine, the following resolution was unanimously adopted:

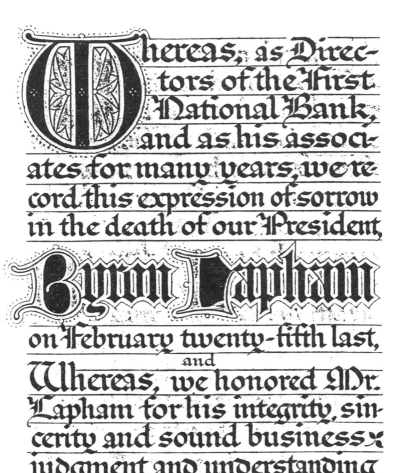

Whereas, as Directors of the First National Bank, and as his associates for many years, we record this expression of sorrow in the death of our President,

Byron Lapham

on February twenty-fifth last, and Whereas, we honored Mr. Lapham for his integrity, sincerity and sound business judgment and understanding of financial conditions, above all we esteemed him for his qualities as a man, his patience, generosity, kindliness and uniform consideration for all with whom he came in contact. Possessed of a keen mind, his exceptional ability, clear judgment and wise counsel, combined with a high sense of honor, commanded the respect of everyone associated with him, and the memory of his cheerful, kind and lovable nature and sterling character will be an abiding inspiration to all who enjoyed his friendship; Now, therefore, be it ❧

Resolved, that deeply aware of the loss sustained, the Directors of this Bank hereby express their heartfelt and sincere sorrow in the death of Mr.

Lapham, and their sympathy for his family in their great bereavement, and be it further Resolved, that this tribute of respect to our late associate be entered upon the minutes of this meeting, and a copy thereof be forwarded to his family.

Board of Directors

[signatures of the Board of Directors]

Cashier

Directors during Presidency of Byron Lapham, 1906-1929

Merritt Ames		1896-1911 May 30 died
George F. Bayle		1915-1933
William McEchron Bowden		1918-1924
Asst to Pres 1931-1932		1931-1968 resigned
VP	1933-1938	
VP	1952-1961	
Senior VP	1961-1963 resigned	
Alfred S. Clark		1928-1968 resigned
Charles W. Cool		1905-1932
George Chahoon Jr.	Oct	1906-1927
Jonathan M. Coolidge		1885-1912 Nov 12 died
VP 1907-1912		
Theodore J. DeLong		1874-1908 May 12 died
John B. DeLong	June	1908-1926 Jan 9 died
Byron B. Fowler		1885-1936 May 2 died age 90
VP 1913-1936		
J. Irving Fowler	May	1920-1937 July 20 died
S. B. Goodman		1908-1920 Mar 9 died
Maurice Hoopes		1915-1949 Feb 15 died
Pres	1930-1942	age 78
Chairman 1942-1949		
Emmett T. Johnson		1894-1907 Feb 3 died
Teller	1859-1864	
Cashier 1864-1907		
Theo F. Kalbfleisch		1906-1934
Byron Lapham		1891-1929 Feb 25 died
VP	1898-1906	
Pres 1906-1929		
Walter P. Leavens	Nov	1906-1922 Oct 11 died
J. R. McMullen		1912-1946 Oct 8 died
		age 75 NYC

Patrick Moynehan		1903–1920 Jan 19 died 17 yrs to the day
Dennis B. Moynehan		1920–1946 Sep 25 died
George H. Parks		1911–1917 June 30 died NYC
Arthur W. Sherman		1894–1916 Feb resigned
2nd VP 1905–1906	July	1917–1930 July 3 died
VP 1906–1907		
Cashier 1907–1929		
Pres 1929–1930		
William J. Townsend	Nov	1906–1917 Aug 23 died
H. McKie Wing		1895–1933 Jan 9 died age 86 in California

24 men served on the Board during the term of Byron Lapham
2 who would become Presidents of the bank

**FIRST NATIONAL BANK OF GLENS
FALLS.**

Notice of Annual Meeting.

The annual meeting of the shareholders of the First National Bank
of Glens Falls will be held at its
banking house, Number 104 Glen
street, Glens Falls, New York, on the
12th day of January, 1915, at 10
o'clock in the forenoon, the polls remaining open until noon, for the
election of directors for the ensuing
year and for the transaction of such
other business as may properly come
before the meeting.

Notice is also hereby given that a
proposition will be submitted to the
shareholders at said meeting to
amend the articles of association by
renumbering Article 'VII' to read as
Article 'VIII', and at the end of Article 'VI' to insert a new article providing for compensation for the directors and discount committee, and
also to ratify the action of the board
of directors heretofore taken in regard to the same."

Dated, December 12th, 1914.

ARTHUR W. SHERMAN,
Cashier.

*Notice of annual meeting of shareholders—the last one to be held in the old bank
building.*

𝕮𝖎𝖒𝖊 𝕱𝖗𝖆𝖒𝖊
History in Headlines
On or about Monday, February 25, 1929

2/3   NYC Report Reveals Business Girls Average $33.50 for a 50-Hour Work Week.

2/17   Universal Airline Shows a Movie During a Scheduled Flight.

2/19   Burglars Accidently Start Fire in C.V. Peters Store.

2/19   State Authorizes Building of Bobsleigh Run at Lake Placid.

2/20   Extensive Repairs Planned for Feeder Canal.

Commodities Then & Now (Year)

	1929	1990
Dow Jones Ind	$311.24	$2,564.14
Gold, oz	20.67	391.19
Silver, oz	1.09	5.21
Copper, lb	0.18	1.03

President: Calvin Coolidge
Vice Pres: Charles G. Dawes

Prices Then & Now (Year)

	1929	1990
Bread, loaf	$ 0.09	$ 1.17
Milk, gal	0.58	2.13
Butter, lb	0.56	1.19
Gasoline, gal	0.12	1.01
New Ford Car	450.00	10,995.00
Annual Income	2,062.00	25,050.00
New Home	7,246.00	91,945.00

On This Day in History

1836—Samuel Colt is granted a patent on his revolver.

1863—Congress establishes a national banking system.

Firsts, Fads, Things

Talkie movies, Academy Awards, bottle of 7UP, foam rubber

Major Events of the Year

Black Thursday stock market crash in October. First coast-to-coast air service (two days, two nights) journey by plane during day—sleep on moving train during night. Graf Zeppelin makes round-the-world trip.

Winners in the Arts

Actor: Warner Baxter for *In Old Arizona*
Actress: Mary Pickford for *Coquette*
Movie: *Broadway Melody* By MGM Studios
Best Seller: *A Farewell to Arms*
Big Movie: *Divine Lady*

This Year in Sports

W. Series: Athletics top the Cubs.
NFL: Green Bay Packers
Indy 500: Ray Keech at 97.58 mph
Stanley Cup: Boston Bruins
Kentucky Derby: Clyde Van Dusen
Rose Bowl: Georgia Tech

Arthur W. Sherman

THE PRESIDENCY OF ARTHUR W. SHERMAN
1929–1930

Arthur W. Sherman's thirty-six-year career with First National was, to say the least, most unique. He began as a Director at age twenty-four, served first as a Director, then Second Vice President, Vice President, Cashier, and finally as President. However, his tenure as President endured for a mere sixteen months before he died, unexpectedly at age sixty-one.

From the very first he was regarded as a personal representative of the Sherman family interests. His uncle, Darwin, was on the Board at the time but found it difficult to be active because of his health and died before the year ended. His grandfather, Augustus Sherman, had been a prime founder of the bank and subsequent longest term President. Paradoxically, Arthur's was to become the shortest.

To those not conversant with the inner workings of a bank, it might seem that most of his career had been devoid of any significance. Quite the contrary. During his era, for all practical purposes, the Cashier was the man vested with major authority and responsibility as relates to the technical and legal aspects of operating the bank.

Essentially the Cashier was empowered to take acknowledgments, execute and deliver any and all papers, instruments and documents to which the name or seal of the bank is necessary or proper, excepting only a conveyance of its banking house and contracts which are executory on the part of the bank.

In effect, the Cashier was the man most consulted on all banking matters and who made things happen, with the approval of the President and the Board of Directors. The position enabled him to administer the daily affairs of the institution, and thereby gain personal eminence among customers and the banking community.

First let's focus on his short term as President and then flash back to various happenings when he was Cashier.

He was elected President on March 4, 1929, one week after Byron Lapham had passed away. The following week, Gray E. Safford was elected Cashier, while J. Albert Koch and George H. Leicht were elected Assistant Cashiers; the first time two men jointly held that title at First National.

His salary was increased to $25,000 a year. He was the sixth man to become President, and apparently the first to draw a salary. At least there had been no prior mention of reimbursement to any of the other five who had held the office.

The office of President gave him additional stature, and he immediately set about obtaining resolutions from the Board which would clearly define the operating authority of the new officers as to signatures on official documents, right of access to the Security Chest in the vault, and combinations to other chests and doors.

He also obtained a resolution conveying the right to borrow up to ONE MILLION ($1,000,000) on behalf of the bank. It read as follows:

"RESOLVED, that the President, Vice President, Cashier, or an Assistant Cashier of this bank be and hereby is authorized to borrow from the National Park Bank of New York, the National City Bank of New York, or from any other correspondent in the name of this bank and for the credit of this bank, any sum of money, not to exceed ONE MILLION ($1,000,000.) dollars in the aggregate from all such correspondents, either by direct loan to this bank or through the rediscounting of notes given to this bank and

"THAT the President, Vice President, Cashier or an Assistant Cashier be and hereby is authorized to pledge and assign as collateral to any such loans, so as to secure the payment of such borrowings, any bonds or other securities or notes belonging to this bank."

A schedule of various kinds of insurance was presented to the Board, including that indemnifying the bank against loss through dishonest acts of any employees for $75,000; robbery, burglary and holdup both within the bank and of the messenger outside for $175,000; burglary or robbery from safe deposit boxes for $100,000; fire insurance on building and contents $150,000; blanket forgery insurance $10,000; limited forgery $20,000; and insurance covering personal injury both to employees and others.

On April 18, 1929, a resolution was unanimously adopted congratulating B. B. Fowler, "our highly esteemed Vice President" on the sixtieth anniversary of his eminently successful business career in Glens Falls and expressing appreciation for his helpful and loyal service as a Director of the bank since January 13, 1885, and its Vice President since January 18, 1913.

President Sherman advised the Board of the approximate earnings for the bank for the past six months, and a regular semi-annual dividend of 8% was declared payable June 1, plus an extra or Special Dividend of 6%.

On August 18, 1929, Byron J. Lapham was elected to the Board to fill the vacancy created by the death of his grandfather, Byron Lapham, six months previously. It merits mentioning that Byron J., at age eighty-nine, (living in Florida in 1990) phoned to happily provide the current President of First National, Dr. William L. Bitner III, with interesting anecdotes, and memorabilia of his years on the Board.

Notable loans in 1929 included those to downtown merchants, to M. Ames Chemical Works Inc., the City of Glens Falls and to Union School District No. 1, as well as substantial loans to individuals with market securities as collateral.

A general discussion was held by the Discount Committee in early September as to whether or not the Bank was justified "under conditions as they exist today" in granting loans to non-depositors. Several instances were cited where "money was loaned to good people" who had no compensating balances whatever on deposit with the bank. It was the sentiment of the committee that the policy of such lending should be continued.

According to reports from some who worked at the bank in the 1920s, Mr. Sherman had a great deal of faith in the man who had been appointed his assistant in 1919, Gray E. Safford. He had seen Safford enter the bank as errand boy and janitor working from 6:30 in the morning until late in the evening everyday. The only assistance Safford had in keeping the bank clean was that of a woman who came in for a couple of hours on Fridays. Ability and ambition won him many promotions.

As the bank grew, Mr. Sherman delegated more and more responsibility to his assistant, to the point where the employees regarded Mr. Safford as the man who was "running" the daily affairs of the bank. In the meantime, Arthur Sherman enjoyed mythical "bankers hours."

"Black Thursday," the infamous stock market crash of October 24, 1929, did not cascade into panic in Glens Falls or at First National as it did in many parts of the nation. In fact, no evidence was found of major problems being expressed in any of the Board minutes. The bank was living up to its own proclamation of being "Strongly Conservative but more than Conservatively Strong."

Resources of the bank, on that day, were reported as $14,140,323; deposits, $11,389,071; capital, surplus and profits, $2,317,068.

First National, of course, could not be completely insulated from the aftermath of the shock waves that emanated from the financial disruption in the securities market during Sherman's remaining seven months as President. Resources of the bank, on June 30, 1930 were reported as $13,888,866; deposits, $11,071,184; capital, surplus and profits, $2,541,389.

It's true that during that period, President Sherman reported several loans as having insufficient collateral to cover the face of the loans. These, for the most part, were loans to leading citizens. And it was decided that the customers should not be disturbed, either for additional collateral or reduction of principal. The bank was relying on the character of the individuals involved.

You may already know that J. P. Morgan, the most eminent banker of the century, subscribed to that same principle of trust. When asked by the Senate during an investigation in Washington, "On what grounds would you lend a person money? What's the most important thing to consider?" Morgan replied, without hesitation, "Character."

Let's digress a bit to review some of the action that was taking place during the many years that Arthur Sherman was preparing himself for succession to the presidency of the bank.

Way back in 1908, one of his earliest acts as Cashier was to establish contact with Continental National Bank of Chicago for a check-clearing relationship that would last for nearly half a century.

In 1912, he was authorized to purchase calendars bearing the bank's name "when suitable copy could be found." He found it. And annually distributed copies to customers for several years. Today they are collector items.

In 1914, he signed and circulated a monthly letter to customers with a two-page centerfold of sharp pictures depicting the progress on the Panama Canal, one of the world's greatest engineering achievements.

Before the new, white marble structure was completed in 1915, it was decided to place a suitable wall tablet in the vestibule of the new building bearing the names of the bank Directors, officers, and members of the building committee.

That was the same year construction of the concrete viaduct connecting Glens Falls and South Glens Falls was completed. Sherman joined others in predicting that never again would this important artery be severed by floodwaters of the Hudson River.

May 1, 1914

Dear Friend :-

      In this letter we would like to briefly mention how people of various occupations derive a profit from the use of a Checking account in this Bank.

      It being generally agreed that all profits originate from the soil, we first mention the farmer who well knows the advantages of the check-book instead of the pocketbook.

      The business man finds it essential to pay by check. He realizes that in commercial transactions it is the only Safe, Sane Method to use.

      The wage-earner who is striving for advancement knows from experience that his wages go farther when he uses the check book; moreover he creates a decidedly favorable impression with his creditors.

      To Professional Men the checking account becomes a valued necessity because most of his financial book-keeping is done at the Bank.

      Thrifty housewives pay by check, realizing they are never bothered to "make change," and because it maintains an accurate record of household expense.

      We could go on and mention every occupation in this community and how it is represented on our books by the names of thrifty progressive people, and tell you how much pleasure it has given us to see their material success recorded in their pass-book.

      If you have delayed opening a checking account in this Bank because you have received no formal invitation, will you not consider this a direct personal invitation, and avail yourself of the uniform SERVICE and COURTESY accorded all people regardless of the size of their account?

C. P.-4   Very truly yours,

               FIRST NATIONAL BANK OF GLENS FALLS, N. Y.

                            Cashier

P.S.- By controlling the raging Chagres River the great Gatun Dam becomes the keystone of the greatest engineering feat in the world. It will be interestingly described in Part V, the next Panama Canal Report

The First National Bank building and its neighbors shortly before the organization was moved into the new white marble building in 1915.

(Arthur S. Fisher Collection)

FIRST NATIONAL BANK, GLENS FALLS, N.Y.

This 1915 view shows the new white marble bank with the four-story Lapham building in the rear.

(Arthur S. Fisher Collection)

In 1916, Cashier Sherman brought up the question of the bank's reserves, calling attention of the Board to the wide distribution of same, inferring that the bank had too many correspondent banks. However, after discussing his proposition thoroughly, the Board decided it was not yet time to make any changes in the bank depositories.

When he distributed the $25 Christmas gift to each employee that year, he reminded them that it was a token of appreciation for their earnest endeavor to do their very best for the interest of the First National Bank at all times.

After the nation had entered the war, (World War I), the Red Cross requested that each bank contribute one-tenth of its gross earnings for one week to the Red Cross. The Board had already decided to contribute $200, which was slightly more than its fair share of weekly earnings. They let it stand.

Amusing that Mr. Sherman, as Cashier, would record the following in the Minutes of August 5, 1920:

"No meeting today of the Discount Committee. For some reason, unknown to the Cashier, there was no one present."

The following year, he called attention to the advisability of providing the bank with a Hold-Up Alarm System. His suggestion was approved and the Padua System was installed. Thankfully, it never needed to be used.

Something that did get used, however, was first printed the next year—1500 copies of a little pocket-sized magazine, self-published in early February 1922 by a Greenwich Village writer with a rare talent for condensing magazine articles. He named it *Reader's Digest*. And the title of the first article in that issue was "How To Keep Young Mentally."

Arthur Sherman knew how to do just that, maintaining his individuality and common sense approach to business throughout his life. He was aware at all times that deposits are debts, often payable without notice, and urged directors to maintain liquidity.

Here's an interesting incident. A gentleman telephoned Mr. Sherman in May 1926 to report that he had fallen into the coal

1917 Series of U.S. Currency.

1917 Series of U.S. Currency

Message on back warns about counterfeiting
(Courtesy John E. Rafferty)

hole in the sidewalk on Lapham Place and skinned his legs. He stated, "My object in reporting it to the bank is to give you an opportunity to safeguard the public and prevent any other accident of a similar nature." How times have changed! Can you imagine the liability in 1990?

By way of explanation, hard coal was used as heating fuel for the furnace in those days. A delivery man would open a steel-covered hole in the sidewalk, insert a chute, and pour the coal into a large room in the bank's cellar. Apparently he had not properly replaced the cover.

Few people today remember the dirty, dusty mess created by coal. But, well into the 1930s, coal was big business in the area for Finch, Pruyn & Co., Griffin's, Singleton's, and Bronk Coal & Lumber in Hudson Falls. Each of them had several large concrete silos either along the canal bank or railroad spurs, or both, for storage and subsequent delivery to customers in 100-pound canvas bags. It required a lot of hard, grimy hand labor from delivery men with horses, wagons, and sleds, and near the end, trucks.

On September 30, 1927 the holder of the World Series record for consecutive scoreless innings pitched, added to his legend, smashing his 60th home run of the season, a plateau never before achieved in baseball. He lives on in baseball fame as Babe Ruth of the New York Yankees.

Earlier that year, another high achiever, Charles A. Lindbergh, won $25,000 and international fame for the first non-stop flight from New York to Paris; a thirty-three-hour hazardous venture in his single-engine plane, the "Spirit of St. Louis," and thereafter they called Lindy, the "Lone Eagle."

Buses for public transportation were introduced to Glens Falls in 1928 to replace electric trolley cars. Len Sweeney, the bank's genial eighty-five-year-old parking lot attendant in 1990, said, "My first job in Glens Falls was as a bus driver in 1928 driving the Beltline, up Glen Street beyond the bank, up Bay, across Roberts Avenue (Lexington), then down Ridge to complete the circle every twenty minutes."

Also in 1928, the last of the canal boats journeyed down the Feeder Canal on October 28 with a load of about seventy-five tons of paper from Finch, Pruyn & Co. In its heyday there had been nearly 100 locally owned canal boats plying the waters for Glens Falls industries. These fourteen by 100 foot powerless barges were tugged along the canal by mules at the end of a 250-foot towline on a towpath. Each boat had a small stable in the front end (bow) for the mules and a small cabin for the captain and a steering rudder in the rear.

Many harbingers of the future evolved during Arthur Sherman's career: the first practical airplane in 1903, the automobile, motor-cycles, motion pictures, talking motion pictures, submarines, vacuum cleaners, wireless telegraphy, radios, color photography, air conditioning, electric refrigerators, oil-burning furnaces, elec-trified business machines, laboratory stages of television, and a great host of contrivances, too numerous to mention, that improved the quality of life for business and individuals.

The population in Glens Falls in 1930 was 18,976.

As the end of Arthur Sherman's career drew nigh, his $25,000 annual salary equaled that of the Governor of New York State, Franklin Delano Roosevelt. On the other hand, the $80,000 a year salary for Babe Ruth was more than that of the President of the United States, Herbert Hoover.

That same year, Glens Falls native Charles Evans Hughes became Chief Justice of the United States Supreme Court.

Arthur W. Sherman's sudden demise came as the result of a stroke while playing golf at the Lake Placid Club with a congenial foursome from Glens Falls (unable to confirm their names).

He became unconscious about one-half hour after he was stricken. He was survived by one daughter, Mrs. Louis P. Brown of Glens Falls, and two sons, T. Coolidge Sherman and Arthur W. Sherman Jr., both of Cleveland, Ohio. They were with him at the time of his death, having hastened to his bedside in the Lake Placid General Hospital immediately after he was stricken.

The Sherman name had long been prominent in Glens Falls. Members of the Warren County Bankers Association, Presidents and Board members representing every banking institution in the county along with business leaders and citizens throughout the area paid tribute to this highly respected banker at his funeral.

Automobiles parked along Glen Street in the 1920s gave testimony to its popularity as a shopping center for the area. In those days, most shoppers walked to "downtown" stores or rode in a trolley car. The trolley cars made their last run on November 30th, 1928 and were then replaced by buses.

(Courtesy Susan B. Stepp)

Directors during Presidency of
Arthur W. Sherman, 1929–1930

George F. Bayle		1915–1933
Wilfred L. Brodeur		1930–1934 May 17 died
Alfred S. Clark		1928–1968 resigned
Charles W. Cool		1905–1932 Sep 24 died
Byron B. Fowler		1885–1936 May 2 died age 90
VP 1913–1936		
J. Irving Fowler	May	1920–1937 July 20 died
Maurice Hoopes		1915–1949 Feb 15 died age 78
Pres. 1930–1942		
Chairman 1942–1949		
Theo F. Kalbfleisch		1906–1934
Byron J. Lapham	Aug	1929–1941 sold stock
J. R. McMullen		1912–1946 Oct 8 died
		age 75 NYC
Dennis B. Moynehan		1920–1946 Sep 25 died
Arthur W. Sherman		1894–1916 Feb resigned
	July	1917–1930 July 3 died
2nd VP 1905–1906		
VP 1906–1907		
Cashier 1907–1929		
Pres 1929–1930		
H. McKie Wing		1895–1933 Jan 9 died Age 86
		in California

13 men served on Board during term of Arthur W. Sherman
1 who would become President of the bank

𝕿𝖎𝖒𝖊 𝕱𝖗𝖆𝖒𝖊

History in Headlines

On or about Thursday, July 3, 1930

7/3   Congress Creates the Veterans Administration. Auto Sales
      Increasing. 150,000 Workers Recalled as Detroit Plants Open.
7/7   Work Begins on the Boulder Dam. The Greyhound Company
      Expands Service Throughout USA.
7/27 Labor Leaders Propose a Ban on Imports of Soviet-made Goods.
7/29 President Hoover Opposes Cutting Trade with Soviets.

Commodities Then & Now (Year)		
	1930	1990
Dow Jones Ind	$222.46	$2,911.63
Gold, oz	20.67	373.30
Silver, oz	1.09	5.15
Copper, lb	0.20	1.03

President: Herbert C. Hoover
Vice Pres: Charles Curtis

Prices Then & Now (Year)		
	1930	1990
Bread, loaf	$ 0.09	$ 1.17
Milk, gal	0.56	2.13
Butter, lb	0.46	1.99
Gasoline, gal	0.10	1.01
New Ford Car	610.00	10,995.00
Annual Income	1,973.00	25,050.00
New Home	7,146.00	91,945.00

On This Day in History

1775—General Washington takes
      command of Colonial troops
      at Cambridge.
1877—Nez Perce Indians kill
      Army patrol in Idaho.

Firsts, Fads, Things

Flashbulb, sliced bread, the "Garbo" look.
Blondie comics

Major Events of the Year

Dow Jones rises 28% from last year's
crash low but unemployment climbing.
Oil prices drop. More people are leaving
the U.S. than are immigrating. Drive to
repeal Prohibition gains.

Winners in the Arts

Actor: George Arliss for *Disraeli*
Actress: Norma Shearer for
      The Divorcee
Movie: *All Quiet on the Western Front*
      by Universal Studios
Hit Song: *Mood Indigo*
Hit Radio: *Lum and Abner*
Big Movie: *Abraham Lincoln*

This Year in Sports

W. Series: Phila beat St. Louis
NFL: Green Bay Packers
Stanley Cup: Montreal
Kentucky Derby: "Gallant Fox"
Rose Bowl: Southern Cal over Pittsburgh

Maurice Hoopes

THE PRESIDENCY OF MAURICE HOOPES
1930-1942

Tumultuous times lay ahead in the banking industry when Maurice Hoopes was handed the presidential reins on July 10, 1930.

Even though Glens Falls had not been heavily hit as yet, great economic uncertainty prevailed nationwide amidst definite signs of a deepening depression in the United States. The aftermath of the stock market crash and the extravagance of the roaring twenties were catching up with industry. In fact, worldwide economic depression was deepening and unemployment was becoming catastrophic in many lands. Pessimism was feeding upon itself, leaving little hope that business would soon curve upward toward prosperity.

With such foreboding, it was indeed fortunate that First National selected a President who was a living symbol of stability, stature and dignity. It was particularly important at that time in history that the bank's leading figure be someone in whom the community would have faith and respect; a man who could instill confidence.

Without question, Maurice Hoopes was the right man for those troubled times. He had already built a reputation for a high sense of honor, understanding and compassion as President of Finch, Pruyn & Co. Inc., and was thoroughly loved and respected by other business leaders and citizens throughout the area. To many, he was not only a man of influence but a father-figure as well; one whose wise counsel was sought on many matters.

According to the recollection of a long-retired former Director, there were very strong feelings among Board members as to who should or should not succeed to the Presidency so unexpectedly vacated by Arthur Sherman. The minutes of July 7, 1930 support that remembrance. They read, "On the subject of Election of a President of the Board to succeed Mr. Sherman, it was the expressed unanimous opinion of all those present that the matter should be very carefully considered for a time before action was taken." G. E. Safford, Cashier, wrote those minutes.

Mr. Hoopes asked to be excused from attendance at the next meeting on the 10th. Normally the Cashier attended and wrote the minutes. But not at this one. Theo. F. Kalbfleisch served as Secretary pro-tem. The vote for Mr. Hoopes was unanimous, dispelling the disquietude among Directors.

Six months later Gray E. Safford was elected to the Board of Directors along with T. Coolidge Sherman (one of Arthur Sherman's sons). William McEchron Bowden, who had been a member of the Board (1918–1924), returned to the Board after six years' absence in Canada.

Two weeks after Mr. Hoopes became President, First National granted a $5,000, four-month loan to a customer of the Ticonderoga Bank as an accommodation to that bank. The bank also loaned on a contract for installing heat in the Washington County Poor House. Some investments were made in high grade convertible bonds, as well as several electric utilities recommended by Moody's. At the same time, the bank sold some mortgages on downtown business buildings to a local individual. Two months later, the bank sold its Fourth Issue Liberty Bonds and invested $400,000 in Railroad and Public Utility bonds.

William McEchron Bowden, a former Director, became a member of the staff on September 1, 1930 serving as an assistant to the President in dealing with investments. Near the end of the year he was given accountability for all the bank's insurance, relieving the Cashier of this responsibility.

The Discount Committee carefully watched the current market value of the collateral on large loans and instructed the

Cashier to endeavor to secure additional collateral or reduction of loans where prudent. Slow and doubtful loans were being carefully and attentively watched by executive officers of the bank.

Near the end of the year, a watchman's clock was placed on the vault. It would register the presence and wakefulness of the night watchman, on a dial, and also sound an alarm in the Police Station in case of his failure to wind the clock at given intervals. Also, a vault burglar alarm was installed, which would sound a different gong in the Police Station. The matter of installing tear gas equipment was postponed.

Statement of the condition of the FIRST NATIONAL BANK OF GLENS FALLS N. Y. *as reported to the Comptroller of the Currency*

December 31, 1930

Resources		Liabilities	
Loans and Discounts .	$9,487,715.75	Capital Stock	$136,400.00
U. S. Bonds and Other Bonds , ...	3,437,974.60	Surplus and Profits . .	2,335,979.13
Real Estate	192,352.96	Circulation	134,000.00
Accrued Interest Receivable	80,102.86	Due to Banks	20,797.62
Cash in Vaults and Deposited in Banks . .	1,182,792.93	Reserved for Interest, Taxes, etc.	222,474.00
5% Redemption Fund .	6,700.00	Deposits	11,537,988.44
	$14,387,639.19		$14,387,639.19

"*P r u d e n c e   P o i n t s   t h e   W a y*"

On December 31, 1930, resources were reported as $14,387,639; deposits, $11,537,988; capital, surplus and profits, $2,472,379.

The first action of the Board in 1931 was to transfer the bank's securities to the custody of the Federal Reserve Bank in New York and to increase the amount of insurance carried in most categories for greater protection of the bank.

The Cashier reported a charge to Profit and Loss of $92,546, because of bond depreciation, and $48,877 on various notes as suggested by the National Bank Examiner and the Examining Committee of the Board.

On March 2, 1931, Mr. Hoopes brought to the attention of the Board his forthcoming vacation. It was voted that George F. Bayle, a member of the Board, would "be in charge" during the absence of the President.

It was determined in late May that the bank should obtain a competent man with experience in some large institution to head the fledgling Trust Department and develop trust business for the bank. Paul Renn was chosen and joined the staff in July 1931 at a salary of $7,500.

Six months later, the Board adopted a three-page resolution stipulating the formal structure of the Trust Department, the duties of the Trust Officer, the form of records to be maintained, the handling of securities and investments, the appointment of five Directors to a special Trust Committee, and the duties of the Examining Committee in its semi-annual review of the department, plus other details. Members of the Trust Committee were to receive $2.00 per meeting.

The first mention of an exchange being charged on Canadian currency by the bank appeared in the minutes of September 25, 1931. The rate was 10%.

Late that year, First National loaned $30,000 to the Hamilton County Bank at Wells, New York.

Following the annual meeting in January 1932, Maurice Hoopes was re-elected President. B. B. Fowler, George F. Bayle, William McEchron Bowden, and Gray E. Safford each became a Vice President. Mr. Safford now had a dual title: Vice President and Cashier.

The 1932 winter Olympics were held in Lake Placid where Sonja Henie won two gold medals in figure skating, exciting spectators with her charm and grace.

It was decided in late May 1932 that messengers or guards carrying securities or currency to and from points outside the bank need no longer carry firearms inasmuch as the insurance companies did not require them to be armed.

Mary Cary and Elise Lareau, bank tellers, were both hospitalized in early summer and were pleasantly surprised and grateful to learn that the bank had assisted them substantially with their hospital expenses. This was before the days of any employee benefit programs at the bank.

During the Fall, the bank distributed 1,000 copies of a booklet, "The Book of Presidents." No copies have been found.

Paul Renn became the instructor for the bank's first group study course offered under the American Institute of Banking curriculum. To provide additional incentive, the Board agreed to pay one-half the cost to those students who successfully completed the twenty-week evening course on their own time. All twenty-two enrollees completed the course satisfactorily, testifying to their interest.

Times were worsening and more customers were confronted with difficulties in making payments on loans and mortgages. The bank was reluctant to instigate foreclosures and deferred such action whenever it was able to make other arrangements, even to the point of sometimes renting a house, with the owner's consent, to keep the mortgage alive.

In November, Franklin D. Roosevelt won a landslide victory for President of the United States by promising "to restore this country to prosperity." Who could foresee his enormous impact on the banking industry?

At the beginning of January 1933, Maurice Hoopes and George F. Bayle Sr. wanted it recorded in the minutes that they were not active "working" officers of the bank and did not have combinations to any of the security chests. Furthermore, they did not wish to have such responsibility.

NTERIOR, FIRST NATIONAL BANK, GLENS FALLS, N. Y.

The bank lobby interior from 1915 until renovated in 1937.

Hubert C. Brown and George F. Bayle Jr. were elected to the Board at the annual meeting, filling the vacancies created by the demise of Charles W. Cool and H. McKie Wing. Mr. Cool, the city's first mayor, had served on the Board since 1905. Mr. Wing, whose distinguished ancestry dated back to the very foundation of the community, had served since 1895.

Acting on the year-end recommendation of the National Bank Examiner, a charge-off of $239,171 relating to loans, investments, and real estate was made to Profit and Loss.

Despite the fact that First National was maintaining a Spartan course with high reserves and a liquid position, it was experiencing its share of problems because of the overall state of the economy.

Then at 9:30 Saturday morning, March 4, 1933, at a specially called meeting of the Discount Committee, a telegram was read from the Federal Reserve Bank of New York, notifying the bank that the Governor of New York State had declared Saturday, March 4, and Monday, March 6, legal holidays.

In the opinion of the bank's legal counsel, the bank had a legal right to remain open. But in checking with banks in neighboring cities, including Albany, they found that the Governor's proclamation was generally accepted as mandatory. Therefore FNB decided to close even though there were already customers in the bank.

To say the least, it was a confusing situation. How were they going to accommodate merchants who needed coin for the weekend, or provide money for payrolls? None of their customers had any prior warning so as to prepare for such a contingency. What about notes that matured on Monday?

The Governor's proclamation was followed up, on Monday, by a notice from the Comptroller of the Currency in Washington, stating that shortly after his inaugural speech, President Roosevelt had issued orders that all banks be closed for a seven-day bank holiday to allow time for emergency legislation by Congress.

Bankers were assured that major banks, found by federal and state authorities to be sound, would be allowed to reopen at the end of the holiday. Then, the holiday had to be extended until the Treasury Department could make new regulations.

What a predicament!

Paul E. Lavine, a teller at that time, recalls that both First National and the Glens Falls National set up teller stations in the old Glens Falls Trust Company building across the street: FNB tellers on one side of the lobby. GFNB on the other.

Lavine said, "A week or so before that, we had gotten in several hundred thousand dollars in cash. That was due to Safford's uncanny foresight, I believe."

Lavine added, "Initially, we were not allowed to take any deposits. Could not cash checks. However stores still needed change. So we took care of their needs. And, we allowed merchants to leave deposits with us for storage in the vault but could make no entries to their accounts."

Further investigation reveals that within a few days the Secretary of the Treasury issued an order permitting the banks to perform only the following functions:

1. Deliver and receive property for safekeeping.

2. Permit free access to safe deposit boxes.

3. Provide money for payrolls, including cashing checks drawn for payroll purposes.

4. Allow limited withdrawals for absolute necessities of life— for the relief of distress.

First National sent telegrams daily to the Comptroller of the Currency seeking permission to open because the bank was in such excellent shape. We had $1,921,461 in capital funds and surplus against $11,144,248 in deposits. This was an exceptionally high ratio of capital to deposits: more than 17%. Those were hectic times for the banks—all banks—because of the uncertainty that surrounded government action. Hundreds of banks in the nation were not allowed to re-open their doors. However, both of the Glens Falls banks were permitted to resume business at the end of the "Bank Holiday."

The conservative philosophy of the local banks enabled them to remain stable in a period when great numbers of their counterparts failed. Once again at First National, being "strongly conservative but more than conservatively strong," coupled with its slogan of PRUDENCE POINTS THE WAY, had paid off.

The many new banking laws during the 1930s brought profound changes to the industry. The most prominent and costly of these was the Banking Act of 1933, which established the Federal Deposit Insurance Corporation. Its purpose was to insure deposits in commercial banks up to $2,500 for each individual customer, the cost of the insurance to be borne entirely by the bank. The amount of insurance coverage per customer account and the cost have increased dramatically over the years.

By May of 1933, the Board decided that continual auditing by someone on the staff was preferable to periodic audits by outside agencies and agreed to try a staff member in that capacity.

In July the bank agreed to participate in Roosevelt's National Recovery Act (the NRA) and added people to the staff in order to operate efficiently under the Code. That was the same month loans to employees of the Glens Falls Insurance Company reached a total of $749,875 under their stock purchase plan.

More governmental regulations were forthcoming. The Warren County Bankers Association was revived and First National agreed to adopt the schedule of service charges authorized by the association's NRA Committee in compliance with the new Bankers Code of Fair Competition.

In February 1934, the Board considered the advisability of increasing capital funds by issuing 10,000 shares of preferred stock at $50 par value. Cashier Safford and Vice President Bowden made two trips to New York to confer with the Chief National Bank Examiner and then with the management of the Reconstruction Finance Corporation.

Then the bank had to apply to the Comptroller of the Currency for approval under Section 301 of "An Act to Provide Relief in the Existing National Emergency in Banking" before calling a special meeting of stockholders in order to be authorized to issue preferred stock, now in the amount of $625,000. This they did.

When issued, the Reconstruction Finance Corporation picked up 9,200 shares, and the Glens Falls Insurance Company subscribed to the remaining 800 shares of preferred stock.

The National Bank Examiners were riding herd on all banks to assure that they were adhering strictly to new guidelines and regulations, of which there were many. First National was subjected to a complete examination in November 1933, and another in February 1934, and was criticized mainly for the spread of collateral value on secured loans. The bank felt that the "write-down" by examiners exceeded the amount of reasonably probable loss. And the bank was right. In due time many loans were "written-up" because of appreciation in market value of collateral securing such loans.

Near the end of July 1934, the Board voluntarily charged off another $200,000 in loans that were questionable. One customer, in fact, was found to be overextended not only with FNB, but also with the Glens Falls National, the Sandy Hill National in Hudson Falls, and the People's National in Hudson Falls. An agreement was reached among the banks whereby the individual assigned his life insurance and a mortgage on his real estate to a Trustee for the benefit and protection of the banks.

Spurred on by many agencies and programs under Roosevelt's New Deal, some signs of recovery from the Great Depression were emerging. One of the most important, being born, was the Federal Housing Administration under the National Housing Act. Its mission was to encourage property improvement by providing credit insurance under Title I through eligible banks.

The Board was notified in August 1934 that it qualified as an eligible bank. Management immediately set about informing the public about the new loan opportunities. Then on December 11, 1934, the first Federal Housing Administration loan approval in the entire United States, was issued to First National—a fact of which it is still proud. The loan of $4,500 was for extensive improvements to a family home on South Street.

The bank capitalized on all the publicity attending the event and soon was granting more loans in this category than any other. It painfully developed expertise in processing the government paperwork. Thus it was amply indoctrinated and prepared for the next upward move by FHA: Title II mortgages. For years, thereafter, First National was the prime housing lender in the Albany District of the FHA.

Concurrent with the encouraging new loans, there were still problem loans on the books. In October, the Board voted to transfer $500,000 from the surplus account to a reserve for contingencies. Then they charged $148,710 to losses as determined by the National Bank Examiner.

Some senior citizens contend that Glens Falls with its wide business diversity and substantial affluence was virtually untouched by the Great Depression. And that was true for some segments of the population. From their point of view, there were no bread lines, no mass unemployment, no homeless, no food riots, none of the dramatic trauma such as was being seen in big cities and many other communities.

However, those with keener perceptions were well aware that there was curtailed employment, cut-backs in pay, substantial layoffs at Imperial Paper & Color, Finch Pruyn & Co. Inc., the cement company, shirt factories, and many others. Some employers forbid any overtime pay, despite heavier workloads.

There were people in town without jobs of any kind and small hope of finding new employment—and no such thing as unemployment insurance. Many depended on relatives for help. People lined up for handouts of food and clothing at the Salvation Army. The WPA doled out part-time work assignments on government projects. Some men enrolled in the CCC (Civilian Conservation Corps) and were housed in barracks. The city and county Welfare Departments required the unfortunate to relinquish radios and other "unnecessary items" before providing any assistance. Merchants were faced with the dilemma of good customers who could not pay their bills, yet had need for the basic necessities of life. Doctors provided medical care full well knowing that they might never get paid.

There were borrowers who could not meet their mortgage payments, and others who were unable to pay even the interest on their loans. Compassion on the part of Maurice Hoopes and other Board members deferred foreclosure and other drastic collection action against many an otherwise good borrower. However, constant harassment from examiners compelled the bank to take action contrary to their own best judgment. In the Cashier's opinion, selling collateral in an already down market and foreclosing mortgages in a distressed real estate market only compounded the problem.

This was reflected in a letter to the Comptroller of the Currency wherein it was explained that officers, as well as some of the Directors, were "endeavoring to sell the Bank's other real estate as rapidly as possible under existing conditions." Also, it pointed out that efforts were constantly being made to secure additional collateral or reduction in debt to provide adequate margin.

The local bankers knew and understood local conditions and local customers. Drugged with the euphoria of newfound bureaucratic power, the mentality of the examiners did not allow for this judgment factor.

More letters ensued.

Finally a letter, signed by all eight members of the Discount Committee, was directed to the Comptroller of the Currency. It explained that the Committee was meeting twice each week to evaluate loans, make recommendations, criticisms, and instructions to officers and record same in the credit file of each borrower. The letter further stated, "It is our purpose to continue this program until all grounds for reasonable criticism of our loans and other assets have been eliminated."

In the meantime, the bank employed the firm of Peat, Marwick, and Mitchell in April to make a complete independent audit of the bank and its operations. Procedural operations suggested by the firm were considered helpful and were adopted. It's interesting to note that "cash totaling $188,157.39 was counted on the morning of April 23 and found to be correct, except for an overage of twenty-five cents."

Despite the loan charge-offs at the insistence of the National Bank Examiners, and a transfer to a reserve for preferred stock dividend, in June 1935 the bank paid its regular 8% dividend and a special extra dividend of 6%. And normal salary increases of $100 a year were granted to most employees, with a few receiving $150 or $200.

In April of that year, the United States went off the gold standard and federal officials said the move was only "for the time being."

Another exchange of letters with Washington transpired. Evidently disgusted with the bureaucratic nonsense, Mr. Safford wrote, "We repeat what we have stated before. The poor loans in this bank date back to the period before 1930. It is true that under previous management and under different business conditions then existing, the bank had a liberal loaning policy, and with the shrinkage of values found itself burdened with slow, doubtful and

Bill redeemable in gold

Silver Certificate redeemable in silver
(Courtesy of John E. Rafferty and Joel A. Barnes)

Today's currency

This Federal Reserve Note is legal tender for all debts, Public and Private. However it is not backed by anything of intrinsic value.

worthless loans in too large a proportion. The work since this time has been to salvage as much as possible from these loans.

"The matter has had competent and vigorous attention, but we cannot always agree with your examiners as to the advantage to the bank of drastic action in cases where we feel that a more tolerant policy is not only more profitable for the bank but saves something to the borrowers. We can promise you our continued vigorous efforts to save the maximum on these loans."

He further explained that the Discount Committee was meeting twice weekly since Board meetings had been changed to monthly meetings. "Each Director on committee gives, in and out of these meetings, a very substantial part of his whole business week to the affairs of this bank."

He also pointed out that if it would be helpful to the Comptroller, the bank would send a committee to New York or Washington to explain more fully what the bank was doing and to discuss the best ways and means of accomplishing the desired results.

He made other salient points in the two separate two-page letters, including, "In our opinion we have by no means neglected the management of this bank or failed to appreciate the responsibility that rests upon us under the law and our oaths of office. We have fixed policies under which the bank has been operating and provide officers competent and willing to conform to such policies."

Evidently someone in Washington took notice. No further letters of criticism were forthcoming.

Perhaps to obtain further insight as to the mentality in Washington, the bank hired Clarence A. Scriver, then in the employ of the Office of the Comptroller of the Currency in the Division of Insolvent National Banks, to become credit manager for First National beginning in November 1935 at an annual salary of $7,000.

Meanwhile at the national level, in 1935 the Social Security Act was enacted as a program of old-age insurance for workers in commercial and industrial jobs. That same year, a simplification of the currency system in the USA was accomplished. All National Bank Notes (currency issued by individual banks) were retired and replaced by Federal Reserve Notes as provided in the Federal Reserve Act of 1913–14. At the time, First National had $134,000 of such notes outstanding.

The frugality of bank management is evident in various expense items for the month of January 1936—travel and entertaining $32.50; light, water and fuel, $61.42; postage, $198.67; salaries, $8,612.22; directors and committee fees, $225. The cost for FDIC insurance was $4,476.05, more than half the cost of salaries.

Foreseeing the possibility of criticism, the Board inserted in the 1936 minute book a formal Certificate of Consent from the Federal Reserve Board, dated November 13, 1929. It stipulated, "The Federal Reserve Board of Washington, D.C., hereby grants a permit to Dennis B. Moynehan to serve at the same time as a Director of the First National Bank of Glens Falls, New York and as a Director of the Hamilton County National Bank of Wells, New York."

Later, in May, First National loaned $50,000 to the Hamilton County National Bank at 3% on a note secured by county certificates of indebtedness. Another $50,000 was loaned to the same bank on the same basis in mid-December, and from time to time thereafter.

In May 1936, a letter signed by H. C. Brown, D. B. Moynehan, and W. H. Barber, members of the Examining Committee, was filed with the Board stating in part, "We recommend that a vote of thanks be given to Mr. Safford for the hard, efficient work done by him to bring about the improvement in the bank's financial and loan condition, and also recommend a vote of thanks to the entire staff for their satisfactory service."

Several recoveries had been made in charge-offs; credit files placed in fine shape; investments improved.

The bank was experimenting with a new type of loan called a Personal Loan, written on a schedule of twelve monthly payments rather than the traditional three-month note form. By mid-year

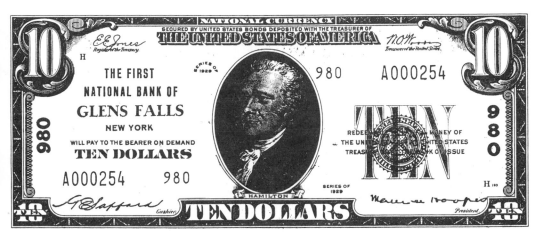

A $10 and a $50 bank note issued by First National and signed by Maurice Hoopes and Gray E. Safford.

(Courtesy George F. Reger Jr.)

there were 346 such loans totaling $59,770, and the Board was satisfied with the performance on these loans. Soon they ventured into the untested field of taking chattels on individual automobiles and permitting monthly payments of as many as fifteen months.

One very troublesome problem in the 30s was that of disposing of property obtained for the bank by foreclosure. Two bank employees did buy at the asking prices. However, many pieces of property, including empty lots, were sacrificed at auctions. Would you believe they found it almost impossible to find buyers for cottages thus obtained on the shores of Lake George?

It took time for the many programs under Roosevelt's New Deal to take hold. But things like the WPA (Works Progress Administration) and the CCC did put many people back to work. The most important effect was that it induced a revised spirit of optimism. Gradually the bank's deposits crept upward from a low of $10,592,000 at the end of 1934 to $11,181,000 at the end of 1937. Nothing spectacular, but at least going in the right direction.

Of course from a longer range perspective of twenty-two years' occupancy in the white marble building, deposits had tripled since 1915, and the volume of paper being processed had increased dramatically. No wonder it had been necessary to build a work balcony above the vault; convert alcoves on the main banking floor into Teller cages; and take over the Directors' room, a second floor area in the front of the bank, for Trust Department space.

Even so, such changes were not adequate to take care of increasing business. Therefore a complete reconstruction of the interior was undertaken in 1937 and completed in June 1938 in order to render more efficient and convenient service to customers.

The most predominant feature was the complete realignment of the main lobby. On the north side, the teller cages extended the entire length of the lobby; first the Savings and Christmas Club windows, followed by individually locked Commercial Teller cages. On the opposite side behind a low railing were desks for

Directors' room prior to conversion for Trust Department.

bank officers, making them more easily accessible to customers. Also a Note Department cage. The bookkeeping department was further extended into a ground floor area of the Lapham Building and fireproofed.

In January 1937, the Board voted to retire $400,000 of preferred stock. The following month, it held a special meeting of the shareholders to increase the common capital stock from $136,400 to $500,000, divided into 20,000 shares. This resulted in a 266% stock dividend with each shareholder receiving slightly more than seven shares of stock at a par value of $25 per share for each share held.

This was the first increase in common capital since the founding of the bank eighty-four years previously with 2,728 shares at a par value of $50 each. A dividend of $1.00 per share on the new stock was declared in December 1937. A month later, more preferred stock was retired and the remainder in 1939.

George F. Bayle Jr. had resigned from the Board in July 1937 following a dispute with the Cashier. The Board agreed with the Cashier. Threats of lawsuits and countersuits followed before the dispute was partially resolved by the courts in favor of the bank in 1939.

William McEchron Bowden resigned as Vice President on February 1, 1938, but retained his seat as a Director.

Sixteen employees signed a petition requesting payment of salary on a semi-monthly basis. No problem. Thereafter salaries were paid on the 15th and end of the month.

In those days, bookkeepers stood all day long at machines posting deposits and checks to individual customer statements. Transit operators and check filers likewise stood. Tellers were required to stand at window stations until the end of customer hours, the contention being that employees could function more efficiently and more quickly on their feet. Receipts for deposits were handwritten in customer passbooks. The general ledger was hand posted in a giant ledger book.

Most employees were allowed only one-half hour for lunch. "Coffee breaks" were unheard of. If you had weak kidneys, you had better look for a job elsewhere. Because of Saturdays, most worked fifty-two hours or more a week. No such thing as overtime. No timecards. You worked until balanced and then helped others prove-up. On the last business day of each month, tellers, clerks, and secretaries helped the bookkeepers until all customer statements were sealed in envelopes ready for mailing, generally around 10:00 P.M. General Ledger people? Forget it. They never could plan on a quitting hour. This was not just because Mr. Safford was a very hard taskmaster, which he was. That's how it was in the industry in those times.

Furthermore, no relatives were permitted to work in the bank. No married women were hired. If a woman married, she lost her job, the argument being she now had other means of support. One excellent worker on the staff postponed her marriage seven years because of this unwritten rule.

About this time there was a noticeable upswing in the economy and profits were improving. Wyman Dean was sent to the annual Savings Conference in New York. And James R. Simpson was hired at $4,000 a year to replace Mr. Bowden as an investment man.

Mindful of opportunities for business expansion, President Hoopes, in 1939, appointed H. C. Brown to head a New Business Committee of the Board and to serve on all other five committees. Earnings tripled in the first six months over the previous year. The Merrill Anderson Advertising Agency of New York was engaged to add further impetus to business development.

The Glens Falls Foundation was created that year to channel gifts for educational, charitable, and benevolent purposes into a plan which would afford flexibility in accordance with the times. First National was designated Trustee.

That year commercial banks were informed that there was a statute on the books which prohibited the use of the word "savings" by other than savings banks. First National changed the nomenclature in all its advertising to "Special Deposits." Interest was paid at 1 1/2% on these accounts up to $10,000; 1% from $10,000 to $35,000.

A local customer, of limited means, cashed a check for $1,650 from an out-of-town estate. The check bounced because his brother apparently had embezzled estate funds and then committed suicide. The local citizen had already spent the proceeds of the check. The bank allowed him to repay the money over an extended period of time.

War was again brewing in Europe. On September 1, 1939, without any declaration of war, German troops invaded Poland in a murderous, motorized lightning war, a "Blitzkrieg." Roosevelt vowed to keep America out of the European conflict which he said "could be long and very deadly."

Personal Loans (monthly payment loans) were still in their infancy in 1940 when Paul Lavine became the first non-officer authorized to grant loans up to $300. He replaced George Leicht, Assistant Cashier, who had been with the bank for the past sixteen years, and resigned to go with a local brokerage firm. That's an interesting tale in itself, reserved for another time.

In order to provide more privacy for borrowers and to handle a greater volume of automobile and appliance financing, the Personal Loan Department was transferred to an office in the rear of the Lapham Building (owned by the bank).

It was pointed out that the existing by-laws of the bank were adopted originally in 1853 and amended from time to time. Therefore it was appropriate for the Board to improve them. And they did. They revised and adopted a completely new set of by-laws in 1940.

In 1940, the population of Glens Falls was 18,836; of New York State, 13,479,142; of the nation, 131,664,275.

It was during the tenure of Maurice Hoopes that First National acquired its first branch bank. But it took ten months of red tape before the small bank at Bolton Landing became merged with FNB on November 9, 1940. Its total assets were $389,000. First National had $13,055,000. Both Bolton employees were retained, Harry W. Liddle as an Assistant Cashier in charge of the branch, at $2,400, and Blanch Lamb as clerk at $1,200 a year.

President Hoopes concurred with H. C. Brown in creating an Officer Call Program in conjunction with surveying existing custom-

The ground floor location of Personal Loan Department at the rear of the Lapham building during late 1930s and early 40s.

ers to better serve their needs. However, it lacked enthusiastic executive endorsement and was only mildly successful. Subsequently, an incentive program for business development was evolved for officers and other members of the staff. It produced fine results.

Old timers remember that Mr. Hoopes would stop at his office in the bank each morning, open his mail, review matters with Mr. Safford or Mr. Bowden, stand in the lobby a moment or two surveying the activity. Then he would stroll down Glen Street to his office near the end of the river bridge to fulfill his responsibilities as President of Finch, Pruyn & Co. Inc. He was a stately figure of a man who greeted nearly everyone he met by their first name. It is said that he knew every mill hand, lumber yard, and retail store employee by name. He was held in such high esteem many a man would proudly say to his wife, "Mr. Hoopes met me on the street today. He remembered me and called ME by name."

Maurice Hoopes was also known as an ardent golfer and one of the founders of the Glens Falls Country Club. He was chairman of the greens committee for twenty-five years and was instrumental in having the course enlarged from a nine-hole to an eighteen-hole course.

By 1940–41 business was expanding everywhere as America became the Arsenal of Democracy for the world. Mr. Hoopes needed to lessen his responsibilities at the bank.

On December 7, 1941, in a sneak attack, Japanese warplanes pulverized the American military base and naval forces at Pearl Harbor. And America was plunged into war.

The First National staff had increased 68% in the past dozen years, and all forty-six employees signed a letter thanking the Board for the $100 Christmas remembrance.

The following month, Mr. Hoopes was elevated to the position of Chairman of the Board at First National. A man with a high sense of honor, he had seen the bank through some very, very troublesome years. A new era was dawning and the Presidency was passed on to a younger man, a man who could devote more time to the daily workings of the bank.

Bolton Landing Branch in 1941.

The Bolton National Bank in Bolton Landing was purchased in 1940, and became our first branch.

THE FIRST NATIONAL BANK OF GLENS FALLS

GLENS FALLS, NEW YORK

December 26, 1941

The Board of Directors
The First National Bank
Glens Falls, New York

Gentlemen:

  We wish to express our sincere thanks
for your kind remembrance of us this
Christmas season.

  May 1942 bring you happiness and
health.

Sincerely yours,

Directors during Presidency of
Maurice Hoopes, 1930–1942

William H. Barber		1936–1966 Feb 19 died
George F. Bayle Sr.		1915–1933
VP 1932–1933		
George F. Bayle Jr.		1933–1937 July 8 resigned
William McEchron Bowden		1918–1924
Asst to Pres 1930–1932		1931–1968 resigned
VP 1932–1938		
VP 1952–1961		
Senior VP 1961–1963 resigned		
Wilfred L. Brodeur		1929–1934 May 17 died
Arthur F. Brown		1940–1968
Hubert C. Brown		1933–1981 Feb 22 died age 78
Pres 1942–1962		
Chairman 1962–1975 *		
Alfred S. Clark		1928–1968 resigned
Charles W. Cool		1905–1932 Sep 24 died
Byron B. Fowler		1885–1936 May 2 died age 90
VP 1913–1936		
J. Irving Fowler	May	1920–1937 July 20 died
Maurice Hoopes		1915–1949 Feb 15 died age 78
Pres 1930–1942		
Chairman 1942–1949		
Theo F. Kalbfleisch		1906–1934
Byron J. Lapham	Aug	1929–1941 May 8 sold stock
J. R. McMullen		1912–1946 Oct 8 died
		Age 75 NYC
Dennis B. Moynehan		1920–1946 Sep 25 died
Paul Renn		1936–1944 resigned
VP & Trust Officer 1933–44		

Gray E. Safford   1931-1967 resigned age 80
  Clerk, etc.   1902
  Asst Cashier   1919-1929
  Cashier   1929-1932
  VP & Cashier 1932-1952*
T. Coolidge Sherman   1931-1968 resigned
H. McKie Wing   1895-1933 Jan 9 died Age 86
                                                         in California

20 men served on Board during term of Maurice Hoopes
 1 who would become President of the bank

 * Retirement mandatory

    We have already told you about the Federal Deposit Insurance Corporation which insures individual customer accounts and that the cost is borne entirely by the banks.

    The FDIC was established in 1933. Coverage began in 1934 at $2,500 per individual customer, but would be increased over the years to the following amounts:

               1934—$ 2,500
               1939—$ 5,000
               1950—$ 10,000
               1966—$ 15,000
               1969—$ 20,000
               1974—$ 40,000
               1980 –$100,000

    Premiums would vary from time to time. The cost to banks would become very heavy indeed.

Time Frame

History in Headlines

On or about Monday, January 19, 1942

1/14 All Aliens Ordered to Register with Government.

1/19 Blackout Aided by Lake George Boy Scouts.

1/19 Principal Walter P. Reichert Announces Schedule for Regents Tests Starting Today in Junior High School.

1/29 Office of Civil Defense Opens.

1/30 Price and Rent Ceilings Ordered.

Commodities Then & Now (Year)		
	1942	1990
Dow Jones Ind	$110.45	$2,677.90
Gold, oz	35.00	391.19
Silver, oz	.71	5.21
Copper, lb	0.12	1.03

President: Franklin D. Roosevelt
Vice Pres: Henry Wallace

Prices Then & Now (Year)			
	1942		1990
Bread, loaf	$ 0.09	$	1.17
Milk, gal	0.60		2.13
Butter, lb	0.47		1.99
Gasoline, gal	0.15		1.01
New Ford Car	920.00		10,995.00
Annual Income	1,885.00		25,050.00
New Home	3,775.00		91,945.00

On This Day in History

1807—Robert E. Lee, is born. Later Confederate General of Civil War.

1840—Expedition claims part of Antarctica for the U.S.

Firsts, Fads, Things

Bazooka weapon. Tubeless tire
Fibber Magee and Molly on Radio

Major Events of the Year

Millions grow Victory Gardens. Allies continue to lose on battlefront. Progress is made on secret atomic bomb. Flags fly throughout the nation. Horse-drawn wagons deliver milk.

Winners in the Arts

Actor: James Cagney for Yankee Doodle Dandy
Actress: Greer Garson for
    Mrs. Miniver
Movie: Mrs. Miniver
    By MGM Studios
Hit Song: White Christmas
Best Seller: Mission to Moscow
Big Movie: Casablanca

This Year in Sports

W. Series: St. Louis tops Yankees
NFL: Washington
Indy 500: Cancelled because of war
Stanley Cup: Toronto Maple Leafs
Kentucky Derby: Shutout
Rose Bowl: Oregon drubs Duke

Depicted above is the framing and door to the main vault which was located at the end of the lobby in the white marble building from 1915 to 1950.

The sixteen-ton, polished-steel door was hung on an eight-ton frame. The small door on the left was an emergency door for use in the event the main door failed to open. It never had to be used.

Four clocks on the inner side of the door are hand-wound at each closing to control the time at which the vault door can again be opened.

This heavy door was removed from the frame in 1950 and relocated (as explained on page 162) at the end of a newly extended lobby.

The interior of the vault is stacked from floor to ceiling with various-sized safe-deposit boxes for customers. Large chests for housing bank securities are located behind a steel grill. Access to any box or chest always requires the presence of two people, each with separate keys or combinations.

The vault is encased in specially hardened concrete separated by different type layers of steel plate. Further protection is provided by noise-sensitive alarms relayed to the police station.

The vault is sealed off by a glass enclosure and is accessible only to those who identify themselves to the ever-present vault attendant.

Hubert C. Brown

THE PRESIDENCY OF HUBERT C. BROWN
1942–1962

Hubert C. Brown became President on January 19, 1942, at age forty, the youngest man ever elected to that post. Maurice Hoopes was elected Chairman of the Board, a new position in the annals of the bank.

When elected, President Brown was paid $5,000 a year for half-time work at the bank. He was also President of Cool Insuring Agency, then located on Ridge Street. It was not long before he spent most of his day at the bank.

It was easy for employees to perceive that Mr. Safford was very displeased that he had not been selected for the Presidency. Evidently he felt that his long years of outstanding service had earned him the right to the position. He became downright discourteous to the new President to the point that he refused to hang his hat on the same hatrack.

Mr. Brown evidently understood and had empathy for Safford's feelings. At least he never publicly displayed any resentment of the Cashier's insolence. It was well known that he had great respect for Safford's knowledge and competence, but not for the man's mood swings, periodic arrogance, and autocratic management style. The young President was a master of diplomacy. Within a short time, a working relationship evolved that was to their mutual advantage and to the bank's benefit. In fact, when Safford retired ten years later, Mr. Brown appointed Mr. Safford to every committee on the Board of Directors.

President Brown envisioned a kinder, gentler work environment long before that phrase became popular. He introduced an "open door" policy that made him readily available to customers and employees alike. His purpose was to listen, to project a friendly neighbor atmosphere, assuring everyone that bankers at First National were easily approachable. In the process, he was very careful not to usurp the authority of other officers.

A very charismatic man, he preferred to be called "Hubie" by everyone, regardless of their social or economic status. He had a marvelous sense of humor and disdained formality. Invariably, he developed an indescribable rapport with individuals at all levels of society.

When Hubie assumed the Presidency, he was besieged by the specter of a wartime economy which was certain to impact heavily on the bank.

Traumatized by the inglorious thrashing at Pearl Harbor, the nation had changed its mood from apathy to anger. Mobilization became paramount. And it came, quickly and furiously in many forms.

Ten days after Hubie became President, the Office of Civil Defense was established in Washington, D.C. One day later, the OPA (Office of Price Administration) came into being to place ceilings on prices and rents.

Next the Federal government halted the production of civilian cars. State speed limits were set at 35 or 40 mph to conserve tires. Congress provided President Roosevelt with nearly every piece of legislation he requested.

Each month, something new was added: the Office of War Information, the War Labor Board, nationwide salvage drives, the rationing of gasoline and heating oil, sugar, coffee, meats, fats, cheese, shoes, tires, and other items.

Coupon books were issued to control purchases. A horrendous chore was placed on the banks to process the coupons for merchants. Prices, wages, and salaries were frozen. The War Labor Board ordered equal pay to women as recognition of their role in the war.

Hubie Brown predicted that, among other problems facing the bank, there was a strong likelihood the staff would be depleted because of young men entering military service. Robert J. Dehais had already done so in August 1941, months before Pearl Harbor. Others were certain to be drafted.

He was right. At one point a dozen employees, including one young woman, ended up in the military. It was no easy task covering their jobs, especially those who had special skills and experience.

Henry E. Durham, Charles F. Potter, and Robert J. Dehais served in Europe. Robert W. Newton experienced heavy action on LST invasions of Japanese-held islands in the Pacific. James R. Simpson became a Lieutenant Armed Guard Commander of Navy gun crews aboard merchant vessels in all theatres except the Pacific.

Robert S. Clarke, Maurice M. Coon, Fabian O. Ducharme, Paul E. Lavine, Patrick E. McCarthy, and George Stillman all served stateside. Elizabeth Strong enlisted in the U.S. Marine Corps Women's Reserve. The bank gave one month's extra pay to any who entered military service.

As soon as Hubie took office, he started signing the minute book after each meeting, thus attesting that he agreed with what the Cashier had recorded. He discontinued this practice at the end of September 1943.

From the very beginning, Mr. Brown was a strong advocate of advanced education for bank employees. Thus Clarence A. Scriver, an Assistant Cashier, and Robert E. Clarke of the Trust Department were enrolled in three-year summer courses at the Graduate School of Banking at Rutgers University.

Early in the war, citizens were called upon to support the war effort by investing in the Nation. Hubie Brown became Chairman of the Warren County War Savings Bond Campaign. He had a very realistic army tank built out of wood, and it became a symbol in every parade in the area during the war years.

The tank, from which attractive young ladies sold bonds, was prominently displayed in the bank's main lobby. The smallest denomination was a $25 bond, which cost $18.75 and matured in ten years. "Everyone" bought Savings Bonds. The paperwork consumed untold hours of bank time which the bank willingly contributed in addition to that of its President as chairman of the war bond drive.

Model tank operated by Mary Heath.
(Picture by George P. Sauter)

Buy A Bond poster at foot of war memorial monument.
Glens Falls Insurance Company building in background.

The million dollar mark in FHA mortgages was reached in June 1942. The Board praised F. O. Ducharme for his tireless work in promoting and processing these housing loans. As a reward, "Duke" and his wife, who were ardent Yankee baseball fans, were treated to three World Series games in New York that Fall. The Cardinals downed the Yankees in five games.

In the late Fall of 1942, President Roosevelt asked citizens to contribute all the scrap metal they could find toward a war materials salvage drive. The bank donated old radiators, old furnace parts, old motors and the like which had been stored in the cellar since renovation of the heating system.

In 1943, the Board changed the name of the Special Department to Interest Department (savings) and adopted a new set of rules and regulations governing all deposits in such accounts. Among other things, the bank would pay 1% interest, credited semi-annually for accounts between $10.00 and $35,000; no interest for balances less than $10.00 nor more than $35,000, owned by any one person. Deposits of less than $1.00 would no longer be accepted. Technically no depositor had the right to withdraw from an interest account without thirty days' written notice. Seldom invoked.

The Personal Loan Department was transferred back into the main lobby, and the space in the Lapham Building leased to Spencer Trask and Company for $100 a month.

That move made it feasible, four months later, to send Paul E. Lavine to manage the Bolton Landing Branch when H. W. Liddle died unexpectedly on September 8, 1943. Lavine had no car and took an early morning bus to Bolton, returning to Glens Falls on a 5:30 bus. Within a few days he found he could complete his duties at Bolton, and grab a three o'clock bus back to the main bank to work another three or four hours on Personal Loan chores.

Maurice M. Coon, an employee of the Ticonderoga Bank, applied for the vacated position two days after Liddle's death. He began working at Bolton one month later at $2,400 a year.

Glens Falls citizens quickly accumulated a fifteen-foot pile of junk metal, covering nearly three-quarters of an acre in the park between City Hall and the Queensbury Hotel. Its reported weight was 400 tons.

(Arthur S. Fisher Collection)

Coincidentally, the Board also considered acquisition of the Ticonderoga bank, but after full investigation, it never came to fruition.

A suggestion box system was adopted with a minimum award of $1.00 and a maximum dependent upon the value to the bank. Harry Whipple and Joe Barnes received the first two awards of $5.00 each. Later, Rose Marie Dolan was one of those to win awards of as much as $150.

The President recommended a cost of living increase to employees, which was adopted by a majority vote.

Temporary Wage Adjustment
to help offset
Increased Living Costs

To Our Employees

Our Board of Directors recognizing that the cost of living has been increasing for several months have voted, and the National War Labor Board has approved, a temporary wage adjustment retroactive to July 1, 1943 for all regular salaried employees, except officers, on the pay roll records of the bank on July 1st. While the directors are pleased to give this aid during the present emergency, they reserve the right to change or discontinue the plan at anytime. Payment will be made on the following basis:

Effective July 1, 1943, and payable in quarterly installments on the last pay day in the months of September, December, March and June

$100.00 per annum to single persons without dependents or married women whose husbands are self-supporting.

$160.00 per annum to other married persons without dependents or to single persons with one dependent.

$180.00 per annum to married persons with one dependent or unmarried persons with two dependents.

$200.00 per annum to married persons with two dependents or more.

FIRST NATIONAL BANK

Paul Renn, Vice President and Trust Officer, resigned on June 30, 1944, after having been on a paid leave of absence for more than ten months due to a nervous breakdown.

The next January, Blake Francis was elected Trust Officer. Hubie Brown became a full-time working President with a salary of $14,000 subject to the approval of the Treasury Department. Salary advances to other bank officers likewise had to be approved under wartime restrictions.

The G.I. Bill of Rights came into being for veterans. And First National established a 4% rate of interest on these loans, even when part of the financing was under an FHA mortgage loan.

President Roosevelt died on April 12, 1945. Then on May 7, Germany capitulated to Allied demands. The war in Europe was over after five-and-a-half years of bloodshed and mass destruction. America's complete wartime strength could now be concentrated against Japan. In the USA, the rationing of gasoline, fuel oil and oil stoves was ended.

On recommendation of President Brown, the Board agreed to pay one-half the annual fees for employees (other than officers) who would join the Glens Falls Country Club. Previously he had introduced the practice of holding an annual Christmas party at the club for all bank employees. Also every employee (and guest) was treated to a summer outing at a variety of area resorts.

Al Egenhofer, the bank's general ledger accountant, was shot and killed while trout fishing in late June on a stream near Bakers Mills. The culprit was an out-of-season hunter who mistook Egenhofer for a deer. The grand jury termed it accidental and did not indict the hunter.

The bank registered mild approval with the New York State Bankers' Association for Saturday closings from June 1st until October 1st, but objected to such closing for the rest of the year. The two janitors, who were paid sixty cents an hour, were very much in favor of Saturday closings because it would give them a full day to clean the bank during daylight hours.

On August 6, an Atomic Bomb was dropped on Hiroshima. A second bomb was dropped on Nagasaki three days later. Then on August 15, V-J Day (Victory over Japan) was declared.

A 1950 view of renovated main lobby and archway to newly-added building. Note historic murals.

A 1950 view looking toward front door. Note marble floor, high ceiling and skylight.

Now came the herculean responsibility for the nation to convert to a peacetime economy as quickly as possible. Money was the vehicle that would do it. Luckily the bank's mortgage officer was one of the first to return from military service. First National prepared itself for an onslaught of GI and FHA mortgages, and other loans. It came, accompanied by an upsurge of $4,400,000 in deposits, between December 1944 and December 1945. This was the biggest single year increase in deposits in the bank's ninety-two-year history. Another sign of the times: the Board decided to engage in the financing of airplanes.

A special, extra dividend of 4% was declared payable December 15, 1945.

Early in January, the Board answered the Glens Falls Jewish Welfare Fund appeal by contributing to the United Palestine-National Refugee service.

Some minor amendments were made to the by-laws including raising Director fees to $10.00 per meeting, $2.50 per appraisal when appraising property, and $40.00 per diem during any Committee Examination of the bank or Trust Department.

A bank-sponsored retirement party for Harry A. Whipple who had joined the staff in 1896. Employees dressed in "old-timer's" costumes for the occasion.

In May, a report from the Bolton Branch revealed that the bank's first branch had increased its deposits in five-and-a-half years from $385,075 to $976,582, and total loans from $18,172 to $150,876.

Lyman A. Beeman Sr., Francis W. McGinley, and Michael C. Linehan were elected to the Board of Directors in January 1947. Clarence A. Scriver was elected a Vice President and Fabian O. Ducharme an Assistant Cashier. This was the year when the bank first budgeted funds for radio advertising; a total of $2,500. The grand total allotted to advertising, including agency fees, amounted to $12,000.

Banks in New York City, the Capital District, and neighboring communities decided to close Saturdays during the entire year, beginning April 1, 1947. After considerable discussion, First National agreed to do likewise.

At Hubie's suggestion, an Employees' Association was formed to encourage athletic and social activities, and to make management aware of any problems that might exist from time to time.

Shortly after he had been elected to his post, President Brown had voiced concern about the fact that some older members of the staff were confronted with the prospect of ending their careers without benefit of any income other than a meager Social Security allowance. True, the bank was continuing to pay head teller LeRoy Behan while on an extended sick leave. (And would continue to do so during a long period of illness.) But President Brown was concerned that a future Board might be less compassionate. He began a personal investigation of available pension plans which would assure protection for employees.

From time to time, informal discussions were held concerning the feasibility of various plans for retirement and pension of employees. Finally, the Board accepted a plan prepared by the actuarial firm of George B. Buck in New York. It became effective January 1, 1947 and provided for mandatory retirement at age sixty-five.

A three-man Retirement Board was appointed to manage the plan. Alfred D. Clark represented the Board of Directors, Clarence

Scriver, the officers; and Joe Barnes, the other employees. All contributions to the fund were made by the bank. The plan has been modified from time to time to meet the needs of changing times.

Ventilators were installed in the main vault and the silver storage vault to prevent suffocation in case anyone should be accidentally or forcibly locked in the vaults.

Marge Kenneally, an eighty-five-year-old retired employee in 1990, reveals a seldom-seen side of Mr. Safford's character.

"I was the telephone switchboard operator, located on the mezzanine, at an old plug-and-tube board in the 1940s. It was an easy spot from which to observe the main lobby, and if need be, report any disturbance to the police.

"I had to learn how to three-finger type so as to type names and addresses on forms when the phones were not busy. Mr. Safford did not condone idle time.

"One day he noticed I was not busy. He came up the stairs and asked me to type something for the Board of Directors because his secretary was ill. He should have known I was not a secretary.

"Anyway, I turned to Barb Celadon, a secretary who sat behind me, to find out the number of spaces I should use between various parts of the report. She told me. I wrote down the numbers and hurried through the typing. Then I hustled down to Mr. Safford's desk without reading what I had typed.

"He started reading it, looked up at me, read some more, then all of a sudden started to laugh and asked, 'What are all these numbers?'

"Oh, my God. That's the number of blank spaces Barb told me to use.

"He leaned back in his chair and roared with laughter until his eyes watered. He would not let me take it to type over. He kept it."

Paul Lavine recommended a more liberal policy on Personal Loans for the purchase of cars, which was adopted as follows:

	Minimum Down Payment	Maximum Term	Rate of Interest
New cars	25%	24 months	4% discount
Used cars	33%	24 months	5% discount
Used cars, more than 2 yrs old	33%	18 months	6% discount

In early September, $500,000 was transferred from the Undivided Profits Account to the Surplus Account. Later a 6% dividend of $1.50 was declared payable December 16, 1947.

At year end, a bankwide total of $7,998 in loan losses was charged to Profit and Loss. Of that amount, $7,612 was from one loan to a downtown merchant. My, how times had improved from the previous decade.

For an individual to work one's way through the ranks and become a bank officer was a long and arduous task in those days. It took Paul Lavine twenty-five years before he was elected an Assistant Cashier in 1951.

Despite all his wealth, Hubie Brown was, in many ways, a workaholic. True he took time to enjoy himself and share in the pleasures of others. In some respects, he was a "big kid." Whenever a circus came to town, he was among the first to appear at the freight yards to witness the unloading of elephants, tigers, and all the circus paraphernalia. He was an enthusiastic fan at all high school sports events and minor league contests as well.

He was a great admirer of the men in the city Police and Fire departments and often sent them letters of commendation for work well done. He also remembered them with boxes of cigars and candy at Christmas time.

In addition to his stewardship of the bank, he spent countless hours as a director on several other boards in the area, including the Glens Falls Insurance Company, the Glens Falls Portland Cement Company, the Glens Falls Hotel Corp., the Family YMCA, the Community Chest, the Glens Falls Country Club, and the Lake George Club.

He served as Chairman of the Glens Falls Foundation, and was a Trustee of the First Presbyterian Church, and the Hyde Collection, and was President of the Glens Falls Hospital Board during periods of expansion and reorganization.

His leadership style enticed people to want to work with and for him. And it was not in expectation of lavish financial reward. He did not "give away the store." The bank paid prevailing wages for the industry. People liked working for Hubie because of how he treated them; with respect and recognition for their individuality and dignity.

Under his leadership, the bank sponsored a Girls' Softball Team, a Men's Bowling Team, and a Little League Team. More important than the financial support was the fact that the President of the bank gave moral support by attending all the games, casually dressed in army fatigues. Hubie clearly demonstrated that he was a man of the people.

GIRLS' SOFTBALL TEAM

Left to right, Front: G. Nelson Lowe, coach. First row: Charlene Raymond Tracy, Veronica Powers, Joan Wood Burch, Phyllis Crippen. Second row: Doris Gillis, Cecilia Husarick Curran, Jane Glacy, Rose Marie Dolan, Greta Ormstrup Monrian, Doris Derway.

It's worth noting that Hubie's, bank-sponsored, Little League baseball team won the local National League and City Championship in 1960. Hubie Brown personally provided a trophy for each boy. Dick Linehan (then a U.S. Postal Carrier, and one of the bank parking lot attendants in 1990), coached that team. Three of the First National players went on to Williamsport to play as members of the Glens Falls All-Star team in the Little League World Series, the only local team ever to be so honored.

Strange things happen to people in all organizations. Banks are no exception. Mary Cary, a retired ninety-year-old teller (in 1990), clearly remembers the following episode:

One day, her co-worker, Ann, suddenly stopped counting money, stared into space, and said, "I can see the writing on the wall." Mary thought Ann was about to tell a joke. However, Ann simply kept staring into space for about five minutes, and then resumed counting money as if nothing had transpired.

Mary recalls that Ann had been the first female commercial teller north of Albany. In those days, each teller was permitted to process only certain types of deposits and transactions.

A commercial teller window was restricted to checking account transactions. Ann, along with the male tellers, accepted deposits of cash and checks from merchants, business people, and individuals. She cashed checks, exchanged currency and coin, and provided merchants with heavy amounts of coin for their cash registers.

She was an attractive young woman, and became very popular. Some customers would wait in a long line to do business with her rather than go to another teller. She counted money faster than any other teller in the history of the bank. She almost never missed a day of work, and was well liked by her co-workers.

Ann loved a spicy story. Male customers enjoyed telling them to her. She, in turn, would exchange equally spicy stories. Tit for tat, as it were.

However, shortly after the above incident, Ann suddenly changed. One day, at noon, she closed her window, locked her cash in the vault, and left the bank without proving her day's work. The following day, when she did not return to work, Mr. Safford went to her home to find out if something was wrong with her.

Ann said, "No, I just don't feel like working today."

Each of the next three days, he visited her to assure her how much she was missed and how much she was needed. In the meantime, her cash had been counted and proved to the penny.

After four days, Mr. Safford's efforts prevailed. Ann returned to work. But she did not seem to be her own pleasant self. When a customer would start to tell her an off-color story, she would back away from her window, obviously insulted. She shocked old friends by demanding an apology.

Then one day, when she heard the ringing of the church bells, promptly at noon, she closed her window, while in the midst of a customer transaction. She retreated behind the heavy drapes that covered the three-story windows directly behind the tellers. There she proceeded to say her rosary for an indeterminate amount of time.

Friends and fellow employees, who tried to talk with her—to reach out a helping hand—immediately became enemies. Paul Lavine seemed to be the only person in whom she any longer had trust.

The episodes of closing her window and secreting herself behind the drapes became more and more frequent. Her work performance and relationship with customers deteriorated. She was urged to seek professional help, but adamantly refused to even consider it. So the bank granted her a leave-of-absence to spend time at home to regain her health. She lived alone in a big house.

At first she seemed to improve. But then, after several months, things went from bad to worse. She refused help from bank officials, other employees, and friends. There were many reports of strange things she would do in the neighborhood.

Her house was on the corner across from the Abraham Wing School. The kids began to pick on her, and this did nothing to improve her condition.

Finally, one day when school was letting out, she strode out into her yard, and paraded . . . buck-naked . . . in front of the kids. That did it! Neighbors and school officials insisted that she be given professional help whether she wanted it or not.

She had been such an outstanding teller, and a lovely person. She ended up in Marcy State Hospital.

Sad!

The bank was again outgrowing its space in 1948. The firm of Hoggson Brothers, Inc., bank architects and builders from New York City and Chicago, was retained with the stipulation that materials be purchased locally and local contractors and labor be hired wherever possible. The four-story Lapham Building, behind the white marble structure, was demolished and a modern two-story steel and brick structure was erected and attached to the main bank in 1949–50. A third story was added later.

Would you ever have expected to see Mr. Safford standing in front of the bank with tears streaming down his cheeks on a sunny afternoon?

Well, you could have in the summer of 1949.

All the other members of the staff were "crying" too.

Joe Anderson, son of the owner of the bank's New York advertising agency, was a summer employee that year. He is credited with bringing tears to everyone.

It seems that Hank Durham was explaining how to trip the foot alarm in a teller's cage. Hank said, "You place your toe under this bar and lift it twice."

Joe, a quick learner, replied, "Like this?"

A loud explosion followed. A cloud of vapor streamed from jets in front of each teller window.

Luckily, it was after the 2:00 P.M. closing time, and there were no customers in the bank.

Instantly everyone in the main lobby felt a stinging, burning sensation in their eyes. Mr. Safford shouted, "Lock your cash drawers."

The lobby was flooded with tear gas. A loud alarm began to clang on the exterior of the building. The police rushed to the scene as did curious spectators.

In the meantime, the switchboard operator sensed what had happened and phoned the fire department. "Bring gas masks."

Mr. Safford stumbled to the front doors to unlock them for the police. But, within seconds, they also became powerless as the gas flooded their eyes with tears.

Most of the employees scurried down the cellar stairs to the large supply vault where the bookkeepers were housed because of the ongoing construction. But that was exactly the wrong move. Tear gas is heavy and soon settles.

Anyway, firemen soon arrived, donned gas masks and led employees, one by one, from the cellar to the outside air. Windows were flung open, fans obtained, and the place aired out. The tellers struggled for hours to prove their cash while wiping freshly created tears from their eyes. The bookkeepers could not return to their machines until early the next morning.

It took weeks for the gas to finally dissipate from its hiding places in crevices, ledger sheets, and drapes. That episode brought an end to the tear gas system at First National.

In conjunction with the expansion, major changes were made in the interior of the white marble structure. Eight low, modern stations with unbarred windows for tellers were installed on the south side. A new cash vault and a new night deposit vault were situated in a workroom area set aside for the head teller. The Interest Department was enlarged and remained on the north side of the lobby.

The other principal change was the removal of the safe deposit and security vault from the main lobby and the elimination of the mezzanine above it.

Removing the massive door from its hinges and moving it 100 feet to the new location of the vault, at the back end of the new building, was a major feat of engineering skill.

Huge timbers were placed in the basement to shore up the floor. It was imperative that the door remain in an upright position at all times. A crew of skilled movers worked night and day during a weekend, literally inching the massive steel door along its path with special block and tackle and brute strength. It weighed sixteen tons and was a sight to behold.

Few people realized that Gray Safford had a sense of humor. But shortly before the door was to be removed from its hinges, he picked up a workman's crowbar, placed it under the door and posed for a newspaper photographer as if he alone, like Atlas, were lifting the entire weight. Too bad it never got published.

Once the door was hung in its cradle in the new location, the construction foreman said to the vault attendant, "Okay, young lady, let's see you close it." With trepidation, she did. The giant door was again hung so precisely that a youngster could swing it closed. The construction foreman's chest swelled with pride as Hubie Brown said, "Well done."

Telling the story about the crowbar reminded Arthur S. Fisher, retired editor of *The Glens Falls Times,* who happened to be present, of another humorous prank performed by Gray Safford. At the completion of each Board meeting, Mr. Safford would stand at the foot of the stairs and hand each Director a $10.00 bill, his fee for attending a Board meeting.

On one particular day, he was going through the usual routine. However, near the end of the line, one Director glanced at his $10.00 bill and exclaimed, "What the devil is this, Gray?" Bystanders joined Hubie Brown and others in laughter, realizing several Directors had hurried to lunch, each with a CONFEDERATE $10.00 bill stuffed into his wallet.

The cathedral-high bare walls of the main lobby were less than appealing to the eyes of customers. So the Board agreed with President Brown in commissioning one of America's leading muralists, Francis Scott Bradford, to paint four murals depicting historic bridges that spanned the river between Glens Falls and South Glens Falls, and were significant to the development and history of the community.

The murals were painted in the artist's studio on strips of hand-woven Belgian linen, eighteen inches high and twelve feet wide. They were then brought to the bank and glued to the walls in the arches that were part of the original structure. They added a significant sense of culture to the spacious lobby.

However, there is a sad story connected with the murals. Two photographers were sent by the bank's New York advertising agency to take pictures of the murals for inclusion in a booklet to be distributed by the bank. Hubie and a small group of employees nervously watched the photographers taking pictures, late in the evening, perched high in the air on free-standing ladders in the lobby.

It was nearly midnight before they finished their task. They were obviously tired. Hubie tried, in vain, to convince them to stay overnight at his home.

Three weeks went by. Hubie had heard nothing from the agency concerning the pictures. So he phoned the agency and was shocked to hear, "Oh, didn't you know? The driver apparently fell asleep and crashed into an abutment. The car was totaled and both men were killed. Only the film survived, in a metal case."

Subsequently, dissatisfied with the material produced by the agency, Hubie asked Joe Barnes to write a new booklet concerning the historical significance of the bridges, and 10,000 copies were distributed to the public.

To further soften the atmosphere in the bank, the President had background music installed for the benefit of the public and bank employees.

Hubie had another way of showing gratitude for work well done. Many a group of employees, who participated in special projects or particularly difficult conversion assignments, was rewarded with a ride in Hubie's boat and a picnic on one of the islands on Lake George.

We are grateful to George I. Davis, who related memories of a fun occasion at which Gray E. Safford played a major role. Crucial to the story is the fact that Safford owned a pet raccoon, and was adding to the enjoyment of the day by bringing his pet "coon" along on a picnic.

Safford was among twenty-five to thirty prominent local business leaders, who journeyed in four powerboats to a picnic site on an island in the Narrows on Lake George, on a beautiful summer day in (we think) 1950.

It was a day of delightful camaraderie among the "top brass" of the area, indicative of the kind of togetherness that prevailed in those days. Gray Safford was among peers. Much to their delight, Safford released his well-trained pet from its leash to perform a series of entertaining antics.

Louis P. Brown, President of the Glens Falls National Bank and Trust Company, was enthralled. He wanted more. He kept egging the coon on. After awhile, the coon tired of the frolic and climbed a tree, scrambling high into upper branches.

All efforts to induce the coon down from his perch were in vain. The group proposed that Safford leave the coon there overnight and return the following morning to retrieve the coon. They believed the pet would stay on the small island and not attempt to swim to shore.

Safford refused to leave his pet. Efforts continued. Finally, when it was growing dark, the coon responded, and Safford promptly leashed his pet. The men hurriedly piled into the four boats and were homeward bound.

But—that's not the end of the story!

Louie Brown was piloting the fourth boat, some distance behind the others. Somehow, he ran his boat over a ledge of rocks. The shaft was severely damaged. They were unable to attract the attention of others in the party.

Captives in a crippled boat, they started "limping" their way toward the Sagamore Hotel. Someone lifted the hatch cover and discovered the hold was filling with water. Then the lights went out.

Now, they were dangerously exposed.

A speeding boat, its bow high above the water, came racing through the darkness. Shouts of warning were in vain. The speedboat climbed aboard the crippled craft like a mating humpback whale. Fortunately, the smaller speedboat hung up before it completed its mount. The speedster throttled his engines in reverse while the picnickers pushed and shoved it off their larger boat.

Then, of all things, the speedster turned and was leaving the scene of the crash. The crippled craft was taking on more water. Phil Peck yelled, "Come back. Come back and help us." The errant pilot circled. A rope was thrown, and he towed the wounded boat, and its passengers, to shore.

Once the men were safely on the dock, they discovered a streak of green paint on the back of Eddie Maloy's neck. He had ducked just in time, and just barely enough to avoid being crushed.

Somehow, they all had escaped a near tragedy.

Few of those men are alive now (1990), but surely there are family descendants who recall the tales of that eventful outing.

It's too much to expect that forty years later a man would remember the names of all those present at a specific fun outing. The important point is that these local "captains of industry" could be avid competitors in their daily business affairs, yet enjoy good fellowship at informal events.

At the annual organization meeting of the Board of Directors in 1950, it was voted to increase the common stock of the bank $500,000 by paying a 100% stock dividend, thus increasing the capital to $1,000,000, divided into 40,000 shares of stock at $25 par value, subject to approval by the Comptroller of the Currency.

A regular stock dividend of sixty cents was also declared, payable February 1. Later, an extra dividend of eighty cents was declared payable December 15.

First National became the first bank in the area to offer a modern drive-in window facility, when it opened its new branch office in South Glens Falls on February 19, 1951. Customers kept bumping into the protrusion, and it was soon realized that the architect had improperly designed the approach lane. It was rebuilt and attracted an ever-increasing number of customers.

In early September, Thursday evening banking hours, from 6:30 to 8:30, were introduced at the main office as an added convenience for customers and downtown merchants.

A regular dividend of sixty cents had been declared August 1, and then a 3.2% dividend of eighty cents on December 14.

In 1951, we opened our South Glens Falls Office—with the area's first drive-in banking window.

South Glens Falls Branch after major expansion in 1986

G. E. Safford

When Gray Safford took mandatory retirement, at age sixty-five, in late February 1952, William McEchron Bowden was again elected Vice President. Mr. Safford was rewarded with a bonus of $10,000 upon his retirement. Proportionate bonuses would be paid to other employees, when retiring during the next eighteen years.

Clarence A. Scriver was promoted to the position of Vice President and Cashier, effective March 1. He was a slow-talking, slow-acting, super-cautious technocrat, who never exhibited the independence shown by the previous Cashier. Whenever he had difficulty convincing others that something should be done, he simply said, "Well, that's the way Hubie wants it." And it was done.

1952 was also the year in which the new Glens Falls High School building was erected on a ten-acre plot at Quade Street and Sherman Avenue. Hubie's son, Philip was vice president of the first graduating class to have spent all three years of high school education in that building. Our son, John, was president.

Phil was a star basketball player on the 1954-55 Northern Conference Championship team, played first base on the baseball team, quarterbacked and co-captained the football team, and was a scholastic honor student. He worked two summers at the bank as mail boy.

In the summer of 1952, Hubie placed a sign on the corner of his desk, in full view of everyone who passed his office door. It read: I LIKE IKE. That November, General Dwight D. Eisenhower won the Presidential election in a landslide victory. He visited the frontline troops in Korea as he had promised.

The fee for attending Directors' meetings was increased to $20.00. Bank Money Orders were introduced to the public, and First National was soon doing a brisk business with these instruments.

By early September, the Board voted to sell $290,000 worth of low-interest GI mortgages to F.N.M.A. (the Federal National Mortgage Association) to free up money to meet the needs of new mortgage applicants. The bank was carrying a mortgage portfolio of $10,388,955, attesting to its willingness to help the area grow.

Patrick E. McCarthy took over the management of the Personal Loan Department, and was the first to become involved in the Yeagan Plan. This was a system whereby the financing of automobiles was done on a direct dealer basis, with car dealers initiating the loan instruments at their places of business, something First National had never permitted before.

After contacting a few store merchants concerning the feasibility of a Merchants Charge Account Service, President Brown sent Barnes to Franklin National Bank on Long Island to learn the details of operating such a system. This service was something very new in the banking world. It was being operated in only a few metropolitan centers. No bank, in a community as small as Glens Falls, was offering this kind of service. First National was on the cutting edge of a credit card system, which was later to become MasterCard and Visa.

George F. Reger Jr., a new employee, was assigned to help me develop the new Charge-Plan program for First National. A prodigious amount of preparatory work was involved.

Then, on February 17, 1953, the new plan was unveiled before a packed audience of area merchants, at a dinner meeting in the main dining room of the Queensbury Hotel. Several merchants were very much in favor of the opportunity to make credit sales under Charge-Plan, and thereby let the bank take all the risks.

However, like pioneers in any venture, the bank ran into unforeseen problems. Several merchants were willing to assign only their difficult accounts to the bank. Others contended that store accounts built customer loyalty. The concept of a credit card usable in many stores was repulsive to them. The other bank mounted a campaign to discourage merchants from joining the plan.

Also, there was the problem of adjusting bank management thinking (and bank examiners) to the merchant view of super-liberal credit. Merchant hours were long and varied. The Charge-Plan Department had to be staffed accordingly, to match late evening and Saturday hours maintained by drug stores and other establishments.

Despite the resistance, the bank signed up many stores and issued a constantly growing number of individual credit cards.

Nevertheless, after five years of persistent effort, the President concluded that the bank was too far ahead of its times. The community simply was not ready to accept such an advanced concept of credit. Charge-Plan was phased out on February 1, 1958.

First Check Credit was another innovation that failed to gain public acceptance. It was introduced in 1959 and abandoned within three years.

The experience, for young Mr. Reger, proved invaluable as he advanced through the years to eventually become the Senior Vice President of Retail Banking Services for Evergreen Bancorp, Inc., and the First National Bank. He also became a Director of the Keeseville National Bank subsidiary.

In order to protect itself from a sizable loan loss, the bank had been paying the premium on one customer's $50,000 life insurance policy for several years. It was a most unusual step for the bank, but it finally resulted in a judicious settlement by the Executrix of the man's Estate in 1953. Problems with that customer had persisted since 1906.

In addition to the regular quarterly dividends of sixty cents, an extra dividend of $1.20 was declared payable December 9, 1953.

People often found themselves short of proper pocket change to feed a parking meter, a pay phone, or vending machine. They would scurry into the bank lobby to make quick change, only to be delayed by long lines at teller windows.

First National placed an unguarded, open-change bowl on a lobby desk inviting customers to "make your own small change." The public was amazed. But the honor system worked. Small shortages did occur from time to time; also an occasional overage.

One week a series of shortages of between five and ten dollars occurred daily. A teller suspected one woman. She was asked not to use the bowl anymore. The shortages ceased, and the change bowl was retained as a convenience service for years.

Always interested in furthering the education of bank employees, President Brown authorized a $300 contribution to the Educational Foundation of the New York State Bankers' Association in February 1954. But that was only a drop in the bucket, compared to the money spent on sending one or more members of the staff to various colleges each summer, others to specialized training sessions, and making American Institute of Banking Courses available to every staff member.

Rare indeed is the occasion when a defalcation occurs in a bank. But the records reveal that one happened in the Trust Department in 1954, and an Assistant Trust Officer was promptly dismissed. The FBI and the Comptroller of the Currency in Washington were immediately notified. From that point on, such a case is out of the hands of a local bank. All prosecution is handled entirely by Federal authorities.

An experienced Trust Officer, Robert Hinds, was hired from another bank, and the department reorganized. Controls on every phase of the operation were severely tightened and strictly enforced. In addition to this, an outside auditing firm was employed to augment the bank's internal auditing staff for a year. No additional irregularities were found.

That year, for the first time, the bank made Personal Loans available on a Payroll Deduction Plan at 4% to employees of large business firms in the area.

The following year, mandatory Life Insurance on Personal Loans was introduced to lighten the burden on survivors. Low, group rates readily appealed to borrowers.

In mid-summer, President Brown discussed the possibility of acquisition of the Washington County National Bank, at Granville with Maynard Goodfellow, President of that bank. Mr. Goodfellow was receptive. Par value of the First National stock was $25 per share. Granville's was $50 per share.

Left to right: Hubie Brown, Mrs. Caroline Leavens Brown, Mrs. Ada Cowles, Frank Cowles.

(Courtesy of Mary Griffin Brown)

First National offered a merger on the basis of 3.75 shares of its stock in exchange for each share of the Washington County National Bank stock. This translated into 7,500 shares of its stock (par value $187,500) in exchange for 2,000 shares of Granville stock (par value $100,000).

Special meetings of shareowners of each bank were held, and the merger unanimously approved effective November 16, 1955. This produced a consolidated bank with capital of $1,187,500, divided into 47,500 shares of common stock at a par value of $25 per share.

Maynard Goodfellow was elected a Vice President of First National; J. Easton Owens and Robert E. Jones, Assistant Cashiers. All nine other members of the Granville staff were retained.

Seven people, who were members of the Granville staff at the time of conversion, each recorded more than twenty years of accumulated service in their banking careers, as follows: J. Easton Owens, forty-six; Olive M. Morris, forty-two; Anna Williams, forty-one; Charlotte Evans Owens, thirty-nine; Robert E. Jones, thirty-two; Iowerth V. Jones and Hortense Munson, twenty-three. Others on the Granville staff at that time were, Irene B. Carroll (Norton), Hazel B. Chornyak, Anita M. Jones and R. Irene Thomas.

While reminiscing in 1990, Olive Morris said, "I took a temporary job at the bank in 1935 as the President's secretary. But ended up being classified as a 'permanent fixture.' I served as secretary to eight successive administrators."

Hubie then encouraged officers to participate in the meetings and activities of the Washington County Bankers' Association, as well as those in Warren and Saratoga counties. This was in addition to Group V meetings, normally held in Albany, and meetings of the New York State Bankers' Association. He firmly believed such contacts were of mutual benefit to all area bankers.

As of December 1, 1955, adjustments were made, throughout the bank, on salaries between $1,650 and $3,500, to comply with the newly revised Wage and Hour Law, which would become effective March 1, 1956.

Washington County Branch at time of merger.

The Washington County National Bank joined our family as the Granville Office in 1955. The present building was constructed in 1972.

$20 BILL ISSUED BY GRANVILLE BANK
(Courtesy A. Max Helm)

The Granville Drive-In Office was constructed in 1974 to serve Vermont and eastern Washington County.

In January 1956, the Board accepted the requested resignation of a Trust Officer, who had been hired fourteen months previously.

G. Nelson Lowe, a member of the regular staff, was then chosen as a trainee for trust work. He was sent to New York to undergo a period of intensive training in a modern, sophisticated Trust Department at Bankers Trust Company. He returned to Glens Falls and, in due time, became the Senior Vice President of Trust Services for First National, and a Director of Evergreen Bancorp, Inc. For several years, he was Secretary of the Board, and continues to serve as Secretary of the Glens Falls Foundation.

Cognizant of the scarcity of parking spaces in downtown Glens Falls, Hubie Brown proposed a parking lot for First National customers. The Hovey lot, between Maple and Washington Streets, was purchased. Buildings were demolished and the area blacktopped, providing spaces for 100 cars.

The lot was opened on November 9, 1956. Customers were allowed one-hour free parking, and were required to pay for additional time. This prevented all-day parking for other than bank employees. It soon became very popular and was appreciated by customers.

At that point in time, First National was actively devoting time and effort to an expanding Business Development Plan, headed by this author. Among other things, an Officer Call Program was initiated again. Each officer was assigned to visit specific customers at the customer's place of business. It was well structured and required individual written reports for each call. It also was carefully monitored. This time it produced very positive results.

An animated advertising display was conceived for use in the Annual Home Show, sponsored by the Lions Club, and held in the New York State Armory on Warren Street.

Max Tupper, a local sign painter and display artist, then constructed a display, consisting of a revolving ring, eight feet in diameter set at a forty-five degree angle. It featured all the major services offered by the bank. It was so unique that it was subsequently pictured in three national business magazines. Tupper won a bronze award in a worldwide International Display contest of 3,587 entries.

During the three-day show, the display was tended by teams of officers and employees, and immediately generated a new flow of business.

Ever alert to possibilities, President Brown called on the Salem National Bank, but was advised that its Board was not interested in selling at that point in time.

That same year, First National became active in granting New Car Floorplan financing to several area car dealers. It also was actively granting FHA mortgages with only a 5% down payment on properties appraised at $9,000 or less.

In addition to this, the bank was carrying a heavy portfolio of Demand Loans, most of them secured either by cash value of life insurance or stock exchange collateral.

In December, the Board voted to place dividend payments on a quarterly basis commencing in 1957. Business was brisk; deposits had grown to $40,092,999. Loans, especially mortgages, were heavy. In order to maintain proper reserves, the bank had to borrow from $400,000 to $800,000 from Federal Reserve on six separate occasions during the next three months.

A more stringent mortgage policy was adopted in the Spring of 1957. Late charges were imposed for delinquent payments on Personal Loans. Interest on Savings Accounts was increased from 2 1/2% to 3%.

Late in the year, employees were delighted to learn that a group insurance plan was soon to be furnished by the bank. It provided for life insurance, hospital, surgical and major medical expenses for each employee. Coverage was also available for dependents. The bank paid all premiums for other than dependents.

Pay-As-You-Go checking accounts were introduced in June 1958, and attracted deposits from individuals who had not previously used checking account services.

In his continuing effort to improve benefits for employees, Hubie Brown won approval from the Board to grant three weeks

Home Show Display

(Courtesy of A. Max Tupper)

annual vacation to employees having fifteen years service on January 1, 1959 and on the first of January each year thereafter. It was required that each employee take at least two consecutive weeks vacation, if entitled to two or more weeks. Needless to say, he won another round of applause from employees.

In January 1959, William T. Clark and Robert P. Crawford were elected to the Board of Directors, and G. Nelson Lowe was elected Assistant Trust Officer.

The bank donated $20,000 to the Glens Falls Hospital Building Fund in February. Later that year, First National provided a New Boat and Motor Plan line of credit to Lamb Brothers of Bolton Landing. This was the first time the bank had engaged in this field of financing.

Internally, the bank established a written schedule of maximum cash limits for each teller, depending upon where each teller was located. The purpose was to eliminate unnecessary risk in the event of hold-ups.

One bank officer committed an unethical (although not illegal act). He feathered his own nest by having himself personally appointed to a fiduciary capacity for a very rich client of the bank. The case has become a classic, which is still used in Trust Schools as a sordid example to be guarded against.

To prevent a recurrence of any such happening at First National, the Board of Directors adopted the following resolution on November 9, 1959:

"RESOLVED that no full-time salaried officer or employee of First National Bank of Glens Falls, including branches, shall from this date forward accept an appointment to act in any fiduciary capacity when this bank has legal capacity to act in the same capacity, except in situations involving relatives of the officer or employee in question, and such prohibition governs cases where a fee or commission is either charged or not charged. The phrase 'fiduciary capacity' shall include, among other things, acting as a committee, guardian, trustee, executor, administrator, or attorney-in-fact.

"THAT violations of the letter or spirit of this Resolution will be summarily dealt with. THAT if there are special circumstances or any uncertainties as to whether or not a specific appointment falls within or without the terms of this Resolution, that the circumstances will be reviewed respecting any individual case upon receipt of written application for the same, but such review must be had and permission granted or withheld before, rather than after, the acceptance of an appointment."

Each member of the staff was required to sign a form affirming his/her notice and understanding of the Resolution.

First National reached an important milestone on September 6, 1960, when it breached the FIFTY MILLION DOLLAR mark with a new high of $52,477,721 in total assets on that date. It had taken 107 years to reach that plateau. It would take less than twenty years more to reach the TWO HUNDRED MILLION mark. And from that point on, the growth became fantastic.

There were 14,871 commercial banks and 517 savings banks in the nation in 1960. John F. Kennedy won the Presidential election by a mere 120,000 popular votes.

Hubie, and his brother-in-law, George I. Davis, who was a Director of the Glens Falls National Bank and Trust Company, as well as Chairman of the Board of the Glens Falls Insurance Company, certainly were well aware of anything of a positive nature that was happening in the city. It is said that these two competitive tycoons always engaged in lively debates, at family gatherings, as to the merits of their respective banks.

In anticipation of the mandatory retirement of Hubie Brown, the bank added F. Earl Bach to the staff as a Vice President, on September 15, 1960. Later that Fall, Robert J. Dehais resigned, effective the end of the year, to become Treasurer of the Federal Trust Company in Waterville, Maine.

William McEchron Bowden became Senior Vice President (without remuneration) at the annual organization meeting in 1961. And Nelson E. Smith was elevated to the post of Comptroller, the second man to hold that title in the history of the bank.

The most difficult moment this author ever experienced at the bank was on January 24, 1961, when he interrupted a meeting of the Board of Directors and said, "Hubie, you're needed on the phone, at my desk."

"What's so urgent?"

"Your son, Phil."

It was Western Union calling to inform Hubie that his son Philip had been killed in the crash of a Navy jet bomber during a training mission near Sanford, Florida. Ensign Brown had resided with his wife of three months near the Sanford Naval Air Station, and would have celebrated his twenty-fourth birthday the following week.

That was tragedy enough. But there was more to come. His wife, Caroline Leavens Brown, died eleven months later, December 21, 1961, with lung cancer. The following November, his nine-month-old grandson died. The community grieved for him. But he remained stalwart and steadfast.

Blake W. Francis, Trust Officer, was authorized to leave the employment of the bank February 15, 1961.

A bill was passed by the Senate, about this time, permitting a bank to build convenience offices within 1000 feet of its current structure. Hubie Brown decided to explore the feasibility of utilizing this concept to place drive-in windows in the bank's parking lot. Approval had to be obtained from the Chief National Bank Examiner and also the Comptroller's Office in Washington. The bank then purchased an empty plot, immediately adjoining the parking lot on the east, from Mrs. Ethel Balcom. The bank also purchased the Queensbury Motors land and buildings on the west side, toward Bay Street.

The facility, composed of a walk-up window and two drive-in windows, was finally completed and opened to the public on April 9, 1962. Barbara Celadon, Shirley Dark, and Glenn Moore were the first tellers to serve the public from those popular booths.

Adjustments in the salaries of twenty-seven employees were made on July 1, 1961, due to the mandated increase in the Minimum Wage Law to $1.15 per hour, which would become effective on September 1.

President Brown and Margaret LeClaire, president of the employees' association, are shown with Dr. E. Yale Clarke, local physician, inspecting part of an extensive coin and currency collection on display at the bank during April 1961. Dr. Clarke was a renowned numismatist and his collection was considered one of the ten best in the United States.

Open House festivities to introduce public to newly renovated lobby in Glens Falls in 1950.

Joe Hannan, Elsie Raynor, Barbara Celadon, and Shirley Dark. Within a few years, the above foursome became the "permanent" crew at the Maple Street location. The three young women worked together for more than fifteen years as Auto Bank tellers. Parking lot attendant Joe Hannan, a retired Postal carrier, was known as the "Mayor of Maple Street" and one of the bank's best public relations emissaries.

Maple Street Auto-Bank

G. Nelson Lowe was promoted to Trust Officer on September 1, 1961, and Edith R. Hughes was promoted to Assistant Trust Officer, the first woman in the bank's 108-year history to hold an officer title.

A special meeting of shareowners was held on October 10, 1961. A stock dividend of 12% was voted, subject to approval of the Comptroller of Currency. This amounted to an increase of $142,500, enlarging the capital to $1,330,000, divided into 53,200 shares with a par value of $25 each. This was in addition to the regular, uninterrupted quarterly dividend of sixty cents.

Hubie Brown presented a proposal for the purchase of the First National Bank of Lake George. The market bid for FNB of Glens Falls stock was $90 a share at that time. However, none was available at that price. Hubie arranged meetings of both Boards of Directors. Much negotiation ensued. Then competition from the State Bank of Albany surfaced. To make a long story short, Hubie continued to pursue the acquisition.

Make no mistake about it, Hubie Brown, with all his gentle ways, was no pushover. He was a keen, tenacious and ethical competitor. But he was in the game to win.

Finally, a merger was consummated, on December 16, 1966. (More about that, later.)

Unpleasant as it is to relate, another sad scenario unfolded in 1961. The bank introduced a new machine-posted passbook to replace handwritten entries in the Savings Department. Within hours a major discrepancy was noted in a customer's account. A very personable and well-liked teller was the culprit. Investigation soon revealed that she had been maintaining a second set of ledger cards on certain customers. Ultimately, a total shortage of $54,000 was unraveled.

She had been able to circumvent the audit procedures, because each of her selected customers preferred to speak their native language. When receiving a balance confirmation on their accounts, they did not follow instructions to report any error to the auditor. Instead they preferred to discuss the matter in their native tongue with the teller, who could speak their language. She consoled them by showing them one of her dual ledger cards, which matched their individual Savings Passbooks.

During her trial, it was revealed that she had used only a portion of the stolen money herself. Most of it had been handed over to an outside individual with whom she had become involved. Nevertheless, she was sent to prison for four years. On top of this, she was confronted with having to pay income taxes on the stolen money. The terrible experience wrecked her health and what otherwise might have been a happy life.

Christmas Club had been introduced to Glens Falls by First National in 1915. That year, it distributed $62,830 to customers. Merchants looked forward to the flood of checks in late November each year. In 1961, First National mailed 6,589 checks to club members, totaling $738,064. This brought the total distributed by the bank to more than $14,000,000 since the inception of the plan.

In April 1962, President Brown proposed erecting a branch in the Queensbury Plaza Shopping Center. A series of delays ensued before the complex was completed and opened on August 19, 1963.

On September 10, 1962, Hubie Brown requested and was granted early retirement. Simultaneously, he was elected Chairman of the Board (without remuneration).

During his nearly twenty-one years as President of the Bank, Hubie Brown did much to bring a warmth and understanding to banking that replaced the austerity that formerly prevailed. This he accomplished without compromise to sound banking principles, as evidenced by the solid growth of the organization under his leadership. Assets increased from $14,578,000 to $55,340,910, and the the staff grew from 55 to 114 people. Branches had been established in Warren, Washington, and Saratoga Counties. Others were in the offing.

He was a strong advocate of promotion from within, and capitalized on providing available educational opportunities for all staff members. He actively promoted the latest in banking methods, equipment and services in a sincere effort to provide liberal and progressive banking to an ever-increasing number of customers. His

Original Queensbury Office

Our Queensbury Office was established in the area's first shopping center in 1963 and now has six drive-ins.

influence for the next thirteen years as Chairman of the Board was substantial and highly valued.

If one looks back, history will show that significant changes came about because of Hubie Brown. Always a visionary, he sowed the seeds that would make it possible for others to reap the benefits of his foresight. He set the stage for expansion into strategic locations. Minor though they may appear, one of the most brilliant moves was to meet the need for parking in downtown Glens Falls and an Auto Bank accommodation for customers. The perimeters of that location would logically become an area of expansion for the bank. He instilled a pioneering spirit that continues to prevail.

His influence to make Glens Falls a better place to live was never ending. Among other things, it included significant expansion of the Glens Falls Hospital. He became a driving force behind the fund drive for Heritage Hall in the Glens Falls Civic Center. And the list goes on.

Everyone loved Hubie for what he was; not just for who he was and his wealth. He always found time to lend an attentive ear and an understanding heart to anyone in the community.

For years, "the White Bank," and Hubie Brown were synonymous. His leadership as President and then as Chairman covered a period of thirty-three years, the longest in the bank's history.

Few people can ever claim to have the legion of friends that Hubie Brown enjoyed. His friendships ranged from busboys to corporate leaders. He was never too busy to talk to or show interest in other people. He earned for himself a permanent place in the hearts of all who knew him.

Directors during Presidency of
Hubert C. Brown, 1942–1962

F. Earl Bach	1962–1978*
VP Sep 1960–1962	
Pres Sep 1962–1970 Mar*	
William H. Barber	1936–1966 Feb 19 died
Lyman A. Beeman	1947–1968 resigned
William McEchron Bowden	1918–1924
Asst to Pres 1931–1932	1931–1968 resigned
VP 1932–1938	
VP 1952–1961	
Senior VP 1961–1963 resigned	
Arthur F. Brown	1940–1969
Hubert C. Brown	1933–1975*
Pres 1942–1962*	
Chairman 1962–1975*	
Alfred D. Clark	1947–1966 Feb 6 died
Alfred S. Clark	1928–1968 resigned
William T. Clark	1959–1981 Dec 31 died
Senior VP Oct 1968–1970	
Pres Apr 1970–1976	
Pres & CEO 1976–1977	
Chairman	
& CEO 1977–1981	
Robert P. Crawford	1959–1966 resigned
Maurice Hoopes	1915–1949 Feb 15 died
Pres 1930–1942	age 78
Chairman 1942–1949	
Michael C. Linehan	1947–1964 Dec 3 died
Harold P. McConnell	1950–1962
Francis W. McGinley	1947–1979*
J. R. McMullen	1912–1946 Oct 8 died
	age 75 NYC

Dennis B. Moynehan   1920–1946 Sep 25 died

Paul Renn   1936–1944 June 30 resigned
  VP & Trust Officer 1933–1944

Gray E. Safford   1931–1967 resigned age 80
  Clerk 1902
  Asst Cashier   1919–1929
  Cashier Mar   1929–1932
  VP & Cashier 1932–1952*

Clarence A. Scriver   1962–1969*
  Credit Mgr   1935–1942
  Asst Cashier   1942–1943
  AVP   1943–1947
  VP   1947–1952
  VP & Cashier 1952–1960
  Executive VP 1960–1962 Aug*

T. Coolidge Sherman   1931–1968 resigned

Dwight A. Symmes   1954–1965 Mar 22 died

21 men served on Board during Presidency of Hubert C. Brown
  2 who would become Presidents of the bank
  * retirement mandatory

Henry E. Durham, the bank's first full-time purchasing agent, works new electric controls for freight elevator (previously hand cranked). Hank became a forty-five year veteran. John Bulman (on elevator) was the bank's last uniformed armed guard.

𝔗𝔦𝔪𝔢 𝔉𝔯𝔞𝔪𝔢

History in Headlines

On or about Monday, September 10, 1962

9/15   Glens Falls Police Plagued by Telephoned Bomb Threats

9/4   U.S. Pledges to Use Any Means to Bar Communist Cuban Aggression.

9/7   Storytown Greets Its 2,000,000th Visitor.

9/17   First Federal Suit Filed to End Public School Segregation.

9/30   Federal Officers Hold Back Protesters as Black Student James Meredith Is Enrolled at University of Mississippi.

Commodities Then & Now (Year)		
	1962	1990
Dow Jones Ind	$602.03	$2,615.59
Gold, oz	35.00	402.10
Silver, oz	1.08	5.25
Copper, lb	0.31	1.03

President: John F. Kennedy
Vice Pres: Lyndon B. Johnson

Prices Then & Now (Year)		
	1962	1990
Bread, loaf	$ 0.21	$ 1.17
Milk, gal	1.04	2.13
Butter, lb	0.75	1.99
Gasoline, gal	0.28	1.29
New Ford Car	2,924.00	10,995.00
Annual Income	5,556.00	25,050.00
New Home	12,550.00	91,945.00

On This Day in History

1623—Colonists load first cargo at Plymouth for England.

1846—Elias Howe is granted first U.S. sewing machine patent.

Firsts, Fads, Things

JFK coloring books. Worry beads. Powdered orange juice.

Major Events of the Year

Telstar satellite is launched. Russia agrees to dismantle missiles in Cuba. "Overdose" kills film star, Marilyn Monroe. U.S. supplies Israel with short-range missiles.

Winners in the Arts

Actor: Gregory Peck for *To Kill a Mockingbird*
Actress: Anne Bancroft for
    The Miracle Worker
Movie: *Lawrence of Arabia*
    By Horizon Pictures
Best Seller: *Silent Spring*
Big Movie: *The Longest Day*

This Year in Sports

W. Series: Yankees top Giants
NFL: Green Bay. AFL: Dallas
Indy 500: Roger Ward at 140.293 mph
Jackie Robinson to Hall of Fame
Kentucky Derby: Decidedly
Rose Bowl: Minnesota tops UCLA

Shown above, (left to right): Ruth Hawley, Lyle Gregory, commercial tellers, and Robert Newton, head teller. During the 1950s, special Express Windows were used to expedite heavy traffic in the downtown Glens Falls lobby. A floor guard assisted in directing customers to five additional commercial tellers on the south side of the lobby; and two savings tellers and a Christmas Club teller on the north side.

F. Earl Bach

THE PRESIDENCY OF F. EARL BACH
1962–1970

F. Earl Bach was elevated from Vice President to President on September 10, 1962, through the graciousness of Hubie Brown, who had chosen to take early retirement from the Presidency.

Hubie agreed to become Chairman of the Board, without remuneration, and was so elected. He enjoyed being at the bank on a daily basis and was provided with a desk in a corner of the officers' platform. Then he attempted to maintain an office in the Board room, adjacent to the President's office. However, neither location proved feasible. His mere presence implied to customers and employees alike that Hubie was still in charge.

In order to give President Bach an opportunity to prove himself, Hubie had to remove himself from the premises except for Board and committee meetings and other special occasions.

Mr. Bach did not have deep roots in the community, as had all his predecessors. So he was presented with the difficulty of gaining widespread community acceptance. He enhanced his chances by maintaining an open-door policy in the office previously occupied by Hubie Brown.

Mr. Bach had a background, heavy in the field of bank investments. He had spent twenty-five years at Plainfield Trust Company, in Plainfield, New Jersey. In 1953, he resigned as Vice President in charge of trust investments and supervision of that bank's corporate and municipal portfolio. Following a short stay with Lehman Brothers in New York City, he became Executive Vice President and a Director of Merchants National Bank and Trust Company in Poughkeepsie. He retained that title when a merger occurred with Dutchess Bank and Trust Company in 1956.

With his background, it was not surprising to see him reviewing the investment portfolio at First National and reading the Wall Street Journal each morning before devoting attention to other Presidential duties.

President Bach had a fetish for tidiness, and early on saw to it that incidental clutter was removed from desk tops, counters, and file cabinets. There was an accumulation of old desks, chairs, and other outmoded furnishings stored in the basement, and he made these available to employees on a highest bid basis. Boy, did they move out quickly at bargain prices. He also instituted a "records retention schedule," conforming with legal requirements, and thus reduced the space allocated to old records storage.

Early in January 1963, Paul Lavine was appointed to represent the interest of First National on the Board of the Financial Computer Center of Eastern New York, Inc. The local bank joined with eight other medium and small size banks to form a computer center to facilitate processing of the mushrooming volume of checks, which was expected to double in the next decade, and to compete with giant banks. It was like David taking on Goliath in the banking industry—this time using the thin magnetic tape of an electronic computer instead of a slingshot.

It meant that each bank had to provide every customer with new checks and deposit slips printed with magnetic, coded numbers, a costly and time-consuming undertaking.

Initially the computer was mutually shared for processing each bank's checking accounts only. Their combined total deposits placed them among the 125 largest banks in the nation. The cooperative was composed of banks located in seven communities within a forty-five mile radius in the Albany-Schenectady area, and included the following: Adirondack Trust Company, Saratoga Springs; Ballston Spa National, Ballston Spa; Citizens Trust Company, Schenectady; City National Bank and Trust Company, Gloversville; First National Bank of Glens Falls; First Trust Company, Albany; Mechanics and Farmers Bank, Albany; Montgomery County Trust Company, Amsterdam; and Schenectady Trust Company of Schenectady.

The Center was located adjacent to the General Electric Company in Schenectady. That first GE 225 computer was a monstrous piece of equipment, occupying a large dust-free and air-conditioned room. GE had a second computer as back-up for emergencies.

The checks and deposit tickets were "read" into the computer at a rate of 50,000 documents an hour, and then posted to individual customer accounts at the rate of 1,500 accounts per minute. Finally, a high-speed printer turned out more than 1,500 complete customer statements an hour. All of this was considered "mind-boggling speed" at that point in the history of data processing.

The local Board reasoned that this method of cooperative operation would result in long-term advantages to First National. That reasoning proved correct. Over the years, countless improvements have occurred, but the concept of a multi-bank processing center still prevails.

As Chairman of the Board, Hubie Brown continued his contacts with other bankers in the area. He revived personal conversations with Clifford W. Higley, President of the First National Bank of Hudson Falls. Then in March 1963, he sent a letter to the Board of Directors of that institution inviting a merger of both banks.

Among other things, the Chairman pointed out that the last sale of First National of Glens Falls stock had been at $94 a share, and that there was a rather large list of persons who had signified their desire to purchase shares as soon as they became available.

He made it known that the South Glens Falls, Bolton Landing, and Granville branches were working well and profitably; that the Maple Street Drive-In facility was proving most beneficial after having been in operation less than a year; that construction of a new branch in the Queensbury Shopping Plaza would begin as soon as weather would permit; and that the Trust Department had grossed six-figure profits during the last three years and should contribute substantially to future earnings.

An Agreement of Consolidation was approved by the Directors of both banks on March 26, 1963. Each bank called a separate meeting of its shareholders on May 17, and the Agreement was approved, subject to approval of the Comptroller of the Currency, and other supervisory authorities.

Par value of First National of Glens Falls stock was $25 per share. Hudson Falls' was $20 per share.

Glens Falls offered a merger on the basis of 1.80 shares of its stock in exchange for each share of the Hudson Falls stock. This translated into 27,000 shares of its stock in exchange for 15,000 shares of Hudson Falls stock.

This produced a consolidated bank with capital of $2,005,000, divided into 80,200 shares of common stock at a par value of $25 per share. On July 12, 1963, a Certificate of Approval was received from the Comptroller of the Currency, and the consolidation was completed.

Clifford W. Higley was elected a Senior Vice President and a Director of the continuing bank. James Gibson also was elected a Director, he having been a member of the Hudson Falls Board. Erskine Paris was appointed a Vice President; Anna M. Bishop, an Assistant Vice President; and James E. LaPan, an Assistant Cashier. All thirteen members of the Hudson Falls staff were retained.

Four people, who were members of the Hudson Falls staff at the time of conversion, each recorded more than twenty years of accumulated service in their banking careers, as follows: Marion E. Wilson, forty-eight years; Frederick Harris, thirty-six years; Lorraine Coughlin, thirty-three years; and Pearl Mayotte, thirty-two years. Two others are still on staff in 1990. Lois S. Oliver has thirty-nine years to date and is the Assistant Vice President and Manager of the Kingsbury Office. Joan Metraw has twenty-seven years to date and is head teller at the Hudson Falls Office.

Concurrent with the conversion, an Advisory Board of the Hudson Falls Office was elected, composed of the following members: Frank K. Bronk, Ambrose Corcoran, Lawrence B. Griffin, John A. Leary, Erskine C. Paris, William J. Reed, Philip J.

Riley, Daniel L. Robertson, and Melville A. Sheldon. This was the first Advisory Board formed by the bank. More would follow. The primary purpose was to assure a high-level liaison between the home office and the individual communities in which the branch offices were located.

On the national scene, the nation was stunned when President John F. Kennedy was killed on November 22, 1963 by an assassin's bullet as he rode in a motorcade in Dallas, Texas. Just ninety-nine minutes after Kennedy's death, Vice President Lyndon B. Johnson was sworn in as the 36th President of the United States.

By 1964, some local and some national firms were being granted sizable lines of credit. Some, including local firms, ranged as high as $500,000, the bank's legally allowable limit at that point in time.

Harry J. Robinson was hired as an Assistant Vice President on August 17, 1964. Previously, he had been associated with the Chemical Bank New York Trust, and was well known in banking circles because of his various functions in the city bank's National Division.

The 1960s were a decade of strife, civil unrest, permissiveness and protest. Dr. Martin Luther King Jr., a young black minister, pressed his crusade for racial equality. And in the summer of 1964, the most sweeping civil rights legislation in history was signed into law. Among other things, it prohibited racial discrimination in employment and required banks to actively recruit, hire and train blacks and other minorities.

The Beatles, a shaggy-haired group of four male singers from Great Britain, invaded America and catapulted to fame.

The miniskirt became a fashion frenzy.

Politicians committed the youth of the nation to a winless war in Vietnam. Protesters picketed the White House, demanding withdrawal of troops from Vietnam. Young men burned their draft cards. Later, a peaceful demonstration in Washington turned violent and 50,000 stormed the Pentagon.

A 1928 view of building which housed the Sandy Hill National Bank and later became the home of the First National Bank of Hudson Falls.

The 1963 merger of the First National Bank of Hudson Falls gave us an important presence in Washington County.

Racial tension plagued the nation and exploded into a blood-bath of rioting, looting, and arson in major U.S. cities. But peaceful Glens Falls suffered no such dire consequences.

In most of the nation, business was good and the economy surged ahead.

But the war begat blights of moral degradation in expressions of protest like the one that attracted 400,000 to a spaced-out weekend at Woodstock, near Bethel, New York in mid-August 1969.

Near the end of the decade, more than 540,000 Americans were engaged in Vietnam; and 250,000 civilians voiced their opposition to the war in peaceful demonstrations in Washington.

On the bright side, the nation was making great strides in space navigation, sending astronauts to orbit the moon, and then in June of 1969 to land Apollo II on the moon. Astronaut Neil Armstrong declared, "That's one small step for man, one giant leap for mankind."

In January 1965, the Board of Directors reviewed, updated, and amended the bank's By-Laws, "consistent with the requirements of the laws of the United States and of the Articles of Association." A certified copy of the amended By-Laws was filed with the Comptroller of the Currency immediately after adoption.

An air-conditioning system was installed for the ground-floor offices of the main bank, prior to the summer of 1965.

Hubie Brown was continuing to pursue a merger with the First National Bank of Lake George, and with the aid of a special committee was considering ways and means of including the Emerson National Bank of Warrensburg in a consolidation.

The interest rate on time (savings) deposits was increased to 4% effective July 1.

In his annual report to shareholders, President Bach summarized 1965 as another year of solid achievement for the bank, which included new records for earnings, loans, deposits, and total resources. He said, "The year was a record for business and banking. Industry and commerce operated at high levels, and a high demand for loans persisted throughout the year."

Earnings per share equaled $6.78 compared with $6.49 for 1964.

During this decade, the bank was involved in what were known as "SBA Participation Loans." Basically, the bank would loan let's say $10,000 to a firm that met the "small business" criteria of the Federal Small Business Administration. The SBA would agree to guarantee up to 75% of a loan should it become in default. This enabled the bank to lend to borrowers who might not meet normal bank standards, but were worthy of credit on a smaller risk basis.

President Bach had the dubious distinction of being the first President in the bank's 113-year history (1966) to have an armed robbery occur during his tenure. Then, lo and behold, six months later there would be a second robbery.

The first one occurred about 10:50 A.M. on July 15, 1966, in the South Glens Falls Office. I remember it clearly, because I was there, substituting for Jack Rafferty, manager. He picked a fine time to be on vacation.

I was on the phone with the main office, providing Paul Lavine with some information. Suddenly a customer's voice demanded, "Step it up, Jack. I ain't got all day!"

My reaction was, "What kind of service are we giving over here?" I stood up to see over the frosted glass partition. A "customer" cradled a large brown grocery bag in his arms and walked quickly out the door, as if he were a Grand Union manager leaving with a day's supply of coin for his cash registers. No one else was in the lobby.

As the door closed, Elise Fenton, a teller, shouted, "Joe! We've been robbed!"

"You've been WHAT?"

She pointed out the back window. "There he goes, running through those bushes."

Scott Tallman, a twenty-year-old teller, explained. "That guy shoved a paper bag across my counter and ordered me to fill it. He had a gun pointed at me, and it was shaking. He ordered the other tellers to gather around me. I had just finished emptying my cash drawer when you stood up with the phone in your hand and startled him. He grabbed the bag and took off, but he did not run."

Immediately, we phoned the FBI, Albany Office, locked the door, and placed a crude sign in the window. "Emergency. Bank closed. Temporarily."

Without talking to each other, each teller wrote down his or her separate description of the bandit. This method is of greatest assistance to the FBI.

Elise Fenton explained that while Scott was being robbed she was pressing the silent police alarm and could not understand why a police car had not yet arrived.

It developed that the robber had used a diversionary tactic. Just before entering the bank, he phoned the police department to report a disturbance at the South Glens Falls Public Beach. The lone officer on duty was dispatched to the beach. He was out of his car trying to locate the reported commotion while the bank alarm was being sounded, and could not be reached by the dispatcher.

The dispatcher then notified the Glens Falls police, and a general police alert was sounded.

An FBI agent, who had been driving north of Saratoga Springs, arrived almost simultaneously with a Glens Falls police car, which was closely followed by South Glens Falls, the State Police, and even Fort Edward police.

The FBI agent took charge. The way he operated was something to behold. He made no notations. He simply coordinated all action, quickly and precisely, as if every move had been programmed in his mind.

He did it all without impinging on the jurisdiction of any local police units. And they cooperated willingly, as if they expected and appreciated his guidance.

He was pleased that we had blocked off the area around the teller's window so as to preserve any fingerprints.

First, a description was obtained and a police sketch of the suspect made by Patrolman Harold Osborne of the Glens Falls police. Roadblocks were already in the process of being set up, and a description of the bandit was radioed to them. The teller area was being dusted for fingerprints.

Police units were dispersed to scour the streets in case the robber was still afoot. Others were assigned to cover bars known to be frequented by troublemakers. South Glens Falls Police Chief Thomas L. Cleland stood by, supplying the FBI agent with local data.

FBI agents kept arriving, one by one. The first two were assigned to knock on doors in the area and ask residents if they had seen anyone who matched the description of the robber; also to gain entrance to each home to assure themselves that no one was being held hostage. As soon as other agents arrived on the scene, they were assigned to a variety of locations, such as bus depots, taxi stands, the railroad depot, the airport, car rental outlets; any spot that would provide a means of escape.

And the FBI agent in charge never had to refer to a note to verify which locations were already being covered.

Bingo!

During the door-to-door search, one agent found a woman who said, "Yes. I did see something strange. A man was looking under a car, across the street, in the NIBCO (Northern Indiana Brass Company) parking lot this morning, a little after 9:30. Then he left the parking lot and walked down the street. A short while later, he returned with a bag of groceries and drove off. Seems strange that he didn't drive the car to the store."

The NIBCO personnel manager said, "Yes. We did have an employee leave work, not feeling well, this morning. But I don't think he has a car. Let's ask the guy who works with him if he loaned him his car."

A quick check revealed that the coworker's car was missing and that his fellow workman was one of three people who knew where a "hideaway key" was kept.

This was a most promising lead. The Glens Falls police knew the individual. They went to his home and found he was not there. Immediately, he became the prime suspect. He matched the description, and he was missing.

A little later, a .22 caliber pistol was found near shrubbery in a garden east of the bank parking lot.

Shortly after noon, a state trooper discovered the stolen car in the village of Lake George. From eyewitnesses, he obtained a description of the man who had left the car. Attendants at a nearby bus depot said it matched the description of a man who had bought a bus ticket.

State Police in Keeseville were notified and secreted themselves in a bus stop restaurant south of the village. When a bus arrived from the south, they immediately spotted the suspect, waited until he was seated at the lunch counter, then arrested him, and recovered $12,331, just $5.66 less than had been stolen. The money was impounded, to be held as evidence at the trial.

State Police Zone Sergeant Edward Pratt was one of two officers assigned to return the robber to the Moreau barracks, where he admitted committing the holdup. Subsequently he was sentenced and served about three years in prison.

Incidentally, after retirement from the force, Ed Pratt worked at the bank for years (until December 22, 1989) as supervisor of collections in the Consumer Loan Department.

Don Metivier was the first news reporter on the scene and did an excellent job of reporting the events of that day, and writing follow-up stories.

Robert E. Powers, a National Bank Examiner, resigned from the force to become an Assistant Cashier at First National in early July, assigned to mortgage and loan duties. He succeeded the only other man to head the bank's mortgage function, F. O. Ducharme, upon Duke's retirement. After twenty-two years of service, Powers took early retirement at age sixty-two because of health conditions.

Albert L. Emerson, who owned controlling interests in both the Emerson National Bank of Warrensburg (87%), and the First National Bank of Lake George (63%), had died on August 8, 1963. However, it was not until three years later that settlement of his estate was pending. This set the stage for Hubie Brown to reopen negotiations for the above banks, this time through the Estate of Albert Emerson.

The Directors of First National of Glens Falls took a most unusual step. They decided to make a CASH offer to purchase the Lake George bank. On September 12, they began to make all the normal preparations to schedule a special meeting of shareholders for November 1, 1966 to vote on the proposal.

However, within a couple of weeks, a National Bank Examiner spent three days in the area studying the proposal, and advised that, as a cash-purchasing bank, it was not necessary to have shareholders' approval. This was confirmed by a letter from the Comptroller of the Currency. So, on October 10, the authorization for such a meeting was rescinded.

Sealed bids were required by the executors of the estate.

First National of Glens Falls submitted the high bid of $351 per share ($667,662) in cash, for 1,902 shares of the Lake George bank stock. Other banks offered exchanges of stock.

It was not an easy victory. Other bidders included the Glens Falls National Bank and Trust Company, the National Commercial Bank and Trust Company of Albany, the Bankers Trust Company of New York City, the Marine Midland National Bank of Troy, and Mrs. Howard LaRose of Lake George.

On the basis of an exchange of stock, the State Bank of Albany paid the Emerson Estate $2,507,287.50 for the Warrensburg bank. Other bidders were Glens Falls National and Marine Midland.

The merger with Lake George became effective December 16, 1966. Howard McKee, who had been Executive Vice President and Cashier of the Lake George bank, was appointed a Vice President and Jean Morris an Assistant Cashier of the continuing bank. As with previous acquisitions, all seven other members of the staff were retained.

Jean Morris recorded twenty-seven years of accumulated service before retiring in 1989. Karen Steeley is still active with thirty years of service as is Janet Spahn with twenty-six years. Two others, Delores O'Rourke and Beatrice Hughes, did not quite make the twenty-year mark.

A Lake George Advisory Board was formed, and included former President Albert Beswick, William Busch Jr., Frank Cotton, Stuart Hawley, Gilbert Lange, Robert Leavitt, Alger Mason, and Walter VanDusen.

This was the first home of the First National Bank of Lake George and is still referred to by local residents as "the old bank building."

The bank was founded in 1907 by a group of local businessmen including summer residents William Shepard and Spencer Trask.

The bank was robbed twice, once in 1916 when a sack of money was taken from a trolley car in which it was being transported, and again in July 1924 when Cashier Emmett Archibald was robbed at gunpoint in front of Shepard Park by two men who got out of a Lincoln touring car. The perpetrators were never apprehended.

To serve growing tourist industry, we acquired the First National Bank of Lake George in 1966.

(Courtesy George F. Reger Jr.)

Howard McKee, retired Vice President, now (in 1990) recalls, ''The transition was very easy. You would hardly know it happened, except that the next morning's reports were headed *The First National Bank of Glens Falls.* The community accepted the new relationship without any hesitation. The employees were especially happy because, prior to the merger, they had been very apprehensive that they might be acquired by a less-understanding bank.''

President Bach, of course, was pleased to see the Lake George deposits and assets added to the footings, creating a more impressive total for the 1966 year-end statement of the total bank.

Something far less pleasing shocked him into action on the morning of January 4, 1967—another armed bank robbery.

Let's tell it first from what was happening at the home office, then we'll go to the scene of the crime, the Queensbury Office.

Marge Kenneally, the switchboard operator in the main office, reported, ''No one has called in the code number from Queensbury. Had I better call them?''

''Yes. But do it, quick.''

She did and replied. ''George answered and said everything is okay. But he sounded funny.''

''Call the police.'' She did.

Several long moments later, the manager of the Queensbury Office, George F. Reger Jr., phoned and reported, "We've been robbed."

Without waiting for details, word of the robbery was immediately phoned to the FBI.

First National had only one bank officer who had any experience in an actual robbery. President Bach immediately sent that Assistant Vice President to the scene.

Meanwhile, here's what had been happening at Queensbury, as related by George Reger:

"Around 8:05 A.M. head teller Lynn LaBarge arrived at work, together with tellers Mary Shea and Alice VanHorne. Once inside they were confronted by two men, who alternately displayed a snub-nose pistol.

"About 8:08 A.M. I arrived and parked near the bank. As I approached the bank door, I heard a woman screaming. I looked through the plate-glass window and could see that a man was holding a gun to the back of Mrs. Shea's head. He motioned me to enter the bank. My other choice was to run for help. If I did, what would happen to the hostages?

"After I was inside and locked the door, one man taped up the women with adhesive tape and placed them in the ladies' room.

"Then they taped up LaBarge and left him in the men's room. They had already forced him to unlock the metal shield that covered the vault combination. Next, they forced me to go to the vault door, placed a gun at the back of my neck and said, 'Get it open.' "

Reger continued: "Have you ever tried to think with a gun at the back of your head? I couldn't remember the combination. I missed on the first try. The gunman said, 'Quit stalling. Open it.' The gun was making me nervous. Thank goodness the combination worked on the second try.

"While the vault door was opening, I asked the gunmen, 'How did you get in?' One answered, 'It's a military secret.' Again I asked, 'Seriously, how did you guys get in here?' The smaller of the two men answered, 'We were trained for this.'

"That morning, we had a surplus of cash which was all bagged and ready for shipment to Federal Reserve. The bandits had a small suitcase with them and stuffed the money in it, all $99,000. Then they hustled me back into the men's room and bound me up with tape. Those guys already had strips of tape on the walls of the rest room with which to do the job.

"LaBarge broke free first. He went into the work area and pressed the police alarm. Then he returned, untied me, and we untied the women. Moments later the police arrived.

"Within another few minutes, an FBI agent arrived, quickly followed by the Assistant Vice President from the main office. Coordinating command was turned over to the FBI agent, following basically the same procedure as at South Glens Falls, adjusted to the different environment."

It was quickly established that the bandits had taken the keys to Lynn LaBarge's new gold Chevy, stolen it and left the scene. A thirteen-state teletype alarm was issued by the Warren County Sheriff's Office, roadblocks established, and the police began combing the area.

The news media converged on the site. Don Metivier and Harold Robillard, of *The Glens Falls Times*, were provided with information as fast as it developed, and they produced a front page story for that evening's edition, plus follow-up stories, later, and a special feature column by Metivier.

However, following the robbery, in the interest of security, the AVP refused to allow cameramen entrance to the bank lobby. The FBI concurred. The branch manager and two women employees did join cameramen on the doorstep outside the bank for a picture session.

No one had been hurt. In fact, everyone commented on how "polite" the two men had been to them during the holdup. Nevertheless, it was a nerve-racking experience.

Soon, LaBarge's stolen car was spotted in the Dunkin' Donuts parking lot on Upper Glen Street. It later was learned that the bandits abandoned it there and drove off in a foreign sports car.

They drove to the West Mountain Ski Center where they planned to spend the day skiing until the "heat" was off. Much to their amazement, the ski area was closed until 3:00 P.M. They had checked it out the previous week, but failed to realize that the extended hours applied only to the holiday week.

They tried to go over the mountain to Lake Luzerne on a back road, but without proper snow tires could not make it. The hold-up men were from Long Island. One of them said, "We can outsmart these 'Keystone Kops.' They'll be looking for two men. You drive and I'll hide in the back."

Imagine their surprise when the ruse itself aroused the suspicions of two local police officers at a roadblock in Lake Luzerne; two pairs of skis, one occupant in the sports car. While questioning the driver, the policemen detected motion under a blanket in the luggage area. They drew guns, and the driver talked the other suspect into coming out without shooting.

The hold-up men were guests at a dude ranch run by the owner of the bank's custodial service and were trying to get back to the ranch when intercepted at the roadblock.

Later, it was learned that the robbers had only one gun. During the hold-up they had passed it back and forth, behind the backs of the victims, to give the impression that each man had a gun.

How had they gained entrance to the bank?

George Reger explained: "The owner of the bank's custodial service was a friend of one of these men while living on Long Island, and apparently the godfather of one of his children. Unable to find work in the city during the summer prior to the hold-up, these two men came upstate. Their old friend gave them temporary work on a night cleaning crew. As a result, they had actually worked nights, for awhile, in the Queensbury Office, completely familiarizing themselves with the interior. That is when they made a copy of the door key, with which they later gained entrance in order to commit the early morning robbery."

All the money was recovered in less than two hours after the alarm had been sounded, thanks to the speedy response and excellent teamwork among police agencies. The robbers pleaded guilty and were sentenced to four-year prison terms.

By way of explanation as to why it takes two people to open a bank vault door: The combination numbers are covered with a metal shield which is locked in position with a padlock. The key is placed in the custody of an employee who has no knowledge whatsoever of the combination. Any bank officer who is authorized to have a particular combination cannot open that vault or security chest alone. The person with the key must be present to unlock and remove the shield. This is an inviolate rule.

Furthermore, a time lock prohibits the opening of the vault until a pre-set time. The clocks are set, at closing time, by one person and checked by a second person as an additional security procedure.

Gray E. Safford decided to resign from the Board of Directors on February 14, 1967, after sixty-five years of distinguished service. As a mark of gratitude and esteem, a laudatory resolution was entered in the minutes of the Board, which read, in part: "His career in various capacities over this long period was always distinguished by his devotion to the interests of the bank, by the utmost diligence and industry, and by creative and constructive contributions to the bank's growth and progress, making his record one unmatched in our annals."

At that same meeting, Gerald J. Buckley, Donald S. Creal, Carl R. DeSantis, and John V. Hallett were elected as new members of the Board, increasing the total to twenty-one members.

A schedule of fees for Directors and Committee meetings was adopted as follows: Board meetings, $50; Discount Committee, $50; Investment, $50; Trust, $35; Examining, $50; Advisory Board, $25.

Window teller machines were installed in the South Glens Falls and Lake George Offices, and later at all teller locations.

Chairman Brown recommended that the officers be empowered to employ help in expediting the Federal Urban Renewal Program in the city. Efforts were made to facilitate including the

YMCA building, which was then parallel with the bank on the opposite side of Lapham Place.

The rate of interest on certificates of deposit was then running at 4%, 4 1/2%, and 5%, depending upon length of time. These were limited to $25,000 for any one individual.

The bank came to the aid of a local firm by storing a half-million dollars worth of sixty-pound, smoke-blackened bars of silver in the bank's silver vault following a disastrous fire at the company's plant. Never before had the bank been called upon to perform that particular service.

On November 3, 1967, at a Special Meeting of shareholders, the capital stock of the bank was increased $401,000 by the issuance of a stock dividend, three for two, thus increasing the common stock to $2,406,000, divided into 120,300 shares at a par value of $20 per share. Because of the increase in capital stock, the bank was required to subscribe to an additional 482 shares of Federal Reserve Bank stock.

Shortly thereafter, the bank's first TV window was installed at an extended drive-in window to accommodate increased traffic at the South Glens Falls Office. Customers were enthralled to see themselves on TV.

The vibrant economy of the 1960s produced additional business for the bank. Expansion and alteration of existing facilities became advisable. In 1968–69, Duplex Construction Company of Glens Falls, as low bidder, added a third floor to the Main Office, lowered the ceiling in the front lobby, installed an air-conditioning system, and enlarged the South Glens Falls Office.

Lowering of the ceiling in the main lobby necessitated the removal of the history-depicting murals. However, thanks to the insistence of Chairman Hubie Brown, they were not lost to posterity. They were stored in the basement until a suitable home could be found for them in Warren County. (That occurred in 1972 when Dr. William L. Bitner III suggested they be donated and hung in the Glens Falls High School Auditorium. Restoration was accomplished by a local artist, Mrs. James K. Kettlewell, and the murals were rehung by Bernard Schlake of Fort Edward.)

President Bach arranged for the Trust Department and the Personal Loan Department to be transferred to temporary quarters in the former Glens Falls Trust Company building at the corner of Glen Street and the entrance to the Elm Street parking lot, during the renovation.

Construction workers did their best to minimize noise, dirt, and debris while bank employees endured the presence of scaffolding, dislocation of work stations and unavoidable interruptions. Yet they continued to serve customers in an efficient and courteous manner. The public tolerated inconveniences with curiosity rather than complaint.

In conjunction with the renovation, the facade of the white marble structure was sandblasted by the J. M. DeCarlo Company of Naugatuck, Conn., to restore the luster of the fifty-three-year-old building. In an effort to keep noise and dirt to a minimum for other downtown merchants and their patrons, the cleaning commenced at 4:00 A.M. each day with all sandblasting stopped by 8:00 A.M.

William T. Clark, who was already a Director of the bank, resigned his position at the Glens Falls Insurance Company to become the Senior Vice President of the bank on October 14, 1968. Clark had been a key assistant to George I. Davis, Chairman of the Board of the insurance companies.

Clark was sorely missed there, because it was during this period that Chairman Davis was informed that USF&G had acquired 21% of their stock and was about to make a tender offer to gain control and move the entire operation to Baltimore. Davis vowed to fight it to the bitter end; got Continental Insurance Company to make a successful counter offer; and saved the jobs of hundreds of local employees. Continental subsequently built a new eleven-story building and, in time, increased the local work force by 20%.

A. Max Helm joined the bank on the same day as Clark, as an Assistant Cashier, to manage the Hudson Falls Office. President Bach introduced new blood into the organization by recruiting eight experienced bankers from other banks during his tenure. Helm was one of three to survive.

Paul E. Lavine

His business is to help your business grow

This quarter-page ad appeared in the Post-Star on Nov. 18, 1964 and produced amazing results.

Inflation was beginning to play havoc, and an across-the-board annual salary increase of $200 was granted to all employees effective November 1, 1968.

Mortgage loans continued to comprise approximately 50% of the bank's loan portfolio. Nearly 400 families obtained home mortgages that year, and more than 100 commercial mortgages were granted.

The total investment portfolio was decreased slightly with the liquidation of some United States Government securities to help meet loan demand.

Important operating income figures were placed on an accrual basis, for the first time, in 1968, placing operating results on a more realistic accounting basis.

In January 1969, the By-Laws were changed, creating an Executive Committee to replace the Discount Committee with essentially the same duties and responsibilities. Also, at that time, arrangements were made with local brokers for the handling of purchases and sales of First National Bank stock.

When William T. Clark came aboard as Senior VP, the previous October, Chairman Brown had admonished him "not to rock the boat." However, with his aggressive management style, Clark could not contain himself. He made his presence strongly felt. Luckily, Earl Bach was a very accommodating individual, and capitalized on Clark's innovations.

In February, a written loan policy was formulated and approved by the Board of Directors. It provided for an Officers' Loan Committee (OLC), composed of President Bach, Paul E. Lavine, William T. Clark, and Harry J. Robinson, with authority to approve loans within prescribed limits, and report approved loans to the Executive Committee, weekly, for their review. Sizable loans, beyond the prescribed authority, were referred directly to the Executive Committee.

Overall responsibility for lending activities of the bank remained under the general supervision of the Vice President and Cashier as set forth in the resolution.

On March 31, 1969, the bank discontinued its contract with Yeagan Associates and began the operation of car dealer financing through its own management.

In April, the bank again began offering credit card services to customers and area merchants when it signed a contract with Marine Midland National Bank of Troy for processing the paperwork. A stainless steel tableware "free gift" promotion was initiated to attract customers to the new MasterCharge credit system.

New drive-in facilities were introduced to the Queensbury Office. Property was purchased at the corner of Main and Washington Streets in Hudson Falls, and construction of a new branch authorized, to be known as the Kingsbury Office. An option was obtained on property in Granville on which to construct a drive-in and walk-up facility.

Robert J. Dehais resigned the presidency of a bank in Maine during a merger and returned to First National on July 1, as a non-officer assigned to special projects.

Five months later, Carter A. White joined the bank as an Assistant Vice President Investment Officer. Activity in that specialized field has continued to increase with the rapid growth of First National. He is now (1990) the Vice President responsible for the investment function.

In October 1969, the New York Mets baseball team won its first World Series by defeating the Baltimore Orioles, in the fourth series game, 5-3. Before the baseball season began, the Mets had been rated 100-1 to win. Someone commented, "If the Mets can win, anything can happen. Even the war in Vietnam can come to an end."

In January 1970, an interest rate of 8 1/2% on FHA and GI mortgages was authorized, with a 10% down payment and a 1% origination fee. Mortgages on houses less than one year old could be written for a twenty-five-year term, and on all others for not more than twenty years.

An increase in interest rates on time deposits was authorized by the Federal Reserve Board, and First National responded by increasing the basic rate on savings to 4 1/2%, premium savings as much as 5 3/4%, and certificates of deposit as much as 7 1/2%, depending on amount and term of maturity.

A new schedule of fees for Director and Committee meetings was adopted, increasing the Board attendance fee to $60, and others were increased proportionately. One new council was organized, namely the Personnel Committee and Retirement Board, whose members were granted a $60 fee.

During Earl Bach's term of office, there was a major upswing in the nation's economy. An important milestone in the bank's history was reached—the $100,000,000 mark in total resources. This occurred in 1968, six years after he had taken office. It had taken the bank 107 years to reach $50,000,000 in 1960.

When Earl Bach took mandatory retirement from the Presidency, on March 31, 1970, total resources of the bank were reported as $103,028,049; deposits, $92,838,309; capital, surplus and profits, $7,515,610.

During his term, assets increased from $55,340,918 to $103,028,049, and the staff grew from 114 to 180 people.

President Bach had worked closely with Senior Vice President Clark, thus facilitating a very orderly transfer of responsibility and command. Earl Bach continued to serve another seven years on the Board until obliged to take mandatory retirement at age seventy-two.

Another man who was of special importance to President Bach was Comptroller Nelson E. Smith. He relied upon Smitty to keep him updated on trends being reflected in daily figures. He even waited until near midnight each New Year's Eve to peruse the final figures of the year with the Comptroller.

Compiling the figures without the aid of computers was a long and arduous task in those days. Smitty worked on the General Ledger when it was a monstrous hand-posted book, later converted to machine-posted sheets, but never enjoyed the luxury of computer-generated printouts. After thirty-nine years of service, he retired in 1979, three years before the ledger was computerized.

Directors during Presidency of
F. Earl Bach, 1962–1970

F. Earl Bach   1962–1978*
  VP   1961–1962
  Pres Sep 1962–1970 Mar*
William H. Barber   1936–1966 Feb 19 died
Lyman A. Beeman Sr.   1947–1968 resigned
Dr. William L. Bitner III   1968–
  Senior VP   1976–1977
  Pres &
  Chief Adm   1977–1981
  Pres & CEO 1981–1982
  Chairman
  Pres & CEO 1982–
William McEchron Bowden   1918–1924
                                               1930–1968 resigned
  Asst to Pres 1930–1932
  VP   1932–1938
  VP   1952–1961
  Senior VP   1961–1963 resigned
Frank A. Bronk   1966–1972*
Arthur F. Brown   1940–1969
Hubert C. Brown   1933–1975*
  Pres   1942–1962*
  Chairman 1962–1975*
Gerald J. Buckley   1967–1989*
H. Glen Caffry   1965–1975 Mar 7 died
Alfred D. Clark   1947–1966 Feb 6 died
Alfred S. Clark   1928–1968 resigned
William T. Clark   1959–1981 Dec 31 died
  Sr VP   Oct 1968–1970
  Pres   Apr 1970–1976
  Pres & CEO   1976–1977
  Chairman & CEO 1977–1981
Robert P. Crawford   1959–1966 resigned
Donald S. Creal   1967–1979*
Carl R. DeSantis   1967–

James J. Fitzpatrick   1963–1972 resigned
James Gibson   July   1963–1974*
John V. Hallett   1967–1986*
Clifford W. Higley   July   1963–1975*
  Senior VP 1963–1967*
Michael C. Linehan   1947–1964 Dec 3 died
Harold P. McConnell   1950–1962
Francis W. McGinley   1947–1979*
Thomas E. Meath   Jan   1965–1975 June resigned
Leonard J. Moynehan   1965–1974*
Gray E. Safford   1931–1967 resigned age 80
  clerk, etc   1902–1919
  Asst Cashier   1919–1929
  Cashier   1929–1932
  VP & Cashier 1932–1952*
Clarence A. Scriver   1962–1969*
  credit mgr   1935–1942
  Asst. Cashier 1942–1943
  AVP   1943–1947
  VP   1947–1952
  VP & Cashier 1952–1960
  Executive VP 1960–1962 Aug*
T. Coolidge Sherman   1931–1968 resigned
Dwight A. Symmes   1954–1965 Mar 22 died

29 men served on board during Presidency of F. Earl Bach
 2 who would become Presidents of the bank

* retirement mandatory

𝔗𝔦𝔪𝔢 𝔉𝔯𝔞𝔪𝔢

History in Headlines

On or about Tuesday, March 31, 1970

3/12   Senate Approves Lowering Voting Age to 18.

3/17   Glens Falls Schools Will Not Open During Winter Recess.

3/18   U.S. Mail Service Paralyzed by First Postal Workers' Strike.

3/20   Crandall Library Prepares Exhibits on Women's Movement.

3/31   Dr. Robert King to Lead Program to Acquaint Parents with School.

Commodities Then & Now (Year)

	1970	1990
Dow Jones Ind	$785.57	$2,702.21
Gold, oz	36.41	391.19
Silver, oz	1.87	5.21
Copper, lb	0.58	1.03

President: Richard M. Nixon
Vice Pres: Spiro T. Agnew

Prices Then & Now (Year)

	1970	1990
Bread, loaf	$ 0.24	$ 1.15
Milk, gal	1.32	2.13
Butter, lb	0.87	1.89
Gasoline, gal	0.36	1.01
New Ford Car	3,379.00	10,995.00
Annual Income	9,357.00	25,050.00
New Home	23,400.00	91,945.00

On This Day in History

1774—England passes "Intolerable Acts" law after Boston Tea Party.

1870—First Negro votes in city election in Perth Amboy, NJ.

Firsts, Fads, Things

No-fault auto insurance in Massachusetts. Floppy disk.

Major Events of the Year

Cigarette advertising banned on TV. Anti-war sentiment erupts against U.S. involvement in Vietnam. U.S. cuts troops in Vietnam. Earth Day is celebrated from coast-to-coast.

Winners in the Arts

Actor: George C. Scott for *Patton*
Actress: Glenda Jackson for
Women in Love
Movie: *Patton*
By 20th Century Fox Studios
Best Seller: *Love Story*
Big on TV: *Marcus Welby, M.D.*

This Year in Sports

W. Series: Baltimore whips Cincinnati
ABA: Indiana Pacers
Indy 500: Al Unser at 155.749
Stanley Cup: Boston Bruins
Kentucky Derby: Dust Commander
Rose Bowl: USC over Michigan

William T. Clark

THE PRESIDENCY OF WILLIAM T. CLARK
1970–1977

William Terry Clark officially took command as President of First National effective at the close of business March 31, 1970.

His was an aggressive, analytical management style.

During the previous year, as Senior Vice President, he had espoused a very structured system of management. He was adamantly opposed to any casual or laid-back approach to any phase of business.

Initially he had planned to hire an outside consultant to help him evaluate the overall state of affairs within the organization. However, he quickly changed his mind.

Why?

Because he visited the Personnel Officer, who was at home convalescing from detached retina surgery. That officer had produced a tape during his ten days in the hospital, which convinced Mr. Clark that there was sufficient talent within the bank to assist him with his analysis of internal operations.

His very first venture was to enlist the aid of the Personnel Officer in developing a complete organization chart patterned after the one used by the Glens Falls Insurance Company. This gave Mr. Clark a better understanding of the work-flow patterns and departmental divisions within the bank and how they related to one another.

He published the bank's first formal Organization Chart on December 1, 1968, just seven weeks after he had joined the staff as Senior Vice President. It was a harbinger of how he would operate.

Analyzing the components of each person's job responsibilities came next. In order to accomplish this, he charged each individual with the task of describing (in writing) his or her own job, as he or she understood it.

This exercise produced many surprises. Daily operations were running smoothly, yet some management-level people could not clearly articulate what they thought was expected of them. Others claimed responsibilities that had little relationship to their daily duties. The accountability for some functions went unclaimed by any management person.

The bank was succeeding in spite of what Mr. Clark perceived as management shortcomings. Long-term members of the staff had an intuitive feel for what had to be done and pitched in as a family team to assure that customers were properly taken care of. All well and good. But the Senior VP envisioned rapid growth for the bank and reasoned that a more sophisticated management approach was necessary. He insisted that, as a prerequisite, every phase of operations needed to be minutely analyzed.

His education and work background influenced his concept of business propriety. He had a degree in Applied Economic Science from Yale University, and an M.B.A. from Harvard Graduate School of Business Administration. He had been a security analyst at Old Colony Trust Company in Boston, and an investment counselor for a major law firm in Boston. Coupled with this, he had five years of tightly regimented, commanding officer experience in the U.S. Navy during World War II.

His own immediate past as a senior officer in the Glens Falls Insurance Company reinforced his thinking. He was accustomed to larger, more departmentalized, and diverse operations with all the attendant problems of "bigness."

The job descriptions, furnished by the incumbents, enabled Senior VP Clark to have a better understanding of how the bank was currently functioning. He empowered the Personnel Officer to develop a standard format for all position descriptions in the bank, and to work with each person in carefully analyzing their jobs. Mr. Clark then meticulously evaluated and refined each re-written job description.

He established clear lines in a chain of command to ensure that activity would not be hampered by overlapping authority (or perceived authority). There was no room for ambiguity. Each officer could see his/her designated area of responsibility and to whom he/she must report. Needless to say, the chart had to be revised and updated constantly.

Long before he became President, it became apparent that Mr. Clark was an advocate of management-by-objective, reinforced by copious documentation. It was obvious to old-timers that more rigid controls were in the offing and that they were entering a new era of banking at First National.

By the time he was granted the title of President, he had created a solid foundation for the building blocks that were to come. There was no question in anyone's mind as to who expected to be in complete control.

It was clear from the very start that President Clark intended to increase the profitability of the bank and improve the productivity of its staff. He was a man with a mission. He imparted a sense of urgency to everything he did and expected others to do likewise.

He was very goal oriented, and insisted that all officers of the bank set obtainable goals for their area of responsibility for the ensuing year—and be held accountable for attaining those goals.

Times had changed in the banking industry. Competition for business was no longer restricted to friendly and intense competition with "the bank across the street." New banking regulations were going to open up the territory to branches of giant banks from New York City and other large banks within New York State.

Chairman Hubie Brown had seen it coming and had started the ball rolling by establishing footholds in crucial locations within the Tri-County area. It was no accident that he had proposed an aggressive, hands-on, seasoned executive like William T. Clark for the President's chair. Battles were looming, and the bank needed a fighter in the front lines.

On the day William Clark became President, the Board authorized a contract for the construction of the new Kingsbury Office in Hudson Falls. The new drive-in facilities at the Queensbury office were now in full operation, and an option had been exercised to purchase property in Granville on which to erect a separate auto bank building. These were the first of several construction contracts that would be granted during his term of office. In fact, some directors were tempted to identify his era as one of brick and mortar.

During Mr. Clark's first week as President, the prime rate was reduced from 8 1/2% to 8% by many New York and large city banks, whereas FNB had just increased its prime rate to 8%. Historically "country banks" lag behind big city banks in interest changes—both upward and downward—because of a different sensitivity in financial climate. At the moment, FNB's available loan money was in short supply. Management decided that an increase in rates was a more effective way to restrict loans than refusal to grant loans and did not lower its prime rate.

Within two weeks after Clark's election, Paul E. Lavine's title was changed to Vice President and Cashier. Robert J. Dehais was appointed Assistant Vice President-Finance. The regular sixty cent quarterly dividend was declared effective May 1.

The supplemental one-time payment to employees at time of retirement was discontinued, as was the practice of bank-sponsored retirement parties. Amendments were also made to the bank's retirement plan to accommodate conditions previously unforeseen.

President Clark was the fourth President to retain Frederick G. Bascom, attorney-at-law, as the primary legal counsel for the bank. Mr. Bascom had drawn most of the legal papers in connection with thousands of mortgages granted by the bank over the years. He was also engaged to execute the duties of Judge and Inspector of Election at the annual meeting of shareholders.

Mr. Bascom built a close relationship with the bank's employees, having taught evening classes at the bank during four decades under the American Institute of Banking program. Mr. Bascom's oratorical prowess was skillfully employed in courtroom presentations and exhibited frequently on public podiums.

Mr. Clark was a dedicated disciple of the great Vince Lombardi, coach of the Green Bay Packers pro football team. Lombardi inspired his teams to championships by preaching "second effort"—the will to "go one more yard despite the odds." Appropriate as it was, President Clark found it difficult to sell such an aggressive philosophy to hometown bankers.

By July 1970, President Clark had created such a plethora of reports, charts, and comparative data that it was necessary to provide each Director with a loose-leaf binder for each meeting.

In August, the alarm system in the Main Office was completely updated by the Mosler Safe Company to bring it in full conformance with security regulations of the Comptroller of the Currency.

The driveway was widened at the Maple Street facility to better accommodate a double lane of traffic at that busy location.

President Clark enlisted the aid of the AVP—Personnel in researching and outlining an Employee Deferred Profit-Sharing Incentive Plan. It was further formulated and, refined by the firm of George B. Buck, Consulting Actuaries, Inc., of New York. It was thoroughly discussed with the Personnel Committee and minor amendments made before being reviewed by the full Board. Then the plan was presented to stockholders for approval at a special meeting on November 6, 1970.

Essentially the plan provided that the bank set aside an amount into a trust fund in accordance with a formula based on net operating income (before security gains or losses) after applicable taxes as a percent of monthly average capital funds. Net operating income had to exceed 8% before any profits would be allocated to the fund. The higher the profits, the higher the percentage of allocation, so it behooved every employee to be constantly conscious of cost-saving techniques and profitability. A ceiling was placed on contributions even if net operating income were to exceed 15%.

Each year each individual in the plan received a report of the accumulation in his/her account, which would become available at retirement. Employees made no dollar contributions to the fund. The plan, of course, included many stipulations pertaining to varying conditions, but members of the plan were protected by vested rights after two years membership.

Improvements were made in the bank's health insurance plan to provide broadened protection for employees and their dependents during periods of illness or accident.

Computation of service charges on checking accounts was changed from a minimum balance to an average monthly balance basis.

Renovation of the basement in the white marble structure created new office workspace and an improved lunch-recreation room for employees.

In October 1970, Warren E. Rouillard became a member of the Board of Directors. During the year, Floyd H. Rourke was added to the Hudson Falls Advisory Board, and Robert F. Flacke and Robert J. Sweet to the Lake George Advisory Board

On November 6, 1970, at a Special Meeting of shareholders, the capital stock of the bank was increased $240,600 by issuance of a 10% stock dividend, thus increasing the stock to $2,646,600, divided into 132,300 shares at a par value of $20 per share. As a result of the stock dividend, 165 shares became available and were sold at $75.15 per share.

In order to remain in a competitive position with the Albany Savings Bank and other Albany banks, First National decided to pay 4 1/2% interest on 1971 Christmas Club accounts. The branches of capital district banks were struggling to gain a foothold in the area by conducting major advertising and promotion campaigns to attract accounts away from the two local institutions and to capture newcomers. The two "locals" met the competition head-on, despite the heavy cost of doing so.

Late in the fall, FNB hit another milestone in its upward progress when deposits reached $100 MILLION and climbed to $100,733,275 at year end.

Aggressive promotion of savings certificates and certificates of deposit contributed substantially to deposit growth. Also FNB offered daily compounding of interest on regular savings, thus providing customers with the highest possible return under Federal Reserve regulations for this type of account.

Demolition of the existing structure and construction of a new building for the Granville Office underwent three months of discussion and review before it was decided, in early December, to postpone the project until the spring of 1971.

Business conditions across the nation precipitated a general decline in loan rates. Also the bank reduced the downpayment on FHA and VA mortgage loans from 10% to 3% with a maximum loan term of twenty years on existing homes.

On December 14, Robert J. Dehais was promoted to Financial and Operational Control Officer, a new title. One month later, A. Max Helm was named Branch Office Supervisor, another new officer title at FNB.

During 1971, Advisory Committee became the new title for each group acting in that capacity at the various branch offices of the bank, replacing the previous designation of Advisory Board. This was as it should be. These individuals act as "advisors" and do not have the voting rights or the legal responsibilities of corporate board members.

On May 10, 1971, the number of Directors was increased from seventeen to eighteen, and Paul E. Lavine was appointed to the Board and continued to retain his title as Senior Vice President and Cashier. G. Nelson Lowe, Vice President and Trust Officer, was given additional responsibilities as Secretary of the Board to become effective June 14. Robert J. Dehais and this author each became a Vice President.

Homer P. Dearlove, District Superintendent of Schools for BOCES, was appointed to the Hudson Falls Advisory Committee.

Robert J. Newton was named Auditor, a bank officer position which he continued to hold until he elected to take early retirement in 1979 after forty-two years of service. He then ran for public office and was elected treasurer of the City of Glens Falls.

The Charles Parks property on Third Street in South Glens Falls was purchased and additional parking space was provided for another dozen or more cars.

Approximately 3,300 feet of land abutting the Bolton Landing Office was purchased for parking space and possible expansion.

The annual fee to Lester A. Pratt & Co., CPA's, Washington, D.C., was increased for the first time since the firm began reviewing the bank's internal auditing program in 1955. This professional outside firm kept the Board apprised of the competency and completeness of the bank's own daily ongoing auditing performance.

It's worth pointing out that the Auditor at First National reports directly to the Examining Committee of the Board of Directors and is not subject to control by any operating officer in the bank, including the President.

The purpose of auditing is to protect the interests of depositors and shareholders. National banks, such as FNB, are subject to the most stringent controls and regulations in the industry.

In the 1970s, National bank examiners, from the Office of the Comptroller of the Currency, were conducting at least two regular examinations of each national bank each year. The Trust Department was examined separately once a year. A pattern of unannounced visits had been refined over a period of forty years. A crew of examiners would suddenly appear at the door before the bank opened for business in the morning, or shortly after the closing hour.

An examiner was assigned to each teller and counted each teller's cash, while the teller stood by. The examiners placed seals on all security chests and cash vaults until an examiner could be freed to check the contents. In the days before branches, the logistics of assigning examining crews to a bank were simple. Multi-locations required a much larger staff in order to hit all offices simultaneously.

All records, ledgers, posting sheets, and loan documents were placed under examiner control. Early morning arrival was most disruptive since it was often difficult to get enough tellers counted and released in time to serve the public properly.

The review of records, credit files, loans, documents, and discussions with officers and Board members took from three to six weeks or more. The bank could not predict when the examiners would return. It might be in three, six, or nine months. Examiners from the FDIC (Federal Deposit Insurance Corporation) could likewise scrutinize records.

Also, the Examining Committee of the Board would conduct surprise examinations of any department. Every employee understood that being subject to examination at any time was to be expected, especially by those in the more sensitive areas of operations.

National banks had grown accustomed to regular review by the above examining teams. More and more governmental agencies were gaining the right to inspect bank records, including the EEOC (Equal Employment Opportunity Commission), OSHA (Office of Health & Safety Administration), Wage-Price Stabilization Board, State Labor Department, and, of course, the Internal Revenue Service along with other minor agencies of the Federal and State governments.

Cognizant that New York State was to become a single banking district as of January 1, 1976, President Clark was already (1971) implementing new programs and services to thwart the foreseeable onslaught of competition from giant banks. He was fiercely committed to seeing that FNB remained a strong **independent** bank, able to provide full-service banking at the local level from every branch.

Frederick R. Shenk Jr. was recruited from a bank in Pennsylvania and assigned as Vice President responsible for developing an overall Marketing Department at First National. Shenk proved to be capable both at administration and innovation of plans that would help build business for the bank. In 1990, he continues to be a very effective member of the senior management team.

Thomas R. Foster was also recruited with business development in mind. President Clark was familiar with Foster's work at the Glens Falls Insurance Company and believed Foster was capable of specializing in developing business for the Trust Division. He came aboard as an Assistant Trust Officer. Clark's faith was justified. Foster ventured forth into virgin territory, initiating contacts that proved beneficial both to the bank and to individuals who had not previously availed themselves of trust services.

Foster proved particularly adept at "finding" and developing customers from areas previously considered barren and devoid of prospects. His enthusiasm became contagious, and in time other officers, staff, and members of the Board, and the Advisory Committees, were providing him with leads.

Assistant Personnel Officer Jean H. Gray (who had been hired as a secretary in the fledgling Personnel Department in 1969), captured the attention of President Clark and spearheaded a crusade to increase the upward mobility of women in the bank. She pointed out that all leadership positions were male dominated. This included head teller and management trainee assignments. Today (1990), Ms. Gray, now retired as the bank's first woman Vice President, recalls. "This practice was not unique to First National, but was applicable to industries throughout the nation."

She remembers that President Clark sent her to major banks in Boston and Albany and to seminars on "Women in Banking" to acquire ideas applicable to First National, and was gratified to discover that FNB was fast outgrowing its "country cousin" status.

The bank had always encouraged its employees to become involved in community activities and to contribute their services to worthy causes. President Clark talked with Jean Gray about a suitable vehicle to signal the bank's commitment to the broader life of the community. So began the bank's VITA program (Volunteers in Team Action), whose broad objective was to develop a pool of volunteer workers for local service organizations needing help.

Full page newspaper ads, radio and TV publicity followed. And an officer's participation in community volunteer activities became a factor on the new "performance evaluation" forms.

Virginia A. Clark, Marketing Assistant; Jean H. Gray, Assistant Personnel Officer; and Frederick R. Shenk Jr., Vice President review the VITA Campaign during the summer of 1971.

That year the bank conducted a seminar for area lawyers on estate planning. It also led an Earth Day Clean-up project in co-operation with city officials. And tickets for area community events were made available through a new Ticketron Reservation Service.

President Clark was gratified that his management team (listed on the next page) had recorded new highs, in 1971, for deposits, loans, investments, capital funds and a 16.1% increase in net operating income per share. He considered 1971 a year of accomplishment due to the restructuring of the management team, the establishment of more formal procedures, evaluation systems, and accountability standards.

OFFICERS

HUBERT C. BROWN .... CHAIRMAN OF THE BOARD
WILLIAM T. CLARK .... PRESIDENT
PAUL E. LAVINE .... SENIOR VICE PRESIDENT
JOSEPH E. BARNES .... VICE PRESIDENT
ROBERT J. DEHAIS .... VICE PRESIDENT AND CASHIER
FREDERICK R. SHENK, JR. .... VICE PRESIDENT
MAURICE R. FRAZIER .... ASSISTANT VICE PRESIDENT
A. MAX HELM .... ASSISTANT VICE PRESIDENT
PATRICK E. MCCARTHY .... ASSISTANT VICE PRESIDENT
ROBERT E. POWERS .... ASSISTANT VICE PRESIDENT
GEORGE F. REGER, JR. .... ASSISTANT VICE PRESIDENT
LEWIS L. VARNEY, JR. .... ASSISTANT VICE PRESIDENT
JOHN R. BREEN .... ASSISTANT CASHIER
CHARLES F. POTTER .... ASSISTANT CASHIER
JEAN H. GRAY .... ASSISTANT PERSONNEL OFFICER
LYLE E. GREGORY .... OPERATIONS OFFICER
NELSON E. SMITH .... COMPTROLLER
ROBERT W. NEWTON .... AUDITOR

TRUST DEPARTMENT

G. NELSON LOWE .... VICE PRESIDENT AND TRUST OFFICER
CARTER A. WHITE .... ASSISTANT VICE PRESIDENT AND
INVESTMENT OFFICER
EDITH R. HUGHES .... TRUST OFFICER
THOMAS R. FOSTER .... ASSISTANT TRUST OFFICER
TIMOTHY D. SMYTH .... ASSISTANT TRUST OFFICER

OFFICES

HUDSON FALLS OFFICE
RAYMOND A. BLAKE .... ASSISTANT CASHIER

KINGSBURY OFFICE
W. PATRICK BUSHMAN .... ASSISTANT MANAGER

GRANVILLE OFFICE
ROBERT E. JONES .... ASSISTANT VICE PRESIDENT
ARTHUR J. GIROUX .... ASSISTANT MANAGER

BOLTON LANDING OFFICE
RICHARD B. DODGE .... MANAGER

LAKE GEORGE OFFICE
HOWARD W. MCKEE .... VICE PRESIDENT
JEAN A. MORRIS .... ASSISTANT CASHIER

QUEENSBURY OFFICE
WILLIAM R. PERRY .... MANAGER
WILLIAM T. CARBOY, JR. .... ASSISTANT MANAGER

SOUTH GLENS FALLS OFFICE
JOHN E. RAFFERTY .... ASSISTANT VICE PRESIDENT

1971 Management Team.

The year 1972 would prove to be a year of important changes and surprises.

William E. Philion and Floyd H. Rourke were added to the Board in February and Henry J. W. Vanderminden III in October.

John F. Carey, E. Roger Dickinson, and Daniel G. Reid were appointed to the Hudson Falls Advisory Committee. William Busch Jr., Charles E. Hawley, William D. Maltbie Jr., and Walter O. Rehm III were added to the Lake George group.

The Directors were pleased by the projections outlined in the 1972 operating plans. Each senior officer had committed himself, in writing, as to what could be expected from his division for the ensuing year. None of the bank's previous presidents had utilized this form of self-imposed pressure and accountability. It appeared that the year would be one of continued progress.

Seeking a new advertising approach, Vice President Shenk engineered a change to Madison North Marketing Communications Agency, Ltd., Schenectady, and severed the bank's thirty-two-year relationship with Merrill Anderson Agency, of New York. The new agency brought forth a new motto, "A Good Bank—A Good Neighbor."

Everyone was both surprised and shocked when President Clark announced that, according to National Bank Examiner Matthew A. Dylis Jr., one of the bank's most promising young loan officers had exceeded his authority by making loans which should not have been made.

This discovery occurred late in January. Paradoxically, a disparaging remark by the young officer aroused the ire and suspicions of the experienced bank examiner.

Examiner Dylis had sensed a more than normal uneasiness among some of the staff in the loan division. He ordered his men to probe deeper. The manager complained. "Big Matt, your crew is wasting time. You're asking too many stupid questions. If you think something is wrong, prove it! But you won't find anything. Our records are perfect."

And they were. Almost. The paperwork was meticulous. The

young man had previously worked in the bank's internal audit division and knew precisely what the auditors looked for.

However, long experience warned Dylis. "This guy complains too much. He's too defensive. Something is wrong."

But finding that "something" was not easy. The young man had granted a loan to his mother's business in good faith. When she was unable to keep up with payments, a new loan was granted and proceeds used to keep the business afloat and keep the original loan current. Other loans followed, each within his loaning authority.

The control cards were, at that time, filed under varying "due dates." Thus it was difficult to detect any relationship between the loans, especially since none of them were in a "past due" category subject to special scrutiny.

Finally the examiners uncovered separate notes, signed by the same person, but filed under different due dates. Their combined total exceeded the officer's loan authority. Dylis alleged that probably there were more irregularities. The bank officer admitted to a mistake in judgment. But no more. He insisted on talking to the man who had hired him.

President Clark arranged a closed-door session with only the three of them present. Clark stifled his own bulldog approach and allowed the other two officers to "discuss" the situation one-on-one. Finally the personnel Vice President prevailed. The accused young man was motivated to accept responsibility for his misguided deeds and assist the examiners in locating the irregularities. Had he not done so, it could have taken months of painstaking investigation to unravel the web of connivance.

He revealed that the pivotal business loans were supported by many individuals' loans to members of the family and to employees of the business establishment. They had been cajoled into signing many individual "temporary" loan instruments to keep the business alive and protect their jobs until business improved. As an inducement, some of them received a portion of the proceeds with the understanding that all payments would be handled by the business.

Because each and every loan instrument had been properly signed and recorded, auditors had no reason to suspect any chicanery. On the surface, the bank was properly protected by a growing number of loans. But, as a matter of fact, true protection was minimal. Most of the signers of the notes did not have the capacity to repay.

Once apprised of the scheme, the bank examiner concluded they were dealing with something more than "questionable loans." In his opinion, most of the loans involved were not collectible and were written off. The combined total exceeded anything the bank had ever experienced.

President Clark reported the situation to the Regional Administrator of National Banks, the Federal Bureau of Investigation, the Continental Insurance Company, the bank's Board of Directors, and the bank's auditor consultant Lester A. Pratt in Washington, D.C.

Prosecution then became the mandate of Federal authorities, and the officer was subsequently tried in a Federal Court in Syracuse. Complicity by at least one other person in the department had made the scheme possible. She also was tried, but on lesser charges.

In the meantime, the President requested the First National City Bank of New York to assist in an evaluation of the practices of the Loan Department as part of their service to a correspondent bank. As a result a shakeup of the department ensued, more sophisticated safeguards were installed, and an experienced loan officer hired from outside the bank.

Early in February, the bank's prime rate was reduced to 5 3/4%, reflecting the change in economic conditions from the previous year.

The highlight of the year was the establishment of a formal Salary Administration Program under which all positions were classified and rated by salary level. It had taken the Personnel Department nearly two years to obtain data, analyze it, compare it with other banks of similar size and with related jobs in local industries.

Under the chairmanship of Dr. William L. Bitner III, the Personnel Committee of the Board had carefully scrutinized all aspects of this program before authorizing its installation. The salary program had been preceded by a job description program which defined the exact nature of each job.

These programs were intended to prevent inequities and to reward people equally for equal performance in given jobs irrespective of race or sex.

The bank was in the process of installing the salary program and explaining its various ramifications to its 194 employees when an inspector from the U. S. Department of Labor appeared on the scene.

This was part of a concerted effort which was being made nationwide under the EEOC (Equal Employment Opportunity Commission) to guarantee equal opportunity and upward mobility for women and other minorities. Banks had become a prime target and many heavy fines were being levied against financial institutions.

The inspector charged the bank with not being in full compliance with EEOC in certain areas of operations. A $300,000 claim was filed against the bank.

Labor attorney Jacob H. Herzog of Albany and Vice President Barnes went to New York and settled with the U. S. Department of Labor for $150,000 of retroactive pay and NO FINE. The labor department concurred that the bank's new Salary Administration Program was in the process of correcting past practices. Some other banks in the area were not so fortunate. They had not developed acceptable plans and were fined heavily.

In March, new teller machines were installed in all locations, necessitating expeditious training in revised methods and procedures.

Shortly thereafter, customers were encouraged to comment on any phase of current bank service. This survey of customer complaints was conducted under the guidance of Vice President Robert Dehais, the operations control officer. He, more than anyone else, was responsible for devising and installing new methods and procedures to improve the profitability of daily operations.

A modern, spacious new Granville Office opened in June. The former bank building had been demolished and the site landscaped with an entry walk, trees, and lawn.

Other major physical changes, in 1972, included the opening of the new Operations Center on Washington Street in Glens Falls, the renovation of the Board of Directors' Room, and the renovation of the Lake George Office to provide better accommodations for customers.

President Clark reported that the possibility of expansion into other areas of Washington County, including mergers and establishment of new branches, was under active study by management.

A program for annual medical examinations of bank officers was introduced in September to help assure the medical well-being of the bank's leaders. The Board required that a confidential physical report be filed with the President each year.

On October 13, 1972, at a Special Meeting of shareholders, the capital stock of the bank was increased $661,640 by the issuance of a 25% stock dividend, thus increasing the common stock to $3,308,240, divided into 165,412 shares at a par value of $20 per share. FNB was required to purchase an additional 637 shares of Federal Reserve stock. At that time, First National stock was selling at $89 a share.

Micro-fiche card readers were placed in key customer service areas throughout the system. This enabled customer service people to provide current information quickly on checking and savings accounts from microfilm cards.

Concern for the well-being of those who had retired before 1972 prompted the bank to provide a supplementary annual pension payment (for that group only). Payments followed a formula which applied a higher percentage factor to those receiving smaller pensions.

The Board also voted a deferred compensation plan for Directors' fees.

By the end of 1972, the staff had increased to 194 people, yet the number of employees had decreased to 1.5 per million dollars of deposits. This was considered an extremely low ratio for a commercial bank, one of the lowest in the nation.

In February 1973, Paul Lavine was promoted to Senior Vice President, and Robert Dehais advanced to Vice President and Cashier. Fees for Directors were increased to $75.00.

The bank's prime loan rate increased to 7%. Individual mortgage rates were set at 7 1/2%, and term loans to corporations were 8 1/2% and up.

The firm of Arthur Anderson Co. Inc. was engaged to formulate a new audit program, conduct audit reviews, and prepare income tax reports for the bank. The firm of Brown, Bridgman, & Miller, Inc. was retained as consulting actuaries.

Early in 1973, it became obvious that competition was intensifying. There was a deluge of advertising by Glens Falls National Bank and Trust promoting "24-hour banking" at its Queensbury branch. This, of course, referred to an ATM (Automatic Teller Machine) which was being installed at that location. The Queensbury branches of State Bank of Albany and the Albany Savings Bank began vigorously promoting Saturday banking hours. To counteract all this promotion and competition, First National provided customers with many additional hours of service by keeping its Auto Bank complex on Maple Street open six days a week, Monday through Friday, 9:00 A.M. to 8:00 P.M., and Saturday, 9:00 A.M. to 5:00 P.M.

Induced by the prospect of a three-day work week, two teller crews agreed to experiment with the new plan. It required arriving at 8:30 A.M. to set up cash for the day and spending at least a half-hour balancing at the end of the day. It meant a twelve-hour day in which tellers were confined in Auto-Bank booths. The booths were furnished with cooking and other accommodating facilities.

The tellers were soon so pleased with the new schedule that they unanimously asked that it be continued. In fact, other tellers began applying for assignment to the three-day work shifts.

During 1973, progress in terms of building for the future would continue to be the order of the day. The area on the third floor was completely renovated to provide spacious offices for the growing Trust and Investment departments.

Enlargement of the Board Room enabled it to also be used as a general purpose meeting room.

A new drive-in unit was constructed in the downtown Glens Falls Auto Bank complex providing access from Washington Street. Land was purchased opposite a shopping center outside Granville for a future drive-in facility.

More importantly, First National increased its presence in Washington County by purchasing the historic Blandy Mansion in Greenwich, renovating the interior, and opening a Greenwich Office on December 26.

We expanded into Greenwich in 1973, restoring the historic Blandy Home for our office.

Richard F. Crozier was recruited from First National Bank of Greenwich and appointed an Assistant Vice President to manage our office. "Rick" was a well-known resident of the community who had worked fourteen years at a competing bank in town.

He, along with members of a newly appointed Advisory Committee, attracted an unanticipated volume of new deposits. Members of the committee included Norman W. Allen, John Crozier, Christie E. Lyttle, Roblee Miller, Charles R. Russell, Donald L. Skellie, Dr. R. Leith Skinner, and Paul Tomlinson.

John W. Bishop was appointed to the Board of Directors in November. One month later, Nancy Veeder was appointed to the Lake George Advisory Committee, the first woman to serve in that capacity.

On the world scene, an Arab embargo on oil shipments to the United States and Britain was causing acute economic problems. Rationing of gasoline and fuel oil was imminent.

President Clark asked department heads to cooperate in national energy conservation measures by setting office thermostats at upper sixties and turning off individual office lights when not needed. Then in the spring of 1974, a bicycle rack was installed in the parking lot, and employees were urged to bike to work where feasible.

It was during 1973 that VP Shenk introduced a new identification symbol for the bank to appropriately picture a corporate image of a growing bank. The new logo was designed by the Madison North Advertising Agency in consultation with the bank's Marketing Department.

T-shirts emblazoned with the new evergreen symbol were given to all employees, and similar parking lot stickers were issued for use on cars owned by employees. The new logo replaced the one ❶ FIRST NATIONAL BANK of Glens Falls in use since 1967.

The bank's total operating income increased by 13.8% in 1973. The chart on this page gives perspective to the distribution of that income.

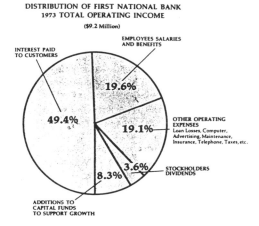

DISTRIBUTION OF FIRST NATIONAL BANK
1973 TOTAL OPERATING INCOME
($9.2 Million)

INTEREST PAID	49.4%	$4,560,217
SALARIES	19.6%	1,805,573
OTHER OPERATING EXPENSES	19.1%	1,760,957
DIVIDENDS	3.6%	330,824
ADDITIONS TO CAPITAL FUNDS	8.3%	768,060

The year 1974 became a year of financial turmoil in which many difficult decisions became necessary in order to keep the FNB financial ship on course.

President Clark became actively involved in voicing opposition to the changes in the New York Banking system as recently proposed by the state's Superintendent of Banks. He objected to the bill's "package" approach to resolve problems in the commercial banking industry, the savings bank industry, and the savings and loan industry.

Savings bank competition increased with the entry of two more branch units into our marketing area. President Clark became more active in dealing directly with regulators, and legislatures, in seeking to eliminate inequities between thrift associations and commercial banks. He joined with other bankers in establishing the Independent Bankers Association of New York State.

Inflation was playing havoc. Effective April 1, FNB raised its prime rate from 8 1/2% to 9%. One month later, it was increased to 9 3/4%. Major banks had already raised their prime rate to 11%. On July 8, FNB increased its prime rate to 10 1/4%.

Federal regulations limited rates on regular savings and dried up what had been the bank's normal source of funds for mortgages. Thus it became necessary to curtail this type of lending by increasing down payment requirements and shortening maturity dates on new mortgages. Also, mortgages on commercial properties were limited to 50% of value at 10% and up.

Certificates of deposit and savings certificates became the prime source of deposit growth at a considerably increased cost to the bank. The spiraling inflation also dictated a conservative investment policy to maintain liquidity.

The cost of protecting individual customer accounts increased when FDIC (Federal Deposit Insurance Corporation) coverage was raised to $14,000.

The bank continued to pay its regular quarterly dividend of $.50 per share, but changed the payment dates to the 10th of the month.

Hans F. Hoenck was added to the Hudson Falls Advisory Committee.

Paul Lavine and Charles Potter retired from the staff with a combined total of eighty-eight years of active service. In the best of Horatio Alger tradition, each began work at the bottom of the banking ladder, climbing along different rungs. Charlie's entire career was devoted to the Savings Department, which had previously been headed by his father. Paul retired as Senior Vice President and continued to serve as a Director.

An association was formed between the Glens Falls AIB study group and Adirondack Community College whereby college credit could be obtained for most AIB courses. For the past forty years, classes had been held at FNB—open to all area bank employees—with credit limited to American Institute of Banking certificates.

At the bank, a formal teller training program was developed to assure that all prospective tellers received precisely the same instructions. Previously, they had been apprenticed to experienced tellers whose methods were not necessarily uniform.

A management training program, aimed at improving supervisory practices, was taught jointly by Max Helm, Vice President of branch administration, and this author over a period of several months. Thirty-two key officers and supervisors completed the course.

"Know Your Money" booklets were made available to merchants to help educate them on methods for detecting counterfeit currency. Historically the summer tourist and Saratoga racetrack season had produced an increased flow of bogus bills (especially $20 and $10 bills). The bank also intensified training of "summer" tellers to combat this scourge, and provided newspaper publicity to alert the general public.

The year 1974 ended with 213 employees and 616 stockholders.

Early in 1975, it appeared that the economy was receding from over-heated inflation and that short-term money rates would trend lower. The bank's prime rate was reduced from 9 1/2% to 9% in March and then lowered to 8 1/2% within less than a month. The new car loan rate was later reduced from 7% to a 6 1/2% add-on rate.

In February, Hubert C. Brown, Chairman of the Board, and Clifford W. Higley, former Senior VP, took mandatory retirement. No one was named to replace Mr. Brown as Chairman.

In April, Alan R. Rhodes was invited to become a member of the Board as successor to H. Glen Caffry, who had died in March, following a long illness. Michael D. Ginsburg was added to the Board in December. John K. Ryder had been appointed to the Lake George Advisory Committee earlier in the year.

President Clark continued his quest for expansion of physical facilities for the bank and kept the Building Committee of the Board busy reviewing and approving plans.

The plans came to fruition in 1976. First to be completed was a major expansion at the Queensbury Office. It included a new building connected to the original structure, six new drive-in facilities, completion of access roads and a new public street named Bank Street.

A building adjacent to the Kingsbury Office was purchased and demolished in order to redesign the drive-in and enlarge the parking area.

The South Glens Falls Office was renovated and expanded.

A Liberty Pole was erected and ceremoniously dedicated at the Queensbury Office to celebrate the nation's Bicentennial.

Following the purchase of a building in Warrensburg and renovation into a new branch office, Calvin C. Engle and Mrs. Millicent B. Lawrence were appointed to the newly named Lake George Regional Advisory Committee.

At the annual meeting of shareholders on February 10, 1976, 138,040 votes were cast in favor of election of the slate of Directors. But for the first time in the bank's history, eleven votes were cast against the election of each Director.

The 1976 Board of Directors: Seated—left to right. Alan R. Rhodes, Floyd H. Rourke, Francis W. McGinley, Dr. William L. Bitner III, William T. Clark, F. Earl Bach, Paul E. Lavine, John V. Hallett, Gerald J. Buckley. Standing— Donald S. Creal, Carl R. DeSantis, John W. Bishop, Warren E. Rouillard, Henry J. W. Vanderminden III, William E. Philion, and Michael D. Ginsburg.

At this same meeting, the capital stock of the bank was increased $827,060 by the issuance of a 25% stock dividend, thus increasing the common stock to $4,135,300, divided into 206,765 shares at a par value of $20 per share.

An amendment was added to the By-Laws requiring Directors to attend at least 50% of Board meetings held each year. This also was applicable to members of the Advisory Committees for their meetings.

Fees for attendance at Board meetings were increased to $100; for committee meetings, $75; and for Advisory Committee meetings, $50.

Elton A. Borden was added to the Greenwich Advisory Committee.

The bank offered employees and members of the Board an opportunity to purchase shares of First National Bank stock by providing for monthly deductions of as little as $2.50 a month from individual checking accounts. An investment firm accumulated the funds and purchased stock at prevailing market rates.

First Check Credit was introduced as a new convenience service enabling qualified customers to "make loans" to themselves (up to a pre-determined amount) whenever desired. This obviated the necessity of going to the bank to make out a loan application form and other documents each time there was need to borrow money.

FNB also introduced "Money-Saver" checking which incorporated a no service charge feature. With the advent of electronic banking, the bank made direct deposit available to Social Security recipients via wire transfer, eliminating the need for a heavy volume of government checks. Other services under EFTS (the electronic funds transfer system) were in the offing.

President Clark was pleased to note in the American Banker (national newspaper) that First National was ranked (by total deposits) in the top 5% of the nation's commercial banks at the beginning of 1976.

However, he feared for continued existence of independent banks and was devoting extensive time and effort to legislative matters at both the state and national level hoping to correct inequities in the system. At the same time, he was confronting the inroads of major commercial banks.

State Bank of Albany, Citibank of New York and Chase Manhattan established branches in Queensbury, and Manufacturers Hanover Bank erected a branch diagonally across the street from our South Glens Falls Office.

President Clark sought and obtained the services of Dr. William L. Bitner III to assist in carrying out various administrative responsibilities. Dr. Bitner was well known in the area, having served nine years as Superintendent of the Glens Falls Schools, and was willing to resign his position as Associate Commissioner of Education of the New York State Department of Education. He had been a very active member of the bank's Board of Directors since 1968.

He joined the bank staff as Senior Vice President on September 16, 1976.

That same week, Patrick E. McCarthy retired as an Assistant Vice President, after forty-five years of service. Pat had worked his way through the ranks and was always popular with his co-workers and customers.

Architects designed a spacious new office for the President, and he soon moved to that third floor location, leaving the ground floor office to the new Senior Vice President.

By freeing himself from a complexity of administrative responsibilities, President Clark was able to increase his participation on the New York State Bankers Association federal and state government relations committees. This was in addition to his growing commitment with IBANY (Independent Bankers Association of New York). He subsequently was elected vice president of IBANY.

It was Bill Clark's decision not to accept the presidency of IBANY because of an increasing concern about an eye problem that proved to be glaucoma.

Mr. Clark also championed causes other than banking. He spent countless hours on community projects, displaying "unflagging determination'' and great zest for the causes he embraced. Most notable were his forceful fund-raising campaigns for the building of the Glens Falls Family YMCA and the Glens Falls Civic Center. The fact that the Civic Center project was mired in controversy did not deter him. He thrived on challenges.

Confident that he had a most capable associate, President Clark quickly transferred more and more responsibility to Dr. Bitner.

Then on February 16, 1977, William T. Clark was elected Chairman of the Board and Chief Executive Officer, assured that a competent successor was already aboard.

Directors during Presidency of
William T. Clark, 1970–1977

F. Earl Bach	1962–1978*	
VP 1961–1962		
Pres Sep 10, 1962–1970 Mar*		
John W. Bishop	Nov	1973–
Dr. William L. Bitner III	1968–	
Senior VP 1976–1977		
Pres &		
Chief Adm 1977–1981		
Pres & CEO 1981–1982		
Chairman		
Pres & CEO 1982–		
Frank A. Bronk	1966–1972*	
Hubert C. Brown	1933–1975*	
Pres 1942–1962*		
Chairman 1962–1975*		
Gerald J. Buckley	1967–1989*	
H. Glen Caffry	1965–1975 Mar 7 died	
William T. Clark	1959–1981 Dec 31 died	
Senior VP Oct 1968–1970		
Pres Apr 1970–1976		
Pres & CEO 1976–1977		
Chairman		
& CEO 1977–1981		
Donald S. Creal	1967–1979*	
Carl R. DeSantis	1967–	
James J. Fitzpatrick	1963–1972 resigned	
James Gibson	July	1963–1974*
Michael D. Ginsburg	Nov	1975–1988 resigned
John V. Hallett	1967–1986*	
Vice Chairman 1982–1986*		
Clifford W. Higley	July	1963–1975*
Senior VP 1963–1967*		

Paul E. Lavine   May   1971-1981*
   Mail clerk etc.   1926
   Asst Cashier   1951
   Cashier   1960
   VP & Cashier   1962
   Sr VP & Cashier 1971
   Sr VP   1972-1974*
Francis W. McGinley   1947-1979*
Thomas E. Meath   Jan   1965-1975 June resigned
Leonard J. Moynehan   1965-1974*
William E. Philion   1972-
Alan R. Rhodes   Apr   1975-
Warren E. Rouillard   Oct   1970-
Floyd H. Rourke   1972-
Henry J. W. Vanderminden III Oct   1972-

24 men served on Board during Presidency of William T. Clark.
 1 who would become President of the bank
 * retirement mandatory

Before proceeding to the next chapter, we should take note that Queensbury Branch Manager, William R. Perry, was showing a particular aptitude for developing new business for the bank. He was later transferred to the Marketing Department and in 1990 would be serving as Vice President/Director of Corporate Business Development—Evergreen, with a twenty-nine year service record.

John S. Porter, another young man adept at producing business, would replace Bill at the busy Queensbury Office, and would be a Vice President and Manager of that office in 1990.

Darlene J. Kosinski was establishing an excellent record in the Transit Department and would later become Branch Administration Assistant.

Many other talented young people were on the staff building careers for themselves and stability for the bank.

𝕯𝖎𝖒𝖊 𝕵𝖗𝖆𝖒𝖊

History in Headlines

On or about Wednesday, February 16, 1977

2/2   Natural Gas Shortages Alleviated by U.S. Allocation Program.

2/12   Lake George Courthouse Damaged When Sprinkler Bursts in Attic.

2/14   Blowing Snow Buries Cars in Record-breaking Blizzard in Buffalo.

2/16   Adirondack Park Agency to Meet Tomorrow.

2/18   Reusable Space Shuttle Makes Test Flight.

2/25   Idi Amin Detains 240 Americans in Uganda.

Commodities Then & Now (Year)

	1977	1990
Dow Jones Ind	$948.30	$2,635.59
Gold, oz	148.30	391.19
Silver, oz	4.62	5.21
Copper, lb	0.67	1.03

President: James E. Carter
Vice Pres: Walter Mondale

Prices Then & Now (Year)

	1977	1990
Bread, loaf	$ 0.36	$ 1.17
Milk, gal	1.67	2.13
Butter, lb	0.98	1.99
Gasoline, gal	0.65	1.01
New Ford Car	4,785.00	10,995.00
Annual Income	15,070.00	25,050.00
New Home	49,319.00	91,945.00

On This Day in History

1869—Boston Harbor freezes over.

1878—Silver dollar becomes legal
      money in U.S.

Firsts, Fads, Things

Bottled water. TV recorder.
Roller disco. Hit song, *Lucille.*

Major Events of the Year

Senate approves tough ethics code. Inflation on the increase at 11%. Carter okays treaty giving canal to Panama. Unemployment dips to 7%. Space shuttle *Enterprise* glides off back of airborne 747.

Winners in the Arts

Actor: Richard Dreyfus for *The Goodbye Girl*
Actress: Diane Keaton for
    Annie Hall
Movie: *Annie Hall*
    By United Artists
Best Seller: *Roots*
Big Movie: *Star Wars*

This Year in Sports

W. Series: Yankees beat Dodgers
NBA: Portland
Indy 500: A. J. Foyt, 161.331 mph
Stanley Cup: Montreal
Kentucky Derby: Seattle Slew
Rose Bowl: USC tops Michigan

Four of First National's eleven Presidents served on the 1972 Board of Directors, namely: Hubert C. Brown, F. Earl Bach, William T. Clark, and Dr. William L. Bitner III.

Shown here are members of the 1972 Board and the Lake George Advisory Committee:

Front row, (l. to r.), Leonard J. Moynehan, Judge James Gibson, Walter D. Van Dusen*, Robert J. Sweet*, Henry J. W. Vanderminden III, Hubert C. Brown.

Second row, Francis W. McGinley, Gerald J. Buckley, Alger Mason*, William D. Maltbie Jr.*, Clifford W. Higley, Wiliam Busch Jr.*, Mayor Robert Blais (guest*).

Third row, Floyd H. Rourke, Carl R. DeSantis, Donald S. Creal, Howard W. McKee*, Charles E. Hawley*, Dr. William L. Bitner III.

Fourth row, Robert W. Leavitt*, Warren E. Rouillard, William T. Clark, F. Earl Bach, Thomas E. Meath.

*Members of the Lake George Advisory Board.

Dr. William L. Bitner III

THE PRESIDENCY OF DR. WILLIAM L. BITNER III
1977–

Dr. William L. Bitner III became the eleventh President of First National when he was appointed both President and Chief Administrative Officer on February 16, 1977. No one else had held this joint title during the bank's 124 year history.

The bank had not yet reached $200 million in total assets despite herculean efforts by his predecessor to attain that goal during his own presidency.

Early on, there were detractors who wondered how a former executive in the field of education could make such a dramatic transition to the intensely competitive world of banking. Some felt he would be "out in left field" on this new playing field. But it was soon realized that he was contributing new perspectives that aided greatly in developing new horizons for the bank. Had they known how the man operated, they would not have been so skeptical in the first place.

When Dr. Bitner first became a member of the Board of Directors he did the same thing in that position that he does in any undertaking today. And that is to become very much involved in what he has agreed to do. For example: To get a better understanding of banking, he thoroughly involved himself in the committees of the bank to understand what each did; why they did it; and what was going on within the organization to make those committees important. That, coupled with prolific reading, helped him obtain a basic banking knowledge before he joined the staff. His administrative capabilities were already well certified.

His approach to dealing with problems was very team oriented and fitted in neatly with Chairman Clark's concept of running an organization. So it was that the major responsibilities of operating the bank were divided between the Chairman and the President to allow the new President time to gain hands-on experience with the ever increasing complexities of piloting a fast-growing bank.

The bank's organization chart was revised, and reporting relationships of division officers were realigned with accountability clearly defined. Dr. Bitner added important depth to the senior management team enabling it to more quickly accomplish its stated goals. His finely honed administrative abilities were readily and effectively transferred from the field of education to the realm of banking.

His adroitness at doing this was enhanced by his expertise as a skilled communicator whether it be at the podium or in face-to-face conversations.

He applied himself assiduously to learning the inner workings of the world of banking, absorbing additional torrents of information in a remarkably short time.

Even though both Chairman Clark and President Bitner were power-oriented individuals, they managed to work closely as a team without a clash of wills. This was to their mutual advantage and to the betterment of the bank.

Chairman Clark was so pleased and impressed with the progress of his replacement that he rather quickly divested himself of most of the burdensome chores he alone had carried. In due time, he felt he was no longer needed on what he called "the bridge" and devoted his time to dealing with legislatures and banking regulators in Albany, in New York, and in Washington.

It became readily apparent that Dr. Bitner firmly believed that PEOPLE—their attitudes and their abilities—are extremely important contributing factors to the success of any organization. Selecting the right people for the right position at the right time is a never-ending responsibility.

He and the Personnel Vice President were very much in accord with what had been accomplished to date when he became

President. But both recognized there was need and room for improvement if the bank was to continue its pursuit of excellence.

Dr. Bitner was willing to recognize, test, and reward talent wherever it could be found in the organization. He did not hesitate to break with convention. For example: a talented young man announced that he was leaving to join another bank at a higher salary. Dr. Bitner fought for and obtained a salary increase sufficient to keep David L. Norris from leaving.

Never before had the bank taken such action to deter others. The investment paid off. David applied himself vigorously and worked his way up through the loan division to now (1990) occupy top status as Executive Vice President of First National and Evergreen Bancorp, Inc., and is a Director of Evergreen Bank and of First National Bank.

Dr. Bitner made another break with custom when he overcame the reluctance of others to let a woman occupy a seat at senior management meetings during the absence of the Vice President of Personnel, who was on medical leave-of-absence. Jean Gray proved herself and in time became Vice President of Personnel. Later, after taking early retirement, she was recalled as a consultant on personnel matters.

Claire L. McCormick and Veronica E. Powers were the first two women officers assigned to rotate among the branches, managing or assisting in managing various offices.

Dr. Bitner not only preached "equal opportunity," he practiced it. Lois Chase worked her way from a secretarial position to eventually head the very active Mortgage Department at FNB. Irene (Rene) Clements became the bank's first woman Credit Manager and is now (1990) an Assistant Vice President dealing with Corporate Credit matters.

However, Kathy Flewelling Duncan was the first to break the Commercial Loan barrier. When Dr. Bitner initially suggested the breakthrough, opponents said, "Our business customers will never go to a woman Commercial Loan Officer." Now they wait in line for her as Vice President of Corporate Loans.

Barbara B. Glenn is Vice President of Personnel, participating in senior management meetings with the advantage that she has worked in nearly every department of the bank and has firsthand knowledge about every job.

Kathleen Martinez holds the highest position as Senior Vice President/ Administration and Corporate Secretary of Evergreen Bancorp, Inc. with full top-echelon responsibilities and authority. She is also Secretary of the Board of the First National Bank.

Kathleen Martinez

There are several other women at varying levels of the officer-level strata, where there was only one, two decades ago. Added to this are those who serve as managers and assistant managers of departments and branches.

Whoa! Let's not let our tale get ahead of the historical course of events.

The year 1977 proved to be a good year with bank examiners complimenting First National on the soundness of its loan portfolio which had now reached a new high of $118,467,046, operating in full compliance with the ten subdivisions of the 1976 Consumer Credit Protection Act.

The Trust Department celebrated its 50th anniversary with commission income reaching a new high. New estates and a variety of other trust accounts were being added to the department as a result of aggressively seeking new trust business.

The Directors approved a Business Code of Ethics developed by the Chairman and the President. It required all officers and key personnel, each January, to certify understanding of and adherence to this policy.

Donald D. Hanks was added to the Board in the spring. Howard McKee was appointed to the Lake George Advisory Board. An automatic Dividend Reinvestment Plan was instituted for stockholders. The interior of the Hudson Falls Office was renovated. The number of employees at year-end was 242, the same as last year.

Most notable in 1978 was the crossing of the $200 million milestone during the bank's 125th year of operation and ending the year with $210,666,089 in total assets.

At the suggestion of Dr. Bitner, the 20 First Club was organized to give annual recognition to employees, directors, and retirees with 20 years or more of active service with the bank. Fifty-six members were eligible to attend the first dinner meeting. Thirteen of the fifty-six inducted had forty or more years of service. Ninety-year-old retiree Mary Cary hasn't missed a meeting yet.*

At the request of a group of Salem residents, First National opened a temporary office in September, and appointed D. Sheldon Brown to the newly designated Greenwich-Salem Advisory Committee. There were major renovations and expansion of drive-ins at the Warrensburg facility.

The year 1978 was also a year of escalating interest rates on loans to offset the higher interest paid to depositors, higher mandated minimum wages, increased Social Security, and higher cost of supplies and equipment. Customer awareness of higher interest rates was reflected in a 67.4% overall increase in certificates of deposit, retirement savings, and savings certificates. Promotion of 5% NOW accounts began in early December.

Five shares of First National Bank stock were awarded to each of the bank's thirty-six retirees at Christmas time, representing one share for each twenty-five years the bank had been in operation.

It's worth noting here that an amendment to Federal Reserve Regulation O in June 1978 prohibited executive officers in member banks from receiving more favorable credit terms than those offered to the general public. This included credit cards, check credit, and credit plans of any kind.

The bank's By Laws were changed to read: "No person originally elected or appointed a Director subsequent to August 14, 1978 who shall attain age 70 shall be eligible to be elected or re-elected a Director."

*Mary arranged to attend the 1990 dinner party but died suddenly five days before the event.

In Warrensburg, we converted a gas station building into this modern office in 1976.

The Bancroft residence, a historic landmark in Salem, was restored and became the permanent home of the Salem Office.

The Comptroller's office in Washington announced a new Uniform Interagency Bank Rating System to be used in examinations of banks in the future.

Members of the 1978–79 Senior Management Team. (Standing l. to r.) William T. Clark, Dr. William L. Bitner III. (Seated l. to r.) Robert J. Dehais, Jean H. Gray, A. Max Helm, G. Nelson Lowe, Frederick R. Shenk, Carter A. White, and George F. Reger Jr.

In a reiteration of the bank's policies and broad objectives, it was emphasized that continued success in the intensely competitive banking environment was dependent upon teamwork throughout the organization.

In May, 1979, a Chief National Bank Examiner reported, "First National is a sound, profitable and well-managed bank with minimal deficiencies disclosed."

For those who wonder about a bank's investments, this is a good place to point out that at FNB "the basic policy shall be to consider the investment portfolio as the residual employment of funds after the reasonable loan demand has been met or the Bank's lending limit has been reached. The portfolio will always be considered as an adjunct to the primary function of providing funds for the legitimate credit needs of the community."

Carlisle W. Shaw was appointed to the Greenwich-Salem Advisory Committee, and the restored historic Bancroft residence became the permanent home of the Salem Office. Donald H. Rozell joined the Hudson Falls Advisory Committee.

The Operations Center on Washington Street was expanded to provide room for additional equipment and more operations staff as well as relocation of Consumer Loan processing.

In June, members of the Hudson Falls and Lake George Advisory groups met with the Board of Directors along with three branch managers and three senior officers. Dr. Bitner had introduced this concept to facilitate more direct exchanges of information.

President Bitner embarked on a campaign of disseminating banking information by personally speaking before civic and service groups in every community served by First National. This included opening the meetings to questions and answers to obtain input from active members of each group.

In April 1980, a "Meet The President Day" program was initiated, wherein the President visited each branch office, inviting residents to voice their opinions personally to the bank President. He chatted casually and informally with individuals and with groups. It continues to be a popular form of exchanging information.

He then stimulated other officers to increase their business calls and to converse with a wide range of residents in addition to being available to speak to homebuilders, civic clubs, and school groups in regard to bank services in general and credit needs in particular.

As a result, a comprehensive Community Reinvestment Act Statement was compiled later by First National and was unanimously approved by the Board of Directors. It was pointed out that in addition to meeting the credit needs of individuals, the bank provided funding for municipal projects as well as commercial ventures that increased the employment base throughout the area.

Lake George, Queensbury, and Bolton offices all showed slight decreases in deposits, probably due to the decline in resort business caused by gasoline shortages during the early summer. Growth endured in other sectors, and the bank continued to pay its regular quarterly dividend.

Dr. Bitner reported a $2,500 weekly reduction in payroll via attrition as a result of consultant Penquite's recommendations and indicated that officer status of some individuals was under review.

All Directors were re-elected at the annual meeting in February 1980, this time with 810 votes being cast against each Director out of a total of 205,545 votes.

At the same meeting, a two for one stock split was voted, increasing the stock to $5,169,120 divided into 516,912 shares at a par value of $10 per share. Creating a greater number of shares intentionally reduced the market price per share and increased the marketability of the stock.

It was noted that there had been a substantial growth in rate-sensitive deposits which accounted for 25% of the bank's deposit structure. The new quarterly dividend rate became $.27 per share.

The Omnibus Banking Law was passed, culminating in deregulation of all consumer credit-rate ceilings for banks.

A new twelve-week investment certificate, secured by U.S. Government obligations, was introduced by FNB, bearing a 10% interest rate in amounts of $3,000 and up. It was the equivalent of a repurchase agreement for small savers and attracted 45% of its buyers from sources normally not served by the bank. More than $5,000,000 worth were readily sold.

G. Nelson Lowe

G. Nelson Lowe, Senior Vice President and Trust Officer, became Chairman of the New York State Bankers Association Trust Division and addressed the group at the Waldorf-Astoria in New York during its annual convention.

FNB offered additional safety for customers when it installed the area's first Drive-up night depository at its Queensbury Office.

On October 14, 1980, Joan M. Kubricky was welcomed as a new member of the Board of Directors, the first woman to be so appointed in the bank's 127 year history. Within two months, she was appointed to the bank's Executive Committee.

What a far cry from the days when J. P. Morgan reigned supreme in the world of banking. It is said that up until the time of his death in 1913, NO WOMAN was permitted to step inside his bank in New York. The first woman secretary was hired two years before his death and was required to sit in an office across the street with one of Morgan's partners.

Obviously such action would not be tolerated today. In fact, it is not unreasonable today to envision a woman as President of the bank, perhaps before the turn of the century.

In October, the subject of establishing a one-bank holding company was brought to the attention of the Directors. It had been considered and dismissed ten years previously as it did not appear to hold any useful purpose at that time.

However, the tempo of acquisitions of smaller banks was again accelerating. Management felt that FNB was vulnerable to an unfriendly take-over. And a holding company would lessen its vulnerability to bargain hunters or at least force any predator to pay substantially more for the bank. No one-bank holding company had been formed since the 1920s.

It was agreed to form a corporation by the name of First Glen Bancorp, Inc. It was organized as such, in 1980, under the laws of the State of Delaware to acquire all of the then outstanding shares of the First National Bank of Glens Falls.

At a special meeting on April 15, 1981, the stockholders of the bank ratified the agreement to merge as a wholly-owned subsidiary of Bancorp, but to carry on the business of the bank as "The First National Bank of Glens Falls."

Following necessary regulatory approvals, it commenced business as a one-bank holding company on July 1, 1981, on which date shares formerly representing ownership of First National became evidence of ownership of First Glen Bancorp, Inc.

It was a time of great uncertainty in the world of banking. Inflation had been raising havoc with interest rates for the past two years. There were thirty-three changes in the Fed prime rate in 1981, and FNB had twenty-three. The rates charged on commercial loans were higher than at any time in the history of the bank. On January 1, 1981, the prime rate was 19%, on March 24—18%, and on July 21—20%. On August 10, the bank granted a $100,000, 25-year mortgage at 15 1/2%. The bank was paying an average interest rate of 14.4% on certificates of deposit.

A new instrument, the All-Savers Certificate, became available on October 1, with the rate being adjusted every four weeks by calculating 70% of the 52-week Treasury Bill average yield. It was one of the most heralded provisions of the 1981 Tax Act and allied regulatory changes. However, it did not appeal to the public and fizzled.

A fundamental change in economic philosophy had taken place in Washington under President Reagan, and it was expected that full scale deregulation would soon become a reality.

The future held promise for considerable change from what FNB had known. And it was in an improved position to meet many of the changes because of the plans that had been laid in the past.

Management recognized that the ATM (automatic teller machine) was a necessary step in the age of electronic banking, but had declined to install early models that did not meet customer needs. In mid-September, the most sophisticated model available was installed at the Maple Street Auto Bank. Within a year, several more units were installed at various branch offices.

Tragic news of the untimely death of Chairman William T. Clark, on the final day of the year, shocked and overwhelmed the community and the banking industry in New York State.

On January 4, 1982, a special meeting of the Board of Directors was held at which Dr. Bitner was appointed Chairman of the Board by a unanimous vote.

On January 11, Samuel P. Hoopes, a grandson of the bank's first Chairman, Maurice Hoopes, was appointed to the Board. At the same meeting, John V. Hallett was appointed Vice Chairman of the Board, the first to hold this post in the annals of the bank.

The annual meeting of stockholders was changed to April, at which time Dr. Bitner was elected Chairman of the Board, President and Chief Executive Officer, positions which he still holds in September 1990 (the date of this writing).

By 1982, the Board was well aware that he was a strong individualist who could influence and motivate others. These were the cornerstones of his management style, enabling him to decisively manage people and work for a profit. He had already shown his willingness to by-pass convention and come up with imaginative and unusual solutions to problems.

His insatiable curiosity gave him a wide range of interests which kept him in tune with the marketplace and the ever-changing environment in which he would be required to operate. He could give dissertations on almost any topic, anytime of day or night.

Becoming Chairman strengthened his hand, and Dr. Bitner began changing the focus of the bank in a manner that carried it from a fair performance bank to a high performance bank. He recognized, like the major banks in the nation, that the real money could be made in the area of commercial lending.

So he shifted the focus from mortgages—which had been one of the largest parts of the FNB loan portfolio (where funds are tied up longer and there is less income)—to commercial lending. It was a carefully calculated step to rather quickly develop a significant increase in income in a field that could basically be plotted out over a period of years.

It necessitated expanding the bank's market beyond the Glens Falls area—through friendly acquisitions—to get into areas where more business could be developed at fairly high income levels.

Since we were not expert enough locally, at the time, to carry that off, the initial thrust was to get involved in participation loans with large banks in the Northeast. Dave Norris was trained in the intricacies of the field and a commercial loan division developed under him.

In conformity with his own management style, Dr. Bitner also got himself educated in the pros and cons of this kind of operation for a bank of FNB's size so as to keep an informed and watchful eye on development of the function.

It became clear it was just as easy and safe to make medium-sized commercial loans as it was to generate $100 million worth of car loans. Furthermore, long-term commercial relationships begat deposits as well as loans. That was part of the bank becoming far more sensitized to the competitive environment.

By diverting emphasis to this field, the bank's performance was taken well over the benchmark of 1% on assets to 1.40%, to 1.46%, to 1.51% and hopefully beyond.

That is not to say that the bank ignored the mortgage field. It did not. When the economy turned good again, inviting land development for housing and other structures, it continued to be the dominant mortgage lender in the area.

For awhile, the bank did gravitate somewhat away from what it was very good at (mortgage lending) and made itself good at something else (corporate lending) that began skyrocketing it to previously undreamed of heights.

That progress did not occur overnight, so we need to take a look at what was happening in the interim.

In 1982, business in our area was described at best as sluggish, or in a negative stance with unemployment at a high level. Yet, FNB was able to report good earnings during the first six months.

Under the new Economic Recovery Tax Act, IRA's (Individual Retirement Accounts) had been introduced early in the year and were attracting a goodly amount of deposits.

In June 1982, the Board discussed alternative locations for the office of its highest-ranking executive and recommended refurbishing of the former Chairman's third floor office. The Board also authorized re-design of the lobby of the main bank.

Senior Vice President and Cashier Robert Dehais was in the process of completing the final conversion of the General Ledger to the computer, which when completed gave the capability of having tellers, ATM's, and vital management information systems "on-line" with one of the most sophisticated banking systems in the Northeast.

As chairman of the Financial Computer Center of Eastern New York, Bob had provided strong leadership and direction at the most critical point in the organization's history in tandem with a heavy workload at the bank.

Throughout most of his thirty-five year tenure with First National, he was the innovator of systems and procedures improvements which kept the bank on the cutting edge of progress in work processing. He took early retirement that year due to a heart condition.

Competition increased from still another institution when Northeast Savings opened in the Aviation Mall. Commercial bankers complained that Money Funds and other "near banks" were draining considerable dollar amounts from the mainstay banking institutions of the country, making competition even more pronounced. There was major concern that interest levels would return to the record high levels of 1981.

A one-time 8% supplemental retirement allowance was granted to existing retirees.

Lyle E. Gregory, who had worked his way through the ranks to the post of Operations Officer, was granted additional responsibilities as the bank's first Security Officer. He continued with these duties until taking early retirement in 1990 after forty-three years of service.

Paul W. Tomlinson and Phillip H. Morse were added to the Board in October 1982.

The First Cash Management Plan which had been launched on June 8 attracted 1,100 customers and nearly $12 million before year-end.

Late in the year, FNB was offering the lowest mortgage interest rates in its service area. Mortgages which had been written the previous year when interest rates were at record highs were reduced from 16% to 12% to the quiet satisfaction and amazement of satisfied customers.

Van Dyke Associates, Inc., was purchased primarily to make appraisals of commercial and residential properties in the three counties served by First National.

Vice President Michael P. Brassel was appointed Cashier effective November 11, 1982. A former Chief National Bank Examiner, who was reared in North Creek, he had joined FNB as an Assistant Vice President on March 31, 1980. He is now (1990) an Executive Vice President of Evergreen Bancorp, Inc., and First National Bank, and a Director of Keeseville, and of the First National Bank.

The phenomenal growth and success of First National (Evergreen Bancorp, Inc.) in the 1980s did not happen by itself.

Someone had to make it happen. It meant getting things done through well-selected people, recognizing and utilizing motivation factors to which each individual would be most responsive. Dr. Bitner was very good at that. Key people were reassigned to areas which would optimize their natural strengths.

This team-strengthening, combined with knowledge, foresight, and a willingness to take calculated risks, allowed him to forge ahead with the endorsement of the Board of Directors. It took a lot of heavy hitters to deliver the kind of earned returns that would impress and attract investors to the growing bank. But let's hold off on that story and not get ahead of the tide of history.

In January 1983, the Board increased the dividend for share-owners of First Glen Bancorp by 12 1/2%, and by year-end revealed an increase of more than 55% during the preceding eighteen months with the market price of its stock increasing 63% during 1983 alone.

It had taken just five years for the bank's assets to move from $200 million to $300 million, whereas it had taken 115 years for the bank to attain its first $100 million. That year mortgages were being written at 11 1/2% with a one-year maturity clause in a twenty-year amortization schedule.

First Glen Brokerage was formed and the bank was provided with a facility for dealing in stocks, bonds, U. S. Government issues and other securities on behalf of its customers.

The Hudson Falls Office became the target of a lone, armed bank robber in a daring and potentially deadly assault shortly before 2:00 P.M. Tuesday, July 19, 1983. Retired new accounts secretary Pearl Mayotte recalls: "I was behind the teller area cutting a check for a mortgage closing. Suddenly I heard a commotion. I turned and saw a black man waving a gun. There were customers in the lobby. He shouted, 'Everybody down! Don't answer that phone!'

"Everyone obeyed. He leaped over a teller's counter, cleaned out the cash, dashed out the door and ran across Maple Street to a car in the parking lot behind the courthouse. Branch manager Ray Blake was in the back room with customers and attorneys closing a mortgage. They never heard the noise in the lobby, and were all stunned when I burst into the room to tell them.

"Anyway, someone had punched the alarm and police arrived almost on his heels."

A high-speed chase ensued up Route 4 with an exchange of gunfire during which the robber emptied his .38 automatic pistol and the police fired back. The fleeing vehicle was boxed in at a sharp corner in Fort Ann, and the robber was apprehended. All the money was recovered.

Memos disclose that the district attorney later phoned the bank President and said, "I don't think we have enough evidence for a conviction."

"What?"

"They'll probably dress this guy up, bring in his grandmother and say he's a good boy and he won't get convicted. So I'm not going to go for anything."

Dr. Bitner firmly replied. "That's out of the question!"

The D.A. was very upset. And even more so when the President added, "I'll tell you what, mister: then the bank will go for a full-page advertisement reciting the facts."

Some folks didn't realize that when push comes to shove, Dr. Bitner was in the big leagues.

Seven charges were filed in the indictment including one count of first-degree robbery, and two counts of first-degree reckless endangerment.

The case went to court. The robber was convicted and sent to prison.

Good news in Hudson Falls that year was that Lois S. Oliver was named "Woman of the Year" by the Hudson Falls Business and Professional Women. In 1990, she is an Assistant Vice President managing the Kingsbury Office.

In October, First National became the first upstate bank to offer personalized Execu-Tel deposit service by appointment. It was of special assistance to commercial customers with complex transactions, at the same time relieving lobby pressure at teller windows in the Main Office.

Genevieve (Bea) Fiore, who had processed night deposit bags exclusively at the Queensbury Office, was selected to introduce this service. She was accustomed to processing large, cash-laden deposits. She later became head teller at the Main Office and took early retirement, in 1990, after a thirty-four-year "interrupted-service" career.

During the 1980s, a mindboggling array of new services and promotion schemes surfaced as a result of deregulation and the efforts of banks to capture increased marketshare. First National carefully evaluated each of these innovations to avoid becoming ensnarled in a whirlwind of trivia that would have little practical value to its customers. That is not to say that FNB was always right. But by maintaining close ties to its customers in every community, it understood and met their needs far better than their big money-center competitors.

Do you want to read about each and every one of these ventures? Probably not. So we will skip most of them.

Most notable in 1984 was the dramatic upsurge in assets when First Glen Bancorp became a multi-bank holding enterprise with the acquisition of Keeseville National Bank, which had offices in Keeseville, Chazy, Peru and Plattsburgh. At that time, Keeseville had $45 million in assets and a total of seventy-nine employees, all of whom continued on staff.

Roger B. Prescott Jr., Chairman of the Board of the Keeseville bank, was added to the First Glen Bancorp Board. He also retained his seat as Chairman of the Board of the new subsidiary, perpetuating the fourth generation of Prescott family association with the bank. Michael P. Brassel, Senior Vice President and Cashier of First National, was added to the Keeseville Board.

Keeseville had been a very sleepy bank in an area that was bursting with opportunity. Among other things, the bank had neglected the mortgage area. Corporate headquarters had just gotten its sales culture in place. It was immediately shared with Keeseville and produced outstanding results.

By now you may be wondering how the banking complex, spawned by First National, became known as Evergreen Bancorp, Inc.

Keeseville National Bank retained its 113-year identity as an "independent bank" when it became affiliated with the "mother" bank in Glens Falls.

Keeseville's Plattsburgh Office, near the military base, as it appears after renovation and enlargement in 1987.

(Courtesy Alan Cederstrom)

Some may contend that it really was conceived when the bank's first ATM was christened "Evergreen," to be put on display in the Queensbury Hotel lobby for the IBANY annual meeting in 1981.

But that's as far as it went—until one day in 1985, after the Keeseville National Bank had been acquired, Dr. Bitner was driving along the Northway enjoying the beauty of all those trees—**evergreen trees**. He asked himself, "Why are we called First Glen Bancorp? Why not **Evergreen?** It would fit perfectly with our green tree logo."

By the time he reached Keeseville, he was convinced and posed the question to the group there. They agreed. He returned to Glens Falls and posed the same question to the Board of Directors. They said, "Sounds good. Let's change our corporate name to Evergreen."

It was thought that the change could be accomplished by some kind of simple fiat. Not so. The stockholders had to vote on it. So management had to wait until the annual meeting in 1986 before making the change to Evergreen Bancorp, Inc.

But that's not all the story. There is an interesting aside.

In 1988, Dr. Bitner attended a meeting of many bankers in Arizona. Each bank representative was called to the podium to be presented with a written report about his bank.

When the name Evergreen was announced, Dr. Bitner stepped forward. So did another banker. For a moment they stood there looking at each other. The stranger said, "I represent Evergreen Financial Corp, out of Evergreen Park, Illinois."

Dr. Bitner replied, "We are Evergreen Bancorp, Inc."

Stunned, the other banker said, "You can't be. Our name is registered as Evergreen."

"So is ours. Our logo is a tree."

The man from Illinois countered, "Our logo is a tree."

But that was not the end of it.

On August 13, 1990, the attorneys finally announced that both parties had agreed to allow the concurrent use of the logo: (Their logo is very close to ours but their tree has many more branches on it.)

Evergreen Bancorp, Inc., has exclusive use of the logo in New York State, Vermont, and Massachusetts. And the Illinois financial institution has all the rest of the states because they filed a Federal Registration in 1967. Our logo was registered in 1973, but only in New York State.

Up until the acquisition of the Keeseville bank in 1984, Vice President Branch Administrator Max Helm exercised dominion over all the branches. He built up a loyal following among his branch managers and zealously protected his people from the intrusions of corporate division heads. This precipitated occasional minor skirmishes over turf. But Max was able to prevail because of his superior knowledge about the total functions of the bank.

At that time, it was decided not to expand dependency upon any one individual for administration of all functions in all branch locations. The concept of "self-ruled" subsidiaries dictated a different method of empowerment.

Twenty years previously, a management succession plan had been developed outlining both immediate and long-range proposals. The Board's Personnel Committee worked closely with Dr. Bitner in keeping the plan updated to conform with the changing needs of the organization and the development of key people.

Fees for Directors and Advisory Committees were raised in 1984 to $175 for Board meetings, $150 for Executive Committee, $120 for other committees of the Board, and $75 for Advisory Committee members.

The two-story building which formerly housed Hall Ice Cream Co. and then Borden's Ice Cream on Maple Street in Glens Falls was purchased for future expansion. Within months the Cool Insuring Agency building, which adjoined the parking lot, also was purchased.

Evergreen Bancorp was committed to maintaining financially sound independent community banks providing equitable returns to stockholders, offering high-quality banking services. It remained vigilant to opportunities to expand business to new geographical areas and into new products.

It was at this stage of development that separate minute books were established for Evergreen Bancorp, Inc. and each of its subsidiaries, each with their own individual Board of Directors.

That seemingly simple step signaled the acceptance of a new philosophy which had been evolving at "company" headquarters in Glens Falls.

Up until that time there was little real holding company mentality in the organization. Everyone knew it existed—was called First Glen Bancorp, then Evergreen. But most people were clinging to the old concept of a hometown bank.

One of the keys to the survival of First National and its associates was the ability of management, through strategic planning, to effectively change the viewpoint of the organization from "A Bank" to a multi-bank holding company. And to develop an organization that fully supported the desire to expand the geographical region of the organization.

But it was more than that. Its prerequisite was a different mind-set—a mind-set that would become far more competitive; far more sales driven; far more aware of what the banking world was beyond the outskirts of the community banks.

Vice President Shenk was empowered to develop a corporate marketing strategy, allowing for individuality at each subsidiary yet adhering to central themes. Sales orientation became a significant force at every level of the organization through the centralization of marketing and training.

The year 1985 became a year of important attainment with a net earnings increase of more than 25%. First Glen Bancorp increased its capital base by 47% with a public offering of 320,000 shares of stock which were fully subscribed on the day of the offering (September 6, 1985) in less than one hour.

The offering was preceded by a two for one stock split. Dividends were increased twice during the year giving stockholders an additional 20% return. The market price of the stock rose more than 75% during the twelve month period, and 260% from 1981.

Dr. Bitner was elected president of the Independent Bankers Association of New York that year and became involved in a great many legislative matters.

Evergreen Venture Capital, Inc. was formed for the purpose of financing small businesses with high growth potential.

At year end, deposits totaled $395,792,000, assets $473,762,000, and staff totaled 341 people.

Teller accuracy—the ability to handle high volumes of cash transactions accurately—is a problem prevalent in all banks. A "teller incentive" program was instituted at First National with the express purpose of rewarding those who exhibit above average performance both in number of transactions and number and size of cash differences.

Coupled with this was the formation of a President's Club with membership open only to those with three consecutive years of outstanding performance. Members, who met all the measured criteria, were invited to breakfast with the President, were publicly praised in the bank's monthly in-house newsletter, and were presented with awards of as much as $1,000 and a gold plate. Some even appeared before the Board of Directors to be given special recognition.

The incentives spurred all tellers to improved performance records. Similarly other groups were stimulated to improve their individual productivity. The normal grumbling by low producers was more than offset by the new pride among those with new excellence. Modifications were made in the program from time to time to the benefit of all concerned.

In January 1986, Kathleen G. Martinez was appointed Secretary of the Board of First Glen Bancorp, Inc. and First National Bank, replacing Vice President Trust Officer Lowe in that assignment. She was the first woman to be so appointed.

Early in the year, Dr. Bitner reported approval of the New York State Banking Board for the acquisition of Peoples Commercial Bank with offices in Albany, East Greenbush, and Hudson, and assets in excess of $19 million. Federal approval soon followed. The merger became effective February 28, 1986, giving the banking complex a strategic foothold in the Capital District of New York State.

G. Nelson Lowe and Anthony J. Koenig were elected to the Peoples Board at a special meeting in March 1986. Within a month, David L. Norris was added to that Board.

At the annual meeting in April, the holding company's corporate name was changed to Evergreen Bancorp, Inc. A three-for-two stock split was voted and the par value of the stock re-valued at $3.33 1/3 per share.

The South Glens Falls Office was again enlarged to include six drive-in lanes, celebrating the 35th anniversary of having introduced drive-ins to the North Country.

Then in 1987, there was major renovation and expansion of the Plattsburgh Office, near the military base. This included the addition of a 4000-square-foot building with four drive-ins and a 24-hour ATM, making it the most modern banking facility north of the Glens Falls area.

Before recommending expansion into carefully targeted new market areas, the two Executive Vice Presidents, Michael Brassel and David Norris, discuss all the ramifications.

In November 1988, a new facility was opened directly across from the New York State Capitol on State Street, utilizing the advantages of construction under the Albany Industrial Development Agency. Such a premier location exemplifies the prestige of Evergreen banks in Upstate New York financial circles.

First National expanded into Corinth and under IDA constructed a new branch office there. Likewise FNB went west on Aviation Road in Queensbury to open a new facility in what later became Evergreen Plaza.

As you can well imagine, moving into the Capital District created new complexities for Dr. Bitner and the corporate senior officers. It is no easy task to sustain the independence of community banks as subsidiaries of a central structure while simultaneously meeting the needs of a major metropolitan urban market. However, the bottom-line figures proved the capability of all concerned in doing so.

That capability was not mere happenstance. It came from educating, training, and developing people at every level, adding to the expertise which many already possessed. Many employees participated in highly specialized courses at colleges and universities across the nation.

Senior Vice President Shenk was vested with responsibility for marketing and training in all locations. This amplified the often overlooked fact that every person in a network sells (or unsells) his/her organization's products and services. The image and attitude of all workers is ultimately reflected in the marketplace.

Assistant Vice President Joseph F. Scriver serves as frontline director of training at all the offices throughout the chain. Training of prospective tellers became a full-time assignment for Barbara Celadon.

Fundamentally, Dr. Bitner himself is a teacher—one who expects students to apply themselves diligently to the best of their individual abilities to whatever their task might be. To him **information** is the key to success in today's world. An informed employee is by far a better motivated employee.

State Street Office, Albany

Central Avenue Office, Albany

Corinth Office

Evergreen Plaza in Queensbury

Kingsbury Office in Hudson Falls

George F. Reger Jr.

George Reger was one of those who kept himself informed and applied himself resolutely to whatever task was assigned. As a result he advanced from a clerk in 1952 to become Senior Vice President of Evergreen Bancorp, Inc. and First National Bank, and a Director of Keeseville National Bank. He took early retirement in 1990 after nearly thirty-eight years service.

The Chief Executive Officer also kept in close contact with all employees via regularly scheduled staff meetings—divided into small peer groups so that individuals would feel free to express their concerns and opinions. This, too, was a valuable two-way teaching process and an effective way to keep his fingers on the pulse of the organization.

Dr. Bitner showed compassion for those who had been "Peter principled" beyond their capacity to perform comfortably and

Strategic planning sessions act as a creative force in the development of innovative ideas and solutions. Dr. Bitner is shown here leading a session with five members of senior management. Seated (l. to r.) Carter A. White, A. Max Helm, Michael Rupeka, Barbara B. Glenn, and John M. Fullerton.

gave them less strenuous assignments. On the other hand, he could and would be rough and tough on chronic grumblers and on upper-echelon people who failed to live up to what was expected of them.

Year after year in the 1980s, the banking complex achieved record levels in deposits, loans, earnings, assets, and capital. Behind it all was the driving force of Dr. Bitner's foresight. He was always visualizing five years ahead, urging the Board to take advantage of opportunities before others recognized them.

He keeps in constant touch, not only with the Board and division heads, but with all the players on the bank team. To him, there is no such thing as an unimportant position or unimportant person on the staff. He knows virtually every employee and speaks to each one by name.

This includes the legion of people "behind the scenes." They are the unsung heroes who provide support for those in the limelight. They toil day after day, unseen by the public, processing endless streams of paper and data vital to serving the public and keeping the bank afloat. They are the secretaries, the operators of transit machines, switchboards, word processors, and a host of others in the financial and operational divisions, as well as the personnel, marketing, trust and investment departments, the guys in purchasing and maintenance—and others.

Few people realized that there were 188 different job classifications among the bank's 354 employees in 1990. The responsibilities were many and varied in an ever-changing world of modern banking methods and technology. It took a lot of synergistic effort to keep the organization functioning smoothly.

In addition to the strategic planning sessions with senior management and with other leaders, the President also conducts quality staff meetings on a quarterly basis so as to maintain open two-way communication channels to keep everyone informed and motivated.

Over and over again, he preaches three things that must be done by every member of the bank family to enable the bank to grow and prosper.

"Number one—get deposits.

"Number two—get DEPOSITS.

"Number three—get **MORE DEPOSITS!**"

In 1988, another major milestone was achieved when total assets exceeded $700 million, having skyrocketed $500 million from the benchmark of $200 million ten years previously.

By now marketing was airing television commercials in Albany and Glens Falls to make the bank's services familiar to the vast audience of the Capital District and beyond.

In the ongoing saga of what had been a tiny country bank in 1853, the corporation known in 1989 as Evergreen Bancorp, Inc. was prospering beyond the wildest imagination of its founding fathers.

Not only were its assets crowding the THREE-QUARTER BILLION DOLLAR mark, its roots were firmly entrenched in a 200-mile corridor stretching from the Canadian border south to Hudson, N.Y.

Dr. Bitner

And its Chief Executive Officer Dr. Bitner was playing a very active role as the 1989–90 president of the New York State Bankers Association. This entailed numerous trips to New York City and Washington, D.C. on major banking matters in addition to delivering speeches to bankers and business leaders in all eight banking districts of the state.

He had taken it upon himself to become conversant with the operations and problems of the state's largest financial institutions. As a former president of IBANY, he was familiar with the smaller independent banks. To this was added his experience of guiding community banks as CEO of the Evergreen complex. Thus he was readily accepted as a knowledgeable banker and exceptionally articulate speaker wherever he appeared.

The annual meeting of the NYSBA was held at the Sagamore at Bolton Landing on July 15, 1990, at which Dr. Bitner gave his farewell speech. The ovation attested to the high regard in which he was held by bankers throughout New York State.

Early in 1989, the use of Gold MasterCard increased as did commercial sweep accounts, Home Equity loans, and the newly introduced Evergreen Investors Account. Evergreen participated in developing the Community Lending Corporation at the suggestion of Governor Cuomo in an effort to coordinate all federal and state subsidized housing opportunities.

Employees were given an opportunity to participate in a Flexible Benefit Plan. Later, a new Employee Stock Option Plan (ESOP) was made available to employees, with the bank making substantial contributions to the fund.

Needing room for expansion, the bank purchased the three-story "Saunders Building" at 234 Glen Street, directly across the street from its white marble structure. It ran into a "hornets' nest" when a misunderstanding arose concerning the removal of terra cotta tiles from the facade of the building.

Once the President was apprised of the historic significance of the tiles, he assured the community that the bank had no intention of removing or damaging the tiles in any way. "The front of the building is being renovated. But the tiles will stay."

During the last half of the year, it became abundantly clear that economic conditions were on the wane.

At the national level, Congress was unable or unwilling to face the issue of budget control. The international balance of trade was worsening, and the United States was becoming the world's largest debtor nation.

The overheated real estate market softened throughout the bank's service area. This precipitated a slowdown in related industries, and lessened the demand for mortgages and other loans.

Nevertheless, the bank increased its net income for the fifteenth consecutive year and produced a three-for-two stock split, making it the fourth stock split in the past five years. In fact, 1989 proved to be the most successful year in the history of the bank, establishing new highs in all important categories. Total assets at year end were $771,970,000.

In the meantime plans were being laid for a merger with Champlain Valley Federal Savings and Loan, in 1990, to increase Evergreen's capacity to serve and broaden its market in the North Country.

However, these plans were later abandoned. Following intensive investigation, the Board of Directors and management concluded that the projected return on money needed to fully capitalize the "S & L" was not sufficient to justify the investment. By mutual agreement, the plan was terminated on July 19, 1990.

First National was pleased to take the lead in helping to solve the affordable housing situation in the Warren, Washington and Saratoga County area. It joined HomeFront Development Corporation in developing a plan (Community Home Buyer's Program) to educate people on the problems associated with buying and owning a home.

Some people think it is easy for banks to make scads of money. Not so. Banking is not all wine and roses. It is a risk business—prudent risk. And, from time to time, bankers are confronted by factors beyond their control.

Such was the case in the first half of 1990.

There was an overall slowing of the economy, coupled with an interest rate squeeze, increased deposit insurance costs, and the need to increase loan loss reserves. These factors caused profits to decline during the first six months of 1990, not only for Evergreen banks but for most banks in the nation.

Furthermore, the industry was plagued by the spillover of the negative news surrounding the savings and loan crisis in the southwest. The news was detrimental to all banks, and caused an unfavorable market reaction on bank stocks without regard for their record or performance.

Unfortunately, during this period, First National found it necessary to make its largest charge off ever (approximately $1.8 million) as the result of a major corporate creditor having filed under Chapter 7 of the Federal Bankruptcy Laws. FNB was one of six bank lenders affected by that bankruptcy.

On the bright side, deposits increased more than $75,200,000, and loans increased $52,200,000 as of June 30, 1990, above the same date in 1989.

Early reports indicate an upward trend for First National and its sister subsidiaries in the third quarter of 1990. Total assets reached $817,000,000 by mid-August.

That is a major accomplishment in view of the uncertainties that prevail in the world today.

What worldwide economic upheavals are going to result from the crisis in the oil-rich Mideast? Will the United States and the leading nations of the world be able to thwart the aggression of Iraq without resorting to war?

First National has weathered many a crisis in its 137 year history. Now as Evergreen Bancorp its capable management will continue to concentrate on the basics of banking—the things they know best—in their own marketplace through the community banks of the North Country.

Characteristically, its current President Dr. Bitner adopts the long-range view. "Lots more to be accomplished between now and 1995 when the offspring of First National will still be the dominant banking force in the North Country."

Nobody ever told Dr. Bitner it would be easy. He wouldn't want it that way.

Directors during Presidency of
Dr. William L. Bitner III 1977–

Edward F. Allard		1988–
F. Earl Bach		1962–1978*
VP 1961–1962		
Pres Sep 10 1962–1970 Mar*		
John W. Bishop	Nov	1973–
Dr. William L. Bitner III		1968–
Senior VP	1976–1977	
Pres & Chief Adm	1977–1981	
Pres & CEO	1981–1982	
Chairman		
Pres & CEO	1982–	
Michael P. Brassel	Dec	1985
Dana S. Bray Jr.		1988–
Gerald J. Buckley		1967–1989*
**Dean V. Chandler		1990–
William T. Clark		1959–1981 Dec 31 died
Senior VP	Oct 1968–1970	
Pres	Apr 1970 1976	
Pres & CEO	1976–1977	
Chairman & CEO 1977–1981		
Donald S. Creal		1967–1979*
Carl R. DeSantis		1967–
Robert F. Flacke	Jan	1979–
John S. Gianto	Jan	1979–1981 Aug resigned
Michael D. Ginsburg	Nov	1975–1988 Sep resigned
John V. Hallett		1967–1986*
Vice Chairman 1982–1986*		
Donald D. Hanks	Apr	1977–
Samuel P. Hoopes	Jan	1982–
Joan M. Kubricky	Oct	1980–
(Joan M. Mannix)		

Paul E. Lavine   May   1971–1981*
    Mail clerk etc.   1926
    Asst Cashier   1951
    Cashier   1960
    VP Cashier   1970
    Sr VP & Cashier 1971
    Senior VP   1972–1974*
G. Nelson Lowe   1984–
Francis W. McGinley   1947–1979*
Phillip H. Morse   Oct   1982–
David L. Norris   Apr   1989
William E. Philion   1972–
**Roger B. Prescott Jr.   July   1984–
Alan R. Rhodes   Apr   1975–
Warren E. Rouillard   Oct   1970
Floyd H. Rourke   1972–
Bjarne G. Soderstrom   1982–1989
Paul W. Tomlinson   Oct   1982–
**Walter Urda   1989–
Henry J.W. Vanderminden III
                                   Oct   1972–
**Daniel B. Walsh   1989–

32 men and one woman have served on the home office Board
during the Presidency of Dr. William L. Bitner III

 *retirement mandatory
**served on Evergreen Bancorp, Inc., Board but not on First
National Bank Board.

CURRENT (1990) DIRECTORS

First National Bank and Evergreen Bancorp, Inc.

Edward F. Allard	Donald D. Hanks	Alan R. Rhodes
John W. Bishop	Samuel P. Hoopes	Warren E. Rouillard
William L. Bitner III	*G. Nelson Lowe	Floyd H. Rourke
*Michael P. Brassel	Joan M. Mannix	Paul W. Tomlinson
Dana S. Bray Jr.	Phillip H. Morse	Henry J. W. Vanderminden III
**Dean V. Chandler	*David L. Norris	**Walter Urda
Carl R. DeSantis	William E. Philion	**Daniel B. Walsh
Robert F. Flacke	**Roger B. Prescott Jr.	

*A Director of First National Bank.
**A Director of Evergreen Bancorp, Inc.
All others are members of both Boards.

Keeseville National Bank

James H. Andre	Melissa W. Davis	George F. Reger Jr.
Michael P. Brassel	Elvin F. Drown	Curtis E. Shipman
Dean V. Chandler	William O. Morgan	Robert C. Smith

Evergreen Bank

Thomas G. Cholakis	Patrick T. Maney	Russell J. Oliver
Anthony J. Koenig	Edward P. McConville	Walter Urda
Ronald H. Laberge	David L. Norris	Daniel B. Walsh
G. Nelson Lowe		

CURRENT (1990) ADVISORY COMMITTEES

Hudson Falls Region

William R. Collins	Richard E. McLenithan	David H. Rozell
E. Roger Dickinson	Michael J. Moran	Gary C. Wilson
Hans F. Hoenck	Daniel G. Reid	

Greenwich/Salem Region

Norman W. Allen	Richard F. Crozier	Donald L. Skellie
Elton A. Borden	Ronald D. Dixson	James C. Tomasi
D. Sheldon Brown	Carlyle W. Shaw	

Lake George/Warrensburg Region

Ronald R. Alcan	John A. Mason	John K. Ryder
Richard K. Berke	John J. Palermo	Nancy B. Veeder
Calvin C. Engle	Walter O. Rehm III	

LEST WE FORGET

There are hundreds of people, past and present, who devoted time, talent, and toil to the success of First National and its satellites during its 137 year history.

If our format had been that of an enormous high school yearbook, we could have related many, many more individual accomplishments and events than space herein permitted.

Hard choices had to be made. Most of them evolved around "being first" in a given activity or some unusual event. Even then, we could not record everything.

Space on this page is reserved for the names of those not previously mentioned, who have (or had) twenty or more years of service at First National. Their deeds and dedication are equally important as those already recorded.

20–24 years of service:

Grace Belstraz
Adela Benson
Elfriede Brickner
William C. Burns
Helen M. Carpenter
Sharon W. Cederstrom
Dympna Corcoran
Lorraine Coughlin
Marie Dagles
Helen D. Dirga
Wallace H. Estill
Regina Every
Donna Frasier
Mary Anne Hall
Barbara A. Helwig
James H. Johnson
May D. Johnston
Darlene Kosinski
Viola Mattison
Hortense Munson
Robert J. Murray
Shirley Parent
Elizabeth Roach
Eileen D. Rozell
Clarence W. Shaw
Virginia R. Shaw
Ann Slade
Marilyn Smith
Aletha Walker
Jean White

25–29 years of service:

Margaret Putnam
Elizabeth Robinson

30–34 years of service:

Margaret Kelleher

35–39 years of service:

Richard B. Dodge
Mary Edmonds
Madeline Heym
Esther Williams

40 years or more of service:

Frances A. Bovee
J. Wyman Dean
Eileen Morrell

ACKNOWLEDGMENTS

The collection of facts, photographs and lore of old Glens Falls was made possible by contributions from many people in the Glens Falls region. We are grateful to each and every one who assisted in any way, most of whom are listed below.

John D. Austin Jr.
Marcia B. Austin
Mrs. F. Earl Bach
Margaret Balcom
Dr. John E. Barnes
Polly Hoopes Beeman
William L. Bitner III
Raymond A. Blake
Michael P. Brassel
Elfriede Brickner
Mrs. Hubert C. Brown
Daniel D. Burke
Sandra G. Butler
Mary A. Cary
Sandra Casey
Alan Cederstrom
Barbara A. Celadon
Joseph W. Cervera
Lois W. Chase
Virginia A. Clark
Bruce Cole
Karl Crannell
William G. Crawshaw
George I. Davis
Marion Brown Davis
Elisabeth B. Day

Robert L. Eddy
Mary Edmonds
Regina Every
Arthur S. Fisher
Thomas F. Foster
Barbara B. Glenn
Jean H. Gray
Lyle E. Gregory
Karin Hathaway
A. Max Helm
Sandra Hughes
Robert Joy
Marjorie Kenneally
Dr. Robert N. King
Byron J. Lapham Jr.
Byron J. Lapham Sr.
Paul E. Lavine
Richard Linehan
G. Nelson Lowe
William Mac Duff
Kathleen Martinez
Michael F. Massiano
Pearl E. Mayotte
Edward McElroy
Aletha C. McGinley
Joan Metraw
Olive Morris

Robert J. Murray
David L. Norris
Mrs. J. Griffith O'Keefe
Lois S. Oliver
Mrs. Frank T. O'Neil
Diane Prairie
Edward F. Pratt
John E. Rafferty
George F. Reger Jr.
Marge Resetar
Elizabeth Roach
Kenneth Romanclli
Penny B. Sandora
Peg Schroeder
Joseph F. Scriver
Elaine Scully
Ralph R. Shapiro
Frederick R. Shenk
Judith S. Sicard
Sanford Silverman
Nelson E. Smith
Viola L. Smith
Joseph J. Stepp
Leonard Sweeney
A. Max Tupper
Carter A. White
Marion Wilson

BIBLIOGRAPHY

Listed below are the primary and secondary sources that were used in preparation of the text.

Minutes of the Board Meetings of:
The Commercial Bank of Glen's Falls, N.Y.
The First National Bank of Glens Falls.
The Evergreen Bancorp, Inc.

Pitchin' Pennies, house publication of the First National Bank of Glens Falls, N.Y.

Evergreen Today, house publication of Evergreen Bancorp, Inc.

Back issues of *The Glens Falls Times, The Post-Star,* the *Glens Falls Messenger,* the *New York Times,* and the *Wall Street Journal.*.

Oral recollections of area history buffs, retired bank employees, their spouses and children, local business people, area citizens—and others.

Books and Miscellaneous Manuscripts

William McEchron 1831–1906 Homely Recollections by Katherine Cunningham. Woodstock, Vt., Elm Tree Press, 1962.

Historical Directory of the Banks of the State of New York, by William H. Dillistin., NYSBA, 1946.

History of Glens Falls, New York, and Its Settlement by Louis Fiske Hyde. Glens Falls, N.Y., Glens Falls Post Company, 1936.

Bridging the Years—Glens Falls, New York, 1763–1978. Published by the Glens Falls Historical Association in cooperation with Crandall Library, 1978

Backward Glances by Howard C. Mason. Glens Falls, N.Y., Webster Mimeo Services, 1963, 1964, 1965.

Chronicle of the 20th Century. Clifton Daniel, Editor-in-Chief, Chronicle Publications Inc., Mount Kisco, N.Y., 1987.

Glimpses of the Past. Historical Museum Notes by Richard C. VanDusen, Walter P. Reichert, and Harold M. Long, editors. Glens Falls, N.Y., Ridgecraft Books, 1970.

History of the Lumber Industry in the State of New York by William F. Fox., Harbor Hills Books, 1976.

The Lime Industry in Glens Falls, 1832–1938 by J. Thacher Sears.

Glens Falls, New York, The Empire City. Glens Falls Publishing Co., 1908.

History of Warren County, New York, William H. Brown, editor. Board of Supervisors of Warren County. Glens Falls Post Company, 1963.

History of the Town of Queensbury by A. W. Holden. Albany, N.Y., Joel Munsell Company, 1874.

The Story of Canals of New York State by John P. Cashion, 1963.

Memorial Biographies. Miscellaneous materials prepared by Alexander Miller and others, deposited in Crandall Library and at the museum of the Glens Falls Historical Association.

The Scout, house publication of Finch, Pruyn and Company, Inc., Glens Falls, N.Y.

One Hundred Thirty-five Years of Community Banking History. Glens Falls National Bank and Trust Company, 1986.

Hospital by the Falls, The History of Glens Falls Hospital 1897–1987 by Joseph A. Cutshall King. Glens Falls Hospital, 1987.

The History of Ballston Spa National Bank 1838–1988 by Ruth W. Roerig, Ballston Spa National Bank, Ballston Spa, N.Y., 1988.

ABOUT THE AUTHOR

Joseph E. Barnes began writing as a "by-line" sports writer for *The Glens Falls Times* in 1933. After joining the bank staff in 1936, he continued his writing by "moonlighting" for newspapers, pulps, slicks, trade journals, and his own syndicated column, *Our People—USA*. He founded and wrote the bank's first house organ *Pitchin' Pennies* for 30 years. For 10 years, he was editor of *Builders' Weekly* for the Glens Falls Kiwanis Club. He wrote a series of folios, booklets, manuals, and books including *SuperPROcrastinators,* and *Writing for Fun and Money.*

He was public relations representative of Group V, New York State Bankers Association, and public relations chairman of the Mohawk division of Kiwanis International.

Mr. Barnes graduated from Glens Falls High School in 1936, as president of his class. He completed 12 years of bank-sponsored courses of the American Institute of Banking, and was a recognized instructor for the local chapter.

Under bank sponsorship, he took summer courses at Syracuse University, Williams College, Rutgers University, and studied Human Behavioral Sciences at Princeton.

Mr. Barnes began his career in banking as mail/messenger boy in 1936. He worked his way up through all departments (other than the trust department). He was the bank's first full-time Personnel Officer and retired in 1977 as Vice President of Personnel.

He served two terms as president of the Warren County Bankers Association, and as an officer in several community groups.

Time Frame

History in Headlines

On or about September 25, 1990

9/17 Divers Locate Warship Sunk in Lake George 232 Years Ago.
9/18 18th Annual Adirondack Balloon Festival Attracts Thousands to Warren County Airport and to Community College Campus.
9/19 Atlanta Awarded 1990 Summer Olympic Games.
9/20 Multinational Military Buildup in Saudi Arabia Ominous.
9/25 Oil Prices Skyrocket.

Commodities Now (1990)

		1990
Dow Jones Ind	(July)	$2,999.25
Dow Jones		2,452.97
Gold, oz		392.50
Silver, oz		5.21
Copper, lb		1.03

President: George Bush
Vice Pres: J. Danforth Quale

Prices Now (1990)

		1990
Bread, loaf	$	1.17
Milk, gal		2.13
Butter, lb		1.99
Gasoline, gal		1.29
New Ford Car		10,995.00
Annual Income		25,050.00
New Home		91,945.00

On This Day in History

1493—Columbus sailed from Portugal on his 2nd voyage.
1513—Balboa discovered the Pacific Ocean.

Firsts, Fads, Things

Nintendo video games, pager, wristwatch, day-glo clothes.

Winners in the Arts

Actor: Daniel Day-Lewis for *My Left Foot*
Actress: Jessica Tandy for
    Driving Miss Daisy
Movie: *Driving Miss Daisy*
    By Warner Brothers
Best Seller: *Memories of Midnight*
    By Sidney Sheldon
Big Movie: *Teenage Mutant Ninja Turtles*

Major Events of the Year

Berlin Wall comes tumbling down. Dollar reverses downward spiral. American troops sent to Mideast to contain Iraq aggression. East and West Germany move to reunify. United Nations back U.S. action in economic sanctions against Iraq. Savings and loan loses incredible.

This Year in Sports

Baseball: Season is delayed by dispute with owners and players.
Indy 500: Arie Luyendyk
Multi-million dollar contracts
Kentucky Derby: Unbridled
Super Bowl: San Francisco 49ers whip Denver Broncos 55–10

Fri. Dec. 14

3:00 + 8:00

Civic Center